Piece By Piece:

My Blended Experience of a Mosaic Family

Dr. Steve Hudgins

Guiding Brilliant Writers

New York, New York

Published by
Guiding Brilliant Writers, LLC
New York, New York

ISBN: 979-8-9996483-0-3 (Paperback)

Library of Congress Control Number: 2025918526

BISAC Subject Categories:
PSY036000 – Psychology / Interpersonal Relations
FAM051000 – Family & Relationships / General
REL012000 – Religion / Christian Living / Personal Growth

Cover design by Dr. Steve Hudgins
Edited by Leslie Thomas Flowers

Printed in the United States of America
First Edition

Dedication

Ralph E.Hudgins
August 1941 – October 2025

Although we did not always see eye to eye, you were the golden glue that held the family together. Our relationship was not without strain—parental attachment wounds, blurred loyalties, and external voices often clouded what could have been clearer. People, systems, and even those closest to us sometimes made it harder to understand one another.

Yet with time and healing, I now see the value in the lessons you tried to pass down the best way you knew how. I remember our lawn mowing contract—what felt like a teenage chore now echoes in my heart as one of your most profound teachings on work, worth, and responsibility. Thank you for that. It stayed with me.

You made it to 84—a quiet triumph of resilience. And though it brings me deep sadness to be kept from seeing you in these later years, I hold on to the eternal hope that one day, we will be reunited in heaven. I want to stand by your side again—not as the boy confused by life's divides, but as the man who now understands. I love you, and there is no substitute for the place you still hold in my soul. Thank you for teaching me life's lessons—spoken and unspoken.

—Your son

Acknowledgment

As I reflect on the journey of writing this book, I am grateful for the countless individuals who have supported me along the way. To my family, thank you for your unwavering love and encouragement. Your understanding and patience have given me the strength to share our experiences.

I also extend my most profound appreciation to my mentors and colleagues in the mental health field. Your wisdom and insights have profoundly shaped my understanding of mosaic family dynamics and inspired me to help others navigate their journeys.

To the families who shared their stories with me, thank you for your vulnerability and trust. Your experiences enriched this work and acted as a guiding light, reminding me of the strength and resilience found within mosaic families.

My special thanks to my editor and publishing team for their dedication and keen eye, which helped to bring this vision to life. Your expertise and support made this project possible.

Ultimately, this book offers the tools, inspiration, and understanding you need to appreciate the unique beauty of your family's mosaic. Together, we can celebrate the diverse and colorful mosaic of family life.

"In the mosaic of family life, each unique piece contributes to a breathtaking whole; within the delicate balance of individuality and respect for boundaries, we find the true beauty of togetherness." - Dr. Steve Hudgins, LPCS, NCC.

Portions of this book were adapted from my doctoral dissertation, *"A Hermeneutical Phenomenological Study Exploring Divorce in Blended Families" (2025), which was* completed at Liberty University.

About this Book

Dr. Steve Hudgins, LPCS, NCC, with his clinical practice, doctoral research, and firsthand experiences, offers a fresh perspective on the vibrant complexities of blended families. The goal is to transition from a blended family to a mosaic family definition. Mosaic art creates individuality and boundaries inherent in the medium. Drawing from his professional background and lived experience, Dr. Hudgins equips readers with insightful tools to navigate the unique dynamics of modern family structures. He challenges outdated terms like "step," "blended," and "bonus," and introduces a more fitting term: "Mosaic Family."

Inside, you will find:

Reflective Questions to engage in self-discovery and deepen your connections with family members.

Key takeaways or strategies to access resources designed to manage change and foster harmony in your home.

Authentic Stories to relate to real experiences that illuminate both struggles and successes.

This book begins by defining key family terms and delving into what it means to fit each unique puzzle piece into the familial mosaic. Dr. Hudgins emphasizes the importance of healing, understanding attachment styles, and recognizing the instant connections we form in these relationships.

Throughout the chapters, readers will explore invaluable lessons in navigating diverse familial roles, setting healthy boundaries, and fostering trust, all while celebrating the contributions of each family member to the larger picture. With years of professional expertise, he provides practical wisdom and strategies for embracing the journey of building a harmonious mosaic family. He emphasizes that while change can be challenging, it often leads to profound growth and connection.

This book is for mothers navigating stepfamily life, for fathers picking up the pieces after divorce, for adult children still wrestling with past loyalties, and for anyone trying to love through brokenness. I did not grow up with a perfect example of marriage as a model. I am deeply thankful my parents remained married for 60 years, yet their relationship included long seasons of strife before settling into a steady and mature love.

My understanding of divorce and blended families came not just from witnessing them, but through becoming a licensed professional therapist and walking through them myself. This is the book I wish had existed before I married into a blended family. Since 2017, I have remained single after my wife left during a season when my health declined. In that time, I have poured myself into writing what I hope will be a source of clarity, comfort, and guidance. This book is sewn together not just from my own experience, but from years of therapeutic work and the powerful, honest voices of others, people like you and me, who found themselves living inside the complexity of a blended family.

You hold in your hands more than a book; it is a mirror, a guide, and a companion. Whether you're grieving what was lost, rebuilding something new, or searching for meaning in the mess, this book will meet you there. You are not alone. Within these pages are stories of failure and resilience, voices of others who dared to hope, and practical tools to help you piece together the family and future you long for. You do not need to be perfect to belong. You only need the courage to begin again — with grace, with truth, and love.

The Mosaic Family Series®

Available Titles

The Journey, Not the Destination
How Broken Pieces Become a Mosaic Life

Piece by Piece
My Blended Experience of Mosaic Family

The Family Mask
Understanding the Roles We Learned to Survive

Forthcoming Titles

Splinters
Why the Wounds We Carry Hurt More Than the Words That Touch Them

When Love Grows Up
Learning to Love with Maturity, Security, and Grace

The Mosaic Life Series explores how the experiences of our lives, both broken and beautiful, become the pieces that shape who we are becoming.

Each book examines a different aspect of the human journey: identity, relationships, healing, and growth. Together, they reveal that life's most difficult moments can eventually become part of something meaningful.

This series is not about perfect lives.

It is about learning to see how the scattered fragments of our experiences can slowly form a mosaic.

Contents

Part One

Part Two

Part Three

Part Four

Definition Of a Mosaic Family

Mosaic Family refers to a family system formed through remarriage, where individuals from previous relationships come together to form a new, integrated family unit. Each member represents a distinct "*piece*," bringing unique personal histories, roles, and relational dynamics. Boundaries function as the "*mortar*" in the mosaic family structure, providing the necessary cohesion, stability, and clarity to manage communication, expectations, parenting responsibilities, financial obligations, and emotional well-being. The mosaic family conceptualization emphasizes the complexity, adaptability, and resilience of second-marriage families, distinguishing them from traditional nuclear or blended families by acknowledging both their individuality and intentional unity. –Adapted from: Liberty University Dissertation, A Hermeneutical Phenomenological Study Exploring Divorce in Blended Families (Dr. Hudgins, 2025).

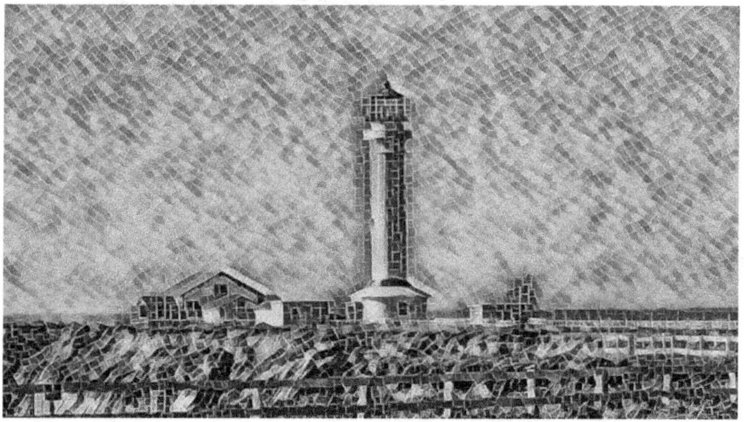

Mosaic lighthouse -Pigeon Point Light Station, Pescadero, CA - ©Steve Hudgins Photograph

PART ONE

ASSEMBLY

Just as a mosaic finds its beauty in the arrangement of broken and imperfect pieces, so too do our scars and flaws weave together to create a richer, more vibrant mosaic of life.

Chapter One

Shards Of Experience

How MY BROKEN pieces became a mosaic

The desire to be the best has always burned brightly within me. It is not solely about crafting the perfect cup of coffee, though that brew, to be honest, is something special too. It is about assembling the intricate mosaic of my life, where each experience adds color, shape, and form. Inside the café, amidst the hum of clinking cups and quiet conversation, I discover a mosaic of human stories; fleeting connections that reveal both vulnerability and beauty.

Over time, I saw that I was not only assembling my own mosaic. I was witnessing one far greater ... God's mosaic art. Each person's story, each sorrow and triumph, is a distinct fragment in a divine work. We are individual shards, imperfect, sharp-edged, uniquely tinted; yet in the hands of the Artist, we are fitted together with intention. Our cracks do not disqualify us. They are where the light slips in.

We are not meant to blend in.
We were made to be placed with purpose.

This book is for those navigating life's fractures; those rebuilding or reassembling their families after loss, divorce, or other significant transitions. Whether you are a parent, therapist, pastor, or someone simply trying to love again after loss, this book is not a manual for healing. Rather, it is a mosaic of stories ... mine, yours, and the ones we are still writing. Each chapter offers a piece of that mosaic, built from memory, mistake, and grace. You will not find easy answers; however, you will find honesty. And hopefully, belonging. Through personal stories, research findings, and lived insights, each chapter will explore a facet of mosaic families: identity, grief, boundaries, belonging, and hope. Like piecing together stained glass, we will discover how broken parts can create sacred patterns.

Before the mosaic is revealed, the table looks like a mess.

The shards were being arranged, sometimes painfully, sometimes beautifully, into something meaningful and whole. Something holy. I remember my mom measuring sugar into her morning coffee while my dad stood silently in his military uniform. Even as a child, I noticed the quiet tension between them, the kind you only learn to name later as disconnection. That moment, so ordinary, stuck with me. Perhaps because I somehow knew even then that family was not just something that we brewed, but rather something that was built with care, and often rebuilt after it breaks.

However, beneath the form of success lies an undertow of doubt. There is constant pressure to outperform the gnawing question: What does it truly mean to be the best? Is it a flawless technique? Recognition? Or is it something more profound, a connection forged over shared moments, a recognition that transcends perfection?

The pursuit of the perfect cup of coffee mirrors my deeper quest: to gather my fractured experiences and understand how even pain was being reshaped into purpose. Beneath the surface of success, doubt lingered. What does it mean to be the best? Is it a technique, recognition, or the deeper connections we forge over shared moments?

Pouring my heart into each cup taught me that mastery is not flawlessness. It is about embracing imperfection, valuing the unscripted moments, and finding beauty in the cracks. This book is a testament to that balance; a journey shaped by ambition, vulnerability, and a relentless pursuit of authenticity.

Growth, like a rich roast, is born in discomfort. Coffee beans must endure heat to unlock their full flavor. Likewise, we must lean into change. Each morning, as I reach for my favorite mug, I am reminded that life, steeped in bitter and sweet experiences, brews the person I am becoming. Growth, like a rich roast, is born in discomfort. For that, I hold deep gratitude.

Life often serves us an overwhelming cup, hot with intensity. Challenges can scald us, yet with time and reflection, they reveal the richness of life. Like coffee cooling, trials deepen our understanding. We may turn to friends, mentors, or faith to temper the heat. And just as we allow coffee to cool, enhancing its flavors, we give ourselves space to process trials reveal life's richness. Patience and reflection become nourishment, prompting growth.

The coffee cools. The story brews. Truth arises.

I remember sitting in the parking lot outside my counseling office one evening, staring at my steering wheel, feeling completely empty. I had just poured everything I had into a client session, while silently managing my own unraveling health, the ache of separation, and the silence waiting for me at home. The irony was not lost on me: the One helping others feel whole had nothing left in his own cup. I learned that night the importance of refilling, not just with rest, but with grace.

Perhaps you have felt that way too; poured out and stretched thin, wondering if there is anything left for you. You deserve a chance to refill your cup. To gather what has been scattered. To be seen. What I have discovered is this: *We do not refill accidentally. We refill intentionally*, with stillness, reflection, community, and God. As coffee needs time to steep, we need spaces to sit, breathe, and let wholeness return.

Wholeness is not the absence of fracture.
It is the honoring of every edge.

True strength is not only about facing challenges, but also about loving deeply and being vulnerable. A ***mosaic family is not a blend*; *it is a masterpiece*** of redemption, built from pieces that were never meant to match. It is within these connections that the essence of our humanity is revealed; in loving and being loved, we find the courage to embrace both our individuality and our shared existence.

Much like a shattered mug reimagined into a vibrant mosaic, what has often been called a "blended family" is not a smooth mixture, but rather, a gathering of unique, jagged pieces, histories, scars, and dreams that create something breathtaking. Each piece holds its own color, texture, and story. The term blended suggests a dissolving of differences and smoothing over individuality. But real families, especially those formed through remarriage and complexity, are not homogenized – they are mosaics.

Mosaic families celebrate individuality while forming connections. They do not erase differences; they *honor* them.

They draw strength and beauty from the visible seams, from the intentional joining of what was once broken or separate. In this way, we phase out the term *'blended,' not out of rejection, but in pursuit of* something more truthful, artful, and resilient. A *mosaic family* is not a blend; it is a *masterpiece of redemption*, built from pieces that were never meant to match, yet together, tell a fuller, richer story.

Life becomes captivating as we piece together who we are. Our experiences, relationships, and disappointments each contribute to a larger picture of our identity. When two people come together, after heartache or divorce, they bring entire mosaics: histories, scars, children, patterns, and lessons. Marriage is not just joining hearts; it is a blending of mosaics.

These pieces may appear random at first, scattered like puzzle fragments waiting to be assembled. As we dive deeper, however, into self-discovery, we recognize that each piece is significant, contributing to a larger picture that reflects our identity. For me, it is the thrill of turning a piece of art in my hand, its edges sharp with potential, and envisioning where it might fit.

The process of self-exploration is much the same. We grapple with questions about who we are, what we value, and how our past shapes our present.

"After my divorce, I took time to heal before even considering another relationship. That changed everything for me," said Joy (Hudgins, 2025).

Challenges become invaluable tools, teaching us about resilience and adaptability. Like that favorite mug we long to piece back together, it can be frustrating when we cannot find all the matching pieces. Life often tests us in overwhelming ways, pushing us to seek clarity amid the chaos. What if, by chance, two favorite mugs are broken and now are mixed?

A beautiful image emerges as we begin to assemble these pieces. We uncover our passions and realize what truly drives us. We identify our strengths, recognizing the traits that make us unique. We gather additional pieces into our understanding through interactions with others, friends, family, and even those who challenge us. Our stories intertwine, enriching our perspective and helping us navigate complexities.

And then, something shifted. I was no longer holding my pieces alone.

When two people come together, especially after heartache, loss, or divorce, it is not just love they bring to the table. It is an entire mosaic: histories, scars, children, patterns, longings, and lessons. Each person arrives with their own carefully gathered fragments ... some still sharp, while others are becoming dull, already beginning to heal.

When Two Mosaics Meet

Coming together after a loss does not mean starting from scratch. It means honoring what each person brings into the relationship and learning how to arrange those pieces with care and consideration. Marriage the second time around is not merely a joining of hearts, but rather a blending of mosaics. Suddenly, your shards meet theirs, your patterns overlap, and sometimes your edges will clash. And if children are part of that sacred mix, the complexity deepens. The artistry of the mosaic becomes more intricate and more delicate.

What I once saw as being broken, I now see as sacred material. Every piece from my past, my identity, wounds, victories, and transformations, is reimagined in a new relationship. Mosaics are *crafted* with time, patience, and a keen eye for detail.

This is how a mosaic family is born, not through perfection, but through intentionality. Intentionally honoring every piece, even the ones we would rather hide, the sharp ones, the ones that carry grief, conflict, and uncertainty. My doctoral research was the light bulb moment that transformed blended families into something more vibrant and alive through the concept of *mosaic*. In God's hands, two broken mugs do not stay broken. Their fragments are gathered to form a new design, preserving uniqueness while creating a new unity.

This mosaic metaphor reminds us that no two shards are alike. Each person contributes a distinct shape to life's mosaic. Our strength lies in loving deeply and being loved in return. Love teaches us to navigate complexity with grace.

"I had to sit with myself for the first time in years. At first, it was terrifying, but then I realized I had no idea who I really was beyond being someone's wife.

– (Tiffany Quote, Hudgins, 2025)

Through these intimate bonds, we uncover our authentic selves and the courage to embrace our unique individuality and shared existence. Love becomes our greatest teacher, guiding us to navigate life's complexities with grace and empathy. As we open our hearts, we invite joy and pain, creating a rich landscape of emotional depth where growth and understanding flourish. In this shared experience of loving and being loved, we illuminate the path toward a more compassionate and interconnected life, awakening a profound and transformative strength within us.

Growing up with a cleft lip and palate and in a strict military home, I felt fragmented in the early years. Those early experiences shaped my search for connection. The disfigurement exacerbated typical bullying, attachment struggles, divorces, remarriages, and cancer; each added a piece to my evolving mosaic.

When the Fractures Begin

Growing up, I learned about fragmentation at an early age. *Fragmentation*, in the emotional sense, refers to a loss of wholeness, when parts of our identity, connection, or safety are disrupted or left unmet. Born with a cleft lip and palate, I underwent surgeries that left me feeling isolated. Raised in a strict military home, I longed for connection yet struggled to find it. Research now confirms that birth defects can impact maternal bonding and attachment, a reality that shaped my early sense of belonging.

My journey has taken me through childhood bullying, then as an adult, attachment struggles, divorces, remarriages, and the experience of raising a Mosaic family, each step adding a piece to my mosaic. I fought for veterans' rights, stood up for fathers, was able to help the governor of Oklahoma create the equal access law in 2001, and stared down cancer twice. Thankfully, cancer has been completely eradicated and will not come back. Through all these battles, I have seen how unresolved wounds, unspoken fears, and hidden traumas shape our attachments, our love, and sometimes falter.

More importantly, I learned to grout the cracks between the shards with faith and compassion. That is the heart of this book: to share my story, clinical stories, and those of divorcees from blended families, and help you recognize and assemble your own unique and personal mosaic. I will provide insight into the new concept of blended families, which I have reframed as *Mosaic Families*. We will explore how mosaic families can shift from fragmented chaos to intentional, vibrant unity.

Wherever you are, whether a parent trying to connect two different families, a partner healing from past wounds, or someone standing among the shards of life's disappointments, know that you are not alone. Every piece has value. Every story belongs. When arranged with care, your mosaic reveals a masterpiece of resilience, love, and hope.

"I went into my second marriage thinking it would fix what was broken in me. Instead, I had to fix myself first." (Mark quote, Hudgins, 2025).

From Brokenness to Design

Before we move forward, let us pause to define what a mosaic truly means, not just as an art form, but as a metaphor for love, family, and healing. So, what is a mosaic? A mosaic is more than just an arrangement of broken fragments; it is an art form where each unique shard is carefully placed, no matter how jagged or mismatched, to create a unified, beautiful design. In the same way, our lives and our families are mosaics, formed by diverse, sometimes imperfect pieces of our individual experiences, relationships, and histories.

Throughout this book, I will reveal pieces of my mosaic by sharing personal stories, research, and the fragmented voices that were vulnerable enough to share their jagged edges of a divorce from "blended families." Pseudonyms are used to protect their true identity. These stories, layered together, offer a deeper understanding of how mosaic families form and how their unique dynamics can be navigated with intentionality, grace, and resilience.

In the next chapter, we will explore what makes a mosaic family distinct and how each piece, no matter how fractured, has the potential to contribute to something greater than itself. As an individual piece of the mosaic, I flourish not despite my cracks and chaos, but because of them; each story of adversity and journey of resilience I carry contributes to the vibrant masterpiece of love and understanding we create together in a mosaic family. And so, with every cup poured and every shard honored, I began to see what once felt like ruins were the raw materials for something sacred. *Not a life blended, but a life mosaicked — intentionally, beautifully, and piece by piece.*

This is not where the story ends.
This is where the design begins.

We spend so much time trying to appear whole. Wholeness may begin when we stop hiding our cracks. In the hands of love, even sharp edges become part of something sacred. A mosaic declares that every shard matters. As we move into the stories ahead, stories of love, loss, loyalty, and repair, remember this: *the art of family is not about having every piece in place; it's about learning how to hold each one with purpose, especially when it cuts.*

Mosaic Truth

You are not less because you have been shattered.

You are more because you dared to gather the pieces.

In the hands of grace, even what was broken becomes beautiful not by hiding the cracks, But by placing them with a purpose.

This is not the end of your story.

It is the art of becoming whole, piece by piece.

Reflective Questions

? *Have you ever looked back on a painful moment and realized you were slowly gathering pieces, even if you did not know it at the time? What did that process look like for you, then or now?*

? *Have you ever felt pressure to appear "perfect" in your roles or relationships? What did you discover when you embraced imperfections instead?*

? *In what ways do your personal experiences, both bitter and sweet, shape the larger mosaic of who you are today?*

Key Takeaways

O┳ **Perfection is not the goal.** Growth and connection often come through embracing life's imperfections and unexpected moments.

O┳ **Every piece matters.** Although life's challenges, relationships, and passions may seem scattered, ultimately each contributes to a meaningful, unique whole.

O┳ **Self-discovery is a process.** It takes time, patience, and a willingness to honor every part of your story, much like assembling a mosaic design.

O┳ **Strength is found in vulnerability.** Opening up to love, even amid brokenness, fosters deeper connections and resilience.

O┳ **Your story belongs.** No matter how fragmented life feels, each piece is vital in crafting a masterpiece of belonging, love, and authenticity.

Chapter Two

What Makes a Mosaic?

A mosaic is not merely a collection of broken pieces bound by mortar or glue. It is a deliberate work of art, each jagged edge chosen, each color placed with care. Mosaic families are like that; they are not accidental blends. They are an intentional reconstruction of love, faith, pain, and healing. They tell a story not of perfection, but of beauty reborn from brokenness.

Like our lives, mosaics reflect beauty born from difference. Each piece, scar, story, and struggle has texture. It is not the perfect color or symmetry that makes them meaningful; it's how they are held together. Each fragment, no matter how jagged or irregular, carries its own story of where it has been and what it has endured. Some pieces are jagged, others worn smoothly, yet all are shaped by time and experience. In the hands of the artist, these pieces are not discarded or hidden. Instead, they are deliberately chosen, placed with care, and joined together with purpose.

So, it is with our lives. The moments that break us open — losses, failures, betrayals, and unexpected changes — become the very pieces that, when viewed through the lens of grace and intention, can form something more substantial and more beautiful than we imagined. A mosaic does not deny the fractures. Instead, it celebrates them, transforming what was once separate into a pattern of unity and meaning.

The Sacred Middle

I remember sitting across the dinner table with my newly blended family, smiling on the outside while feeling completely lost on the inside. The kids were quiet. The tension was thick. My identity felt scrambled. For those working with stepfamilies, internal identity dissonance is often misread as resistance or behavioral defiance. But in mosaic families, it is usually just grief without language.

Was I doing this right?

Was I allowed to feel unsure?

These questions did not come at the beginning; when everything feels fresh or at the end, when healing takes hold. This was the middle.

Not the hopeful beginning.

Not the resolved, redemptive end. Just the raw, unfiltered space in between — the uncertain middle where you silently ask:

Will this new family ever feel like home?

As we gather the fragments of our experiences, we begin to see that the cracks and contrasts are not signs of weakness; instead, they are signs of resilience. They are the lines where healing and hope take shape. And in that intricate, imperfect design, we find a reflection of both our journeys and the greater story of belonging, love, and renewal.

Throughout my years working in telecommunications engineering, I marveled at the invisible connections that formed complex patterns. These connections mirrored human relationships; fragile yet vital. Hardship led me toward a career in mental health, where I learned the true significance of connection and healing.

As I pursued my doctoral degree, one image kept resurfacing: the mosaic. Blended families (mosaics), often reduced to terms like "step," "blended," and "bonus," deserve language that captures their true complexity and beauty, especially in clinical contexts, where complex family relationships are frequently reduced to mere categories in the mental health field.

The Framework Behind the Art

If you are not a clinician, stay with me — this model will help make sense of what you feel in your own family.

Through my research, I developed the Mosaic Family Systems Theory (MFST) (Hudgins, 2025). This framework builds on Bowen's family systems theory, emphasizing boundaries as the grout that holds diverse pieces together. MFST recognizes that mosaic families thrive not by erasing differences, but by celebrating them while creating healthy connections. Boundaries define the form while supporting individuality. Healthy boundaries allow family members to remain distinct yet interconnected, reinforcing the strength and integrity of the entire system. Building on these findings and inspired by the lived experiences of divorcees from Mosaic families, MFST expands upon Bowen's foundational concepts by accounting for the complexities inherent in Mosaic families, particularly those formed through multiple prior family systems. It underscores the need to establish clear, healthy boundaries not only within the immediate household; also across split family relationships, co-parenting dynamics, and extended relational ecosystems. By doing so, MFST reduces conflict, role ambiguity, and emotional entanglement, common challenges faced by those navigating Mosaic family life.

Drawing from grounded theory principles, MFST integrates practical insights directly informed by those who have lived these realities. Participants in my study shared how a lack of support and undefined roles impacted their emotional well-being and family stability. MFST offers clinicians a structured, adaptable approach, highlighting how intentional boundary-setting and honoring everyone's story can alleviate relational tensions, triangulation, and attachment-related struggles.

MFST offers clinicians a structured and adaptable approach. It highlights how intentional boundaries reduce role ambiguity, triangulation, and attachment struggles common in mosaic families. This model reflects both my research and my faith: that unity is found in diversity, as in Romans 12:4-5 and 1 Corinthians 12:12-27. It invites families to see their mosaic not as broken fragments hastily assembled, but as a beautiful, resilient whole.

Understanding families as mosaics revealed the transformative power of acceptance and intentional connection. Each carefully placed shard contributes to a larger narrative, one of resilience, healing, and love. When we view families through this lens, we recognize that even our broken pieces have a place. Together, we can create a breathtaking masterpiece that celebrates the diversity, challenges, and triumphs that shape us all.

In the mosaic of family, each soul is a shard of color, imperfect yet vital; together they create a masterpiece, where the beauty lies not in uniformity, but in the harmony of our unique shapes. Every crack and crevice tell a story; each glimmering piece reflects a shared joy, reminding us that vulnerability and strength intertwine to form the breathtaking design of love.

"Healing was not immediate, but over time, I realized that I deserved a relationship where I felt valued and respected." (James's quote, Hudgins, 2025).

That is what mosaics teach us: transformation does not happen all at once. It occurs in stages. There is the shattering, the scattering, and then, eventually, the assembling. The middle is messy; however, it is also where colors start to emerge again.

Being 'in process' does not mean you are broken.

It means you are becoming.

What is a Mosaic?

In the vibrant heart of ancient civilizations, mosaics emerged as captivating works of art, each one a dazzling collage of colored glass and stones that whispered timeless tales. These intricate pieces adorned majestic buildings, streets, Roman bathhouses, and bustling public squares, breathing life into the stories of culture and belief. Every tile and shard were carefully chosen, reflecting the collective spirit of the communities that crafted them. As each mosaic piece comes together to create a stunning image, so do families evolve, intertwining their narratives in a beautiful dance of history and tradition.

It is time to shift our perspective and move beyond negative terms like *"step," "blend,"* and *"bonus."* These labels can overshadow the beauty of what families truly represent. Instead, let us celebrate families as a colorful mosaic, where each piece and each member interacts and connects with others, held together by the potent bonding agents of love, respect, and understanding.

In this way, families create a breathtaking picture of unity and diversity, highlighting the intricate interplay of individual stories coming together to form something extraordinary. Such connections remind us that family, in all its forms, is a vibrant color woven from shared experiences, emotions, and aspirations, creating a dynamic masterpiece of human connection.

Notre Dame Mosaic: A Story of Fire and Restoration

The iconic Notre Dame Cathedral in Paris is an unforgettable testament to the beauty of mosaic art. I was fortunate enough to see this cathedral in the 1990s, before the 2019 fire. This architectural marvel, a shining example of Gothic grandeur, is celebrated for its breathtaking stained-glass windows and intricate mosaics that tell stories of faith and history. However, on April 15, 2019, tragedy struck when a catastrophic fire ravaged the cathedral, leaving a charred landscape and a legacy hanging in the balance.

Amidst this heart-wrenching devastation, the precious mosaics, many of which date back centuries, were at risk of irreversible damage. It was a bittersweet moment, a reminder of how beauty can be fragile and fleeting. Yet, hope flickered like the flames that had threatened to consume it. A dedicated restoration process commenced, led by skilled artisans and conservators dedicated to preserving these artistic treasures. Even after tragedy, careful restoration can honor the past while creating something new and meaningful. Like families after loss or divorce, the restoration process is slow, intentional, and sacred.

Mosaic families are not haphazard gatherings. They are intentional creations where each person's story and strength contribute to the greater masterpiece. In both cases, the repair process honors what came before and paves the way for a renewed, more profound connection to the past. Through restoration, art and love can rise again, stronger, and more beautiful than ever.

Life often presents us with moments when we must face the cold truth that some things are beyond repair, much like a beautiful mosaic shattered into countless shards. Families can become these delicate fragments, splintered by circumstances that feel insurmountable. Each piece represents a part of our shared history, imbued with memories and love, yet unable to fit together seamlessly again.

In the wake of such loss, we instinctively gather the scattered fragments, yearning to reconstruct what once was. We seek to create something new amidst the brokenness, driven by a profound hope for the future. Time and again, the participants in my research described feeling as though their lives had split into sharp, disconnected pieces after divorce — memories, routines, and relationships were fractured.

Yet, even in that fragmentation, there was an undeniable pull to piece something meaningful together. One participant put it poignantly: *"It felt like I had been shattered, but I knew I could not stay broken forever. I had to figure out how to rebuild—not just for me, but for my kids."* Their words remind us: Families are mosaics of connection, resilience, and belonging, not smooth blends, but vibrant assemblies of uniqueness.

This is where the concept of blended families comes into play; they emerge as a new mosaic carefully arranged from the remnants of past connections. Mosaic families are not merely haphazard combinations of individuals. Instead, they represent a fusion of once-separate lives, each carrying stories of love, loss, and hope. Several participants shared how boundaries shifted during this blending process, as biological ties intersected with new partnerships, step-siblings formed bonds in shared spaces, and chosen connections took root.

One interviewee remarked, *"It was not easy learning to let go of the old picture of family. Nevertheless, slowly, piece by piece, a new image started to form, one I never expected, but one that felt like ours."* It is through this delicate assembly that resilience emerges, transforming fractured beginnings into something unexpected and beautiful.

Just as an artist can take broken pieces and craft a stunning new work of art, families can reshape their identities through shared experiences and unconditional love. Many individuals I interviewed spoke about how, over time, the once-disjointed pieces of their lives began to fit together in unexpected ways. We began to see how each person brought something valuable to the table.

Each joyful moment acts as a new tile, binding the family together in a way that transcends previous definitions. A client reflected on this transformation, saying, *"My stepdaughter's quirks used to seem foreign to me, but now, they are part of the fabric of who we are."* Everyone's unique traits are no longer merely oddities; they become cherished contributions to a greater, vibrant story; a mosaic of connection, resilience, and belonging.

While some creations may be irrevocably altered, picking up the pieces carries the *potential* for transformation. The mosaic formed by blended families illustrates how, despite past scars, connection and community can flourish, crafting a new narrative that honors the beauty of each shard while celebrating the vibrant, unified whole they create together.

Blended Families: A Mosaic of Connections

As diverse pieces form artistic mosaics, blended families are living mosaics of intricate relationships, histories, and dynamics. Each blended family member brings a unique background, experience, and perspective, contributing distinct pieces to the larger family unit. The beauty of Mosaic families lies in their ability to create something cohesive and beautiful from diverse elements.

In a Mosaic family context, the various pieces may include:

Parents: Each has a unique parenting style, values, and traditions from previous relationships.

Children: Stepchildren and biological children, each bringing their backgrounds and experiences to the family dynamic.

Extended Family: Grandparents, aunts, uncles, and cousins who also become part of the intricate network of relationships. and

Shared Experiences: Traditions, memories, rituals, and challenges faced together bond family members and create a unique family culture.

The Mosaic Grout: Boundaries and Connections

Just as grout binds the mosaic pieces, boundaries bind mosaic families. Emotional, physical, role, parenting, and cultural boundaries give stability while respecting individuality. Participants reflected:

"I learned to acknowledge my emotions and have real conversations."

"I recognize childhood traumas that still trigger me. Now, I am working to cope."

These voices underscore the importance of clarity, empathy, and shared understanding in mosaic families.

Emotional Boundaries

Emotional boundaries are crucial in respecting individual feelings and fostering healthy relationships. Open communication and empathy help families navigate the emotional complexities of blending different familial backgrounds. Individuals I interviewed, or clients, shared the following sentiments: *"I did not share my emotions or feelings ... I have since learned to acknowledge them and have real conversations." "I recognize the traumas from my childhood and how they still trigger me. I understand them better now, and I am working toward coping with those things."*

Physical Boundaries

Physical boundaries encompass personal space and privacy. Each family member must understand and respect the individual time and space needs of their fellow family members. Others shared: *"Physical boundaries encompass personal space and privacy. Each family member must understand and respect individual time and space needs."*

Role Boundaries

Clearly defined role boundaries within the family help prevent overlaps and conflicts. Children must understand their parents' positions and the expectations surrounding stepparents, thereby creating clarity in their relationships. Participants described *"triangulation, where stepchildren became caught between biological parents and stepparents. Weak or permeable boundaries facilitate triangulation and role ambiguity, destabilizing the family unit."*

Parenting Boundaries

Parents need to establish consistent parenting boundaries in Mosaic families. Aligning discipline methods and household rules fosters unity and stability, ensuring all children feel equally valued. Individuals have expressed: *"I have learned the importance of presenting a united front when it comes to correcting children. Biological parents need to take the lead in discipline. This approach helps eliminate ambiguity and reduces the potential for misunderstandings."*

Cultural Boundaries

Each family member brings unique cultural practices and traditions into the mosaic. Recognizing and respecting these differences enriches the family dynamic while fostering inclusivity. Tori's interview revealed how her Amish community disowned her after divorcing and remarrying a second time. Reflecting on her first divorce, she shared, *"My family kept telling me to work through it, even when I was suffering."*

Mosaics, whether in art or the dynamics of blended families, are defined by the harmonious integration of diverse elements into one unified whole. The process of restoring the Notre Dame mosaics serves as a metaphor for the complexities, challenges, and beauty woven into the lives of Mosaic families. Each stone, shard, and boundary contributes to the larger picture, creating a vibrant mosaic of experiences, emotions, and relationships.

Blending shards of mosaics does not mean losing one's identity; rather, it enhances the design's overall beauty by showcasing the uniqueness of each piece. Each tesserae, with its distinct shape, color, and texture, contributes to the harmonious whole without sacrificing its individuality. Similarly, each person's background, culture, and experiences contribute to enriching the collective identity within a Mosaic family or community.

Coming together encourages individuals to share their distinct traits and stories, fostering a sense of belonging while honoring who they are. Rather than erasing their identities, the blending process celebrates diversity, creating a more complex and vibrant mosaic that reflects the richness of each person's contribution. In this way, blending is not about conformity, but about building strength and beauty through unity in diversity.

Several participants in my research described emotions like *"outsiders"* in their Mosaic families, initially struggling to integrate their unique histories into the family structure. Labels like "step" and "bonus" often miss these emotional realities. They can box people in, ignoring the richness of their stories and connections. The mosaic metaphor invites us to see beyond labels and honor what families are building together.

As one participant shared, *"I felt like I had to hide parts of who I was to keep the peace, but over time, I realized those pieces made me who I am."* Another remarked, *"When we finally stopped trying to fit into predefined roles and started listening to each other's stories, which is when things shifted. Our differences became our strengths."*

Their reflections underscore how honoring individuality, rather than forcing uniformity, fosters a resilient and interconnected family. Recognizing each person's quirks, scars, and gifts is the key to a flourishing mosaic family.

In listening to stories like Tori's, we are reminded that culture is not just a backdrop; it shapes our beliefs about love, shame, obedience, and identity. And when those cultural values clash with personal healing, the fracture runs deep. This is where clinical insight becomes not just helpful, but essential. It helps us name the unseen forces driving emotional tension in families that hold diverse identities and histories.

By understanding the art of mosaics, we appreciate the craftsmanship and the intricate connections that bind the pieces together. Every tile in a mosaic, regardless of its shape, color, or texture, plays a vital role in creating a larger, harmonious picture.

Mosaic families can celebrate their individuality while embracing unity, recognizing the uniqueness of each person.

When we turn to the field of mental health for guidance on Mosaic families, we often find something missing. The approach can feel cold, almost mechanical, as though families are puzzles to be solved rather than living, breathing relationships to be nurtured and cherished. The language used terms like *"step-sibling," "bonus parent,"* or *"blended unit,"* tries to fit people neatly into categories; however, families, especially those forged through blending, rarely fit into tidy boxes.

What I noticed, both in my own life and in my research, is that these labels often fall short. They reduce people to roles instead of recognizing the richness of their stories, the depth of their emotions, and the struggles they quietly carry.

Several people I spoke with during my study shared how these terms felt limiting, even dismissive. One participant described feeling as though the title "stepmother" carried a shadow, as if she were forever standing outside the circle of true belonging. Another mentioned how being labeled a *"stepchild"* seemed to highlight what they had lost more than what they were building. Those labels might serve paperwork, but they rarely capture the complexity of living day-to-day in a family where love, loyalty, grief, and hope all blend.

That is why I began to see blended families differently, not as fragmented units patched together, but as mosaics — complex, yet unified. Each person brings their unique color, their rough edges, their cracks, and their shine. Instead of boxing them into predefined roles, we can celebrate how each piece fits together to form something entirely new, something beautiful because of its diversity, not despite it.

When Language Becomes a Lens

It is one thing to redefine family in our hearts. It is another to give that redefinition a name. Language matters. The labels we inherit shape not only how others perceive us, but also how we perceive ourselves. For mosaic families, the power to rename and reclaim identity is not a luxury; it is a lifeline. This is where story meets system, where emotion meets insight, and where clinical language must rise to meet lived experience.

The identity constructs within mosaic families involve navigating boundaries that might not fit neatly into established frameworks. Each individual's personal narrative deserves recognition and respect, as it contributes to the overall health and well-being of the family unit.

For example, participant Joy shared how she constantly felt she was walking a tightrope, trying to create stability for her children while assuring her new spouse was not being pushed aside.

"I constantly felt like I was walking a tightrope, trying to create stability for my children while making sure my new husband did not feel pushed aside."— Joy (Hudgins, 2025)

Sarah echoed similar struggles, balancing the demands of being both a mother and wife, often feeling like she was failing at both. These stories underscore that when mental health services focus solely on roles or categories, they risk missing the emotional realities these families face.

Instead, what families crave is recognition of their complexities, the mosaic of relationships, unresolved pasts, and hopes they bring to the table. Moving toward an integrative, empathetic approach means listening for these nuances. It requires stepping beyond rigid definitions and acknowledging that no two Mosaic families are the same; their identities are layered, their dynamics fluid.

By doing so, therapists and counselors can foster spaces where individuals feel truly seen, not boxed in, but supported in weaving their unique family narratives into something cohesive and meaningful. Acknowledging the nuances and relationships between these identities, we can move toward a more integrative and empathetic approach to mental health services.

Like in a mosaic, where every piece has its place and importance, each family member must have their own space to thrive, express their feelings, and establish their identity. By embracing this perspective, we can help foster a supportive environment that promotes mental health and emotional resilience, a true testament to the beauty of diversity and connection. In doing so, we create a framework that acknowledges the complexities of Mosaic family dynamics and champions the individuality of its members, allowing them to flourish within a loving and inclusive environment.

Let the art of blending families inspire you! Cultivate creativity, understanding, and respect for each person's story, and you will create a loving and inclusive atmosphere where everyone feels valued and heard. By advancing mental health conversations to reflect this complexity, we can cultivate environments where every family member feels valued, heard, and integral to the family's collective journey.

Perhaps the most incredible masterpiece is not the one without cracks, but the one that dares to embrace them. Mosaic families thrive not by hiding differences, but by placing them with purpose, thereby creating a sacred, resilient whole. Maybe you're in the middle right now, grieving the past, questioning the present, unsure of what's next.

Don't rush through it. The middle is where clarity begins to rise from the confusion. It is where hope quietly returns.

Stay with it. There's beauty coming, even if all you see right now are pieces. *God is not finished with your mosaic.* Not even close.

Where Fragments Become Frameworks

Clinical Insight: Applying the Mosaic Frame

- Role ambiguity is typical in the early stages of mosaic family development. Do not force identity; allow roles to form organically.
- The "middle" is often when families seek therapy, not because they failed, but because the friction finally surfaced.
- Avoid quick-fix language in treatment. Instead, name the sacredness of the process: building family, piece by piece.

Mosaic Truth

Mosaic families are not defined by how perfectly the pieces match — they are determined by the care with which they are placed.

It is the intention, not the origin, which holds them together.

Boundaries are not barriers; they are the grout that builds strength.

Love does not erase difference; it honors it.

And in doing so, it creates something more meaningful than sameness ever could.

Reflective Questions

- ? Have you ever felt like a piece that did not quite fit within a family or community? What helped you find where you belong?
- ? In what ways can honoring the unique stories and traits of those around you strengthen your relationships?
- ? Are there rigid labels or roles in your own life that feel limiting?
- ? How might reframing those allow more connection and understanding?

Takeaways

- **Mosaic families thrive on diversity.** Each member brings a unique history, personality, and perspective, contributing to a vibrant, interconnected family system.
- **Labels like "step" or "blended" often fall short.** A genuine connection arises from recognizing the emotional depth that transcends clinical or societal categories.
- **Boundaries are the grout.** Healthy boundaries allow family members to stay distinct yet united, reinforcing both individuality and togetherness.
- **Mental health approaches need to evolve.** Supporting blended families requires acknowledging the nuanced and dynamic nature of their relationships, rather than trying to fit them into predefined boxes.
- **Every piece has a purpose.** Whether jagged or smooth, each life experience adds to the rich, resilient picture of the family mosaic. understanding the Mosaic Blueprint

The Mosaic Blueprint

One of the significant differences between the Mosaic Family Systems Theory (MFST) and Bowen Family Systems Theory is their perspective on where a family's story begins. Bowen's model does a great job explaining concepts like keeping your sense of self, noticing when people emotionally cut off, and spotting patterns that run through generations. However, Bowen's work is based on the idea of a steady, continuous family structure that has never been fractured.

Mosaic families rarely start there. They are built from fragments — pieces of different histories, roles, loyalties, and even unhealed traumas, often coming from two or more completely separate family systems. That changes everything. It means we have to approach boundaries differently and be honest about how old wounds can shape the way we relate to each other right now.

In this blueprint, you'll see three main areas to look for in your own story.

Fragmented Piece Burdens are the emotional wounds and core beliefs we carry from our past.

Boundary Keeper Roles are the ways we protect ourselves, sometimes by holding people at arm's length, sometimes by stepping in too far.

Grout Rescuer Roles are the ways we try to fill in the gaps, some of them healthy, some of them exhausting.

This is not about blame. It is about awareness. Families are living mosaics, which means the pieces and the roles can shift as we grow, heal, and choose differently. Once you can see the whole design, you can decide what's worth keeping, what needs reshaping, and what you're ready to let go of.

Mapping the Mosaic Family: Roles and Burdens

A visual guide to the emotional burdens, protective roles, and connecting strategies found in Mosaic Families

MFST: The Strains Your Mosaic Family Carries

FRAGMENTED PIECE BURDENS

Emotional wounds carried from prior family systems

PAINFUL FEELINGS

- Grief from divorce or separation
- Guilt over divided loyalties
- Anxiety about belonging
- Resentment toward step-relatioyns
- Insecurity abouut role and value
- Loneliness in a crowded home
- Fear of more relational loss

PAINFUL BELIEFS

- I do not fit anywhere in this family
- "Love is conditional
- "T| trust, I will be hurt again"
- I am an outsider in my own home

BOUNDARY KEEPER ROLES

Protective strategies to manage connection and prevent hurt

- Over-functioner Over-helper
- Peacekeeper at personal cost
- Emotional gatekeeper (deciding who gets access to feelidngs)
- Parentified child /aduitified role
- Controiler of schedules and traditions
- Loyaltymonitor between households
- Slient absorber of tension
- "Prove-my-worth" performer
- Deflector through humor or distraction
- Avoider of deep topics

GROUT RESCUER ROLES

Ways family members try to 'fill the gaps'—healthy or unhealthy

- Overcompensating with gifts or experiences
- Aligning with one "side" for safety
- Numbing througih work, busyness, or screens
- Using spirituality as avoidance instead of healing
- Hypervigitance to others' moods
- Self-sacrificing to keep uulty
- Seeking outside affirmation over internal stability
- Repeating old relaional patterns despite cost
- Acting out to test loyalty
- Emotional withdrawal to avold rejection

When you step back and see your family through this blueprint, you start to notice patterns you might have missed before. You might recognize a burden you have been carrying for years. You might see a role you slip into without thinking. You might even realize that some of the ways you have tried to keep the family together have been wearing you down instead of building you up.

The point is not to get it perfect. The point is to start seeing it. Because once you can name it, you can change it. That is the beauty of a mosaic; pieces can be lifted, reshaped, and placed in new ways. They can be moved, reshaped, and placed in ways that create a design worth keeping.

I think of one evening with a family in counseling. The stepdad sat on one side of the couch, arms crossed, quiet. His wife sat in the middle, leaning forward, speaking for both of them. On the far end, her teenage son scrolled on his phone, never looking up. They were all in the same room, but in three different worlds. Each was holding their own burdens, keeping their boundaries, and trying in their own way to hold things together. None of them were wrong — they could not see how their pieces might fit.

In the next chapter, we are going to look at what happens when those pieces do not seem to fit. The jagged edges. The gaps you cannot quite close—the moments when you wonder if this family will ever feel like home. And we will talk about how those places, as uncomfortable as they are, can also be where the real work of building a mosaic family begins.

The pieces that do not seem to fit are often the ones that teach us how to build with more grace, patience, and love.

Chapter Three

When Pieces Don't Fit

This chapter explores the fragments, the broken, unspoken, and unresolved pieces of our lives that often shape us more than we realize. These pieces don't disqualify us. They form the raw material of our mosaic. By understanding the source of our fragmentation, we can begin to place each shard with care and intention.

Have you ever wondered why some patterns keep repeating in your life?

Why does love feel fragile after heartache?

This chapter invites you to trace those cracks — not to hide them, but to heal them.

Experience is the silent teacher that shapes our understanding, guiding us through the labyrinth of life. Wisdom is born not from success, but from the truths revealed through failure. Our stories are made of joy and pain. Every experience, every hurt, every relationship becomes a piece in the mosaic of who we are. Often, we fail to reflect on the colors and contours of those pieces, especially when they carry the hues of childhood hurt. Those early cracks, like the jagged edges of a cherished coffee mug chipped over time, leave marks, whether we realize it or not.

The Scars We Carry

Some of the most powerful wounds are the ones we never had words for.

My research revealed how these early fractures, unseen yet deeply felt wounds, influenced how people approached relationships later in life. One participant shared, *"I did not realize how much my childhood trauma shaped my reactions until it was too late."* That recognition mirrored my discovery.

The shards we hide often hold the most apparent truth.

As I traced back the intricate threads of my own story, I saw how my foundation had been poured while navigating the turbulence of a strict military household, childhood bullying, and physical scars. Those experiences shaped my search for connection, leaving cracks that I did not fully understand until I reached adulthood. It was through this connection that I transitioned from my military and engineering career to becoming a licensed therapist.

From Silence to Systems

What I discovered in my own story, I would later see mirrored in others. Emotional fractures from childhood do not disappear with time; they echo. And unless we understand the systems we inherited, we risk repeating their pain. Therapy gave me a language for what I had long felt but never named. Now, let's look more closely at how those early cracks become patterns and how we can interrupt them.

Participants in my study echoed similar patterns. They described how unhealed childhood wounds shaped their reactions, how they carried emotional baggage into new relationships, trusting like they were holding something fragile, and always bracing for it to break.

These stories remind us that unless we pause to examine and reassemble the shards of our past, we risk recreating the same painful patterns, spilling unresolved pain into new relationships like a cup already too full.

Nevertheless, like the right amount of heat brings out coffee's richness, our painful past can become a catalyst for transformation. **The beauty comes not in hiding the cracks**, but in placing them with care. That is how we build something more substantial, because of the fractures, not despite them. Many participants recognized this; they spoke of patterns they repeated until they paused to heal.

"I learned by attending individual therapy that healing must happen before stepping into something new," said Joy.

Growing up in a strict, legalistic Christian home brought its own set of challenges. I often found myself questioning how I fit into my family's mosaic puzzle, with my role unclear, and my edges not quite matching the rest. The bruises and brokenness of my early years left cracks that I did not fully understand until much later. Yet, I began to realize that the shards of my past, though sharp, carried intricate designs, each one telling a part of my story.

What if the same is true for all of us?

They spoke of fractured beginnings, hidden wounds, and unresolved childhood traumas — shards of their stories scattered across time, carried into adulthood without knowing how to piece them back together. Tiffany shared how the shadows of her past shaped the very reactions that later unraveled her marriage:

"It took me years to understand how much my childhood trauma shaped how I reacted. By the time I saw it, damage had already been done." — Tiffany (Hudgins, 2025)

Their words remind us that the hurt we experience early on does not stay confined to the past; it quietly weaves itself into how we attach love and trust.

What if those jagged, mismatched pieces were not meant to be discarded? What if our brokenness, like in mosaic art, is essential to the design? How do these unique fragments create a picture of who we are today? Where do they belong in the grander design?

James reflected on how his wounds led him to repeat painful patterns: *"I kept making the same mistakes because I never healed properly."* He was not alone in that realization.

Some wounds stay silent until the mosaic begins to speak.

Therapist Insight: Healing Before Rebuilding

Clients often bring old wounds into new relationships without realizing it. Therapy helps surface loyalty and bind with childhood pain that silently sabotages second marriages. Naming pain is the first step in reframing it. Healing does not begin with the next person; it begins with the following honest conversation. Many participants spoke of the moment they recognized that healing had to happen, not after the next relationship, but before. Joy's voice still resonates with me: *"I learned by attending individual therapy that healing must happen before stepping into something new."*

Their stories, much like mine, point to something powerful.

Life does not hand us a finished picture; it offers us pieces to assemble. And it is up to us to fit them together with grace, honesty, and time. We must pause, reflect, and intentionally fit those pieces together, honoring each fragment's role in shaping our journey.

This is not a blended life; it is a '*mosaicked*' life. Every broken part tells a story, and every story belongs.

A mosaic declares that every shard matters.

So, as you sip your coffee and reflect on your mosaic, ask yourself:

Which pieces have I overlooked?

Which shards, though painful, have taught me resilience, compassion, or strength?

Moreover, how can I start arranging them in a way that reflects where I have been and who I am becoming?

The past often leaves tender scars, quiet echoes of pain and disappointment that linger long after the events have passed. These wounds subtly inform how we perceive ourselves, how we interact with others, and whether we permit ourselves to hope. They can keep us cautious, hesitant, and trapped in self-doubt, quietly whispering that we are defined by the hurt we have endured. Nevertheless, here is the thing: it is not the wounds that shape our potential; rather, it is the courage we muster to face them and how we respond to them that defines us.

I often wonder how many of us are still carrying pieces of our childhood without realizing it. How many of us silently ask: *Am I worthy of love beyond the bruises life has left behind?* These thoughts resonated with me before I became a therapist.

One participant in my research, Sarah, spoke to this tension beautifully. She shared, *"I kept thinking I had failed, but then I realized divorce was not the end of my story. It was the beginning of me choosing myself for the first time."* For her, as with so many others, it was not the breakup that marked her growth; it was the bravery to sit with the shards of disappointment and reshape them into something stronger, more beautiful. Sue confided, *"I have many traumas from my childhood, and I have yet to unpack. Moreover, some things trigger me. I recognize them, I understand them, and I am working toward where I need to be and how to cope and deal with those things."*

Her honesty reminds us that we all carry hidden hurts that surface when life unpacks them. Healing begins when we stop running from the broken pieces and place them in perspective, and with purpose.

I cannot count how many times I have asked myself these quiet questions:

How much of who I am today is shaped by wounds I never intended to carry?

Have I let those old hurts dictate how I love, parent, and connect with others?

As well, when will I finally feel whole, not because the scars are gone, but because I have learned to embrace them?

The journey to healing does not happen in a straight line. It often begins in the quiet, painful moments when we realize the patterns we have repeated incessantly, the emotional baggage we have carried from childhood into adulthood, and how those unhealed parts of us color everything. Whether it is clinging too tightly in relationships, fearing abandonment, or struggling to trust, those old wounds have a sneaky way of resurfacing. I refer to these painful moments not as triggers or baggage but as splinters.

James's realization was not unique; it was deeply honest. He finally saw the repeating cycle and admitted what many of us fear: healing does not happen by accident; it requires us to stop and examine what hurt us. And isn't that something we all grapple with at some point? The realization that healing is not just about moving on; it is about looking inward, acknowledging the tender places, intentionally choosing growth, and learning to recognize and pull out these splinters of the past.

I remember sitting alone in my house after the divorce, staring at a box of old photos. Each one felt sharp, too painful to look at, too meaningful to throw away. That is when it hit me: I did not need to erase my past to move forward. I needed to find where those pieces still belonged. Not all in the same place, but in the right place. That is where healing begins, in choosing not to discard your story, but to rearrange it.

I do not want to sugarcoat the process. Confronting the splinters of the past, whether childhood traumas, broken trust, or personal failures, is messy and uncomfortable. However, it is in that messiness that fundamental transformation happens. With all its cracks and sharp edges, the past holds the pieces of a mosaic we are still building. The past leaves scars, subtle and powerful. These shape how we view ourselves, engage with others, and risk hope; however, it is the courage to face them, not the wounds themselves, that defines our potential. Sarah's story stayed with me. Her insight reminded me: healing does not erase the past. It invites us to reframe it — and start again. *"I kept thinking I had failed, but then I realized divorce was not the end of my story. It was the beginning of me choosing myself for the first time."*

Have you ever felt like your life has been lived in pieces?

Sometimes, I wonder what would happen if we stopped running from those broken pieces. What if we arranged them tenderly instead of hiding them, honoring each fracture as proof that we survived?

Reclaiming your story does not erase the past; instead, it allows it to inform how you build your future with more intention and self-compassion. Healing is messy and uncomfortable, yet that is where transformation happens. The past holds the pieces of a mosaic we are still building. Reclaiming your story allows it to shape your future with intention, instead of pain.

We do not start life with pre-assembled images. We are handed pieces, some smooth, some jagged; it is our task to fit them together with intention and grace. Ask yourself:

Which pieces have I overlooked?

Which painful shards have taught me resilience?

How can I arrange them to reflect growth?

Could my pain be part of a design — not a flaw, but a feature in the mosaic?

The art of our lives lies in gathering fragments. They are part of our vibrant, intricate design. It is time to place them with purpose, creating something resilient, beautiful, and uniquely ours. You were never meant to blend into something you are not. You were made to mosaic, piece by piece, story by story, grace by grace.

The beauty of a mosaic life is not in how perfectly the pieces fit, but in how intentionally they are placed.

You are not a mistake.

Your story is not wasted.

And the middle, the fractured, in-process, not-quite-there-yet middle becomes holy ground. Keep building. Keep believing. The masterpiece is still unfolding.

As we begin to recognize the sacred work of assembling mosaic families, it is helpful to step back and examine the individual pieces and what holds them together. Every family has its mix of people, pasts, and pressures. Each element brings color and complexity, yet without grout, the values, boundaries, and intentional practices that bind them, those pieces remain scattered.

The chart below offers a way to visualize these mosaic pieces in your own family. What roles are represented? What emotional glue is still forming? As you read, consider where your family mosaic is strong, and where healing or support might still be needed.

Assembling the Mosaic: What Holds a Family Together

Each family brings unique elements, but without the grout—values, communication, boundaries—those pieces remain disconnected. This chart helps visualize your mosaic in real terms.

Family Mosaic Pieces

Mosaic Piece (Unique Family Elements)	Grout (What Binds & Supports Each Piece)
Biological Parent	Respect for prior relationships & clear parental roles
Stepparent	Patience, acceptance, and gradual trust-building
Stepchildren	Open communication & emotional safety
Ex-Spouse	Healthy boundaries & co-parenting agreements
Siblings (Biological & Step)	Conflict resolution skills & shared experiences
Grandparents / Extended Family	Inclusive traditions & respect for diverse family ties
Cultural/Religious Backgrounds	Mutual respect & openness to learning each other's traditions
Past Traumas / Emotional Baggage	Therapy, self-reflection, and healing practices
Family Traditions from Previous Families	Blended new traditions honoring old, while creating shared meaning
Different Parenting Styles	Unified parenting strategies & consistent boundaries
Unresolved Loyalties or Conflicts	Transparent dialogue & space for children to express feelings freely
Individual Identity (for each family member)	Affirmation of uniqueness & encouragement of self-expression
Emotional Needs	Empathy, active listening, and emotional Availability
New Family Milestones (marriages, births, moves)	Shared rituals and flexibility to adapt together

Mosaic Truth

Healing does not mean forgetting the fracture.

It means learning to place it with purpose.

Our broken pieces are not proof of failure; they are proof we survived.

The mosaic of our life is not formed by perfection, but by the grace to begin again.

Even the jagged edges belong.

Even the pain can find its place.

Furthermore, it is often through those very shards that light shines through.

Reflective Questions

- ? Which childhood experiences, whether joyful or painful, do you still carry as shards in your mosaic?
- ? How have past wounds, left unexamined, shaped the way you trust, love, or engage in relationships today?
- ? Are there pieces of your story that you have hidden away because they felt too jagged or painful to face? What would happen if you gave them a place of honor instead?
- ? In what ways can you begin to intentionally rearrange the fragments of your life to reflect growth, healing, and self-compassion?

Key Takeaways

- **Unhealed wounds silently shape us.** Childhood trauma and past experiences often influence how we approach relationships and life decisions well into adulthood.
- **Patterns repeat until addressed.** Without reflection and healing, we risk carrying unresolved baggage into new relationships, recreating old cycles.
- **Strength lies in the broken pieces.** Each crack, scar, and jagged edge has the potential to be transformed into something resilient and beautiful.
- **Intentional reflection fosters growth.** Taking time to examine the shards of your past allows you to create a cohesive, meaningful life mosaic.
- **Your mosaic is uniquely yours**. Honoring every part of your journey gives you the power to redefine your narrative.

PART TWO

CREATING THE MOSAIC

"Just as a mosaic transforms scattered fragments into a stunning masterpiece, our diverse experiences define the essence of who we are — love, resilience, and connection. Each piece, though distinct, contributes to a greater narrative, illustrating that our identities are shaped not by solitude but by the beautiful interplay of community and shared journeys."

Chapter Four

The Language of Family

This chapter examines the labels we use to describe modern families, terms such as "step," "blended," and "bonus." While these words are familiar, they often fall short of describing the beauty and complexity of families built after loss, divorce, or transition. These are the labels we use to shape the way we see ourselves and others. That is why this chapter examines honestly where those labels can be helpful, where they are hurtful, and why the metaphor of a Mosaic Family might offer something more honest, hopeful, and whole.

Think about coffee beans. At first glance, they seem simple; however, under pressure and heat, their true richness is released. Family names carry a similar story, transformed by experience, shaped by what they've endured, and deepened by time. Just like the names in families, each one carries a history, a transformation, a story of belonging. It is not until they are roasted, transformed through heat, that their authentic flavors emerge. Each light, medium, or dark roast changes the bean's identity. What started as a humble seed now becomes something entirely different, richer, more complex, more aromatic.

They are not just about shedding old labels, but about deliberate transformation. A new name carries layers of history, loss, growth, and possibility, much like each coffee bean carries its journey from seed to cup. How we redefine ourselves, or how others redefine us, shapes how we belong, how we connect, and how we relate to others, just as each roast influences how the coffee will taste and be experienced.

Name changes are not just labels; they mark significant shifts in identity. They reflect grief, growth, and new beginnings. In Family life, redefining ourselves shapes how we connect and where we fit.

This is not theory. It is personal. I remember the first time someone introduced me as a "stepdad." It hit me harder than I expected. Not because it was inaccurate, but because it felt like the title came with a story I hadn't lived yet and wasn't sure I would ever live up to. I didn't feel like a stepfather. I felt like a man trying to earn trust in a house full of fragile hearts, mine included. In that moment, I realized how quickly a label can both define and distance us from one another.

Each shift in identity, whether self-chosen or assigned by others, carries weight. These aren't just circumstantial changes; they are invitations to reimagine what it means to belong and connect. This is especially true when it comes to family.

Labels reduce. Mosaics restore.

Imagine, for a moment, crafting a vibrant mosaic from the fragments of your past, with each tile representing a family member, a life experience, or a personal history. Some pieces may be smooth and colorful, others jagged, marked by loss, trauma, or transition fractures. Forming a family means piecing individual shards together with grout to create an overall picture, while honoring each piece. Blending a family is not like mixing paint or folding batter. It is not seamless — it is sacred. What does it truly take to merge families while honoring everyone's identity?

I once sat with a couple in counseling who were navigating life after remarriage. The wife spoke of how her stepdaughter called her by her first name, while the biological children referred to their father simply as "Dad." It wasn't a point of conflict; it was just how things were. However, underneath, both adults admitted they felt uncertain about where they fit. "It is not about the title," the wife said, "it is about whether we matter." That conversation stuck with me. Many families are undertaking the delicate task of forming trust without clear language to describe what they are building.

That is when I realized we aren't blending identities; we are assembling them.

We are honoring history while forming something new. That is not a blended family. That is a mosaic.

In today's world, traditional family structures, once dominated by patriarchal or matriarchal models, are no longer the standard. Families today are beautifully messy, intricately interconnected, and often defy simple categorization. These evolving dynamics led me to reframe how we describe them. I coined the term Mosaic Families, a concept born from my journey and the patterns I uncovered through years of counseling and doctoral research.

In my research, one reality stood out starkly; second and subsequent divorces occur at alarmingly higher rates, 65% higher, to be exact, than first marriages. This statistic is not just a number; it reflects the real stories of individuals struggling to merge their histories, heal old wounds, and build something lasting. The existing language, terms like *"stepfamily," "blended family,"* and *"bonus family,"* often fall short of capturing the complexity, fluidity, and emotional weight involved.

Through examining over thirty different typologies and definitions, it became clear that the fragmented nature of two nuclear families uniting into one was not adequately addressed. Each person in a blended family enters with their mosaic of experiences, attachments, losses, and roles, yet the terminology tends to flatten or 'collapse' these dynamics rather than celebrate them.

Consider the concept of web families, often used to describe modern families, characterized by interwoven, fluid relationships. Biological parents, stepparents, adoptive figures, and close friends may all form part of this web, where roles evolve, and emotional bonds may transcend biology. Web families reflect the reality many of us inhabit, a reality where rigid definitions do not bind connection, but rather by the emotional glue of shared experience and intentional belonging.

While the web family framework highlights interconnectedness, I found it lacked one essential ingredient: the recognition that brokenness itself becomes part of the beauty. The Mosaic Family model emphasizes interconnectedness and the delicate art of piecing together fragments from two or more prior family systems.

Each piece matters.

Each history has a place.

In my research, participants spoke candidly about how the terms applied to their families often felt limiting, as they failed to capture the nuances of grief, loyalty conflicts, or the delicate process of redefining love. Several described the experience as standing at the threshold of something new yet feeling misunderstood or confined to roles that did not accurately reflect their reality.

One participant shared, *"Being called a 'stepmother' felt like I was always standing outside the circle, never fully accepted."* Others echoed similar sentiments, struggling to reconcile societal expectations with their own evolving family identities.

These reflections compel us to ask:

How do the labels we use shape our experience of family?

What would it look like if we discarded the need for tidy definitions and instead embraced the mosaic nature of modern families?

I invite you to pause and reflect:

What labels, imposed by others or self-chosen, have shaped your understanding of family?

Do they honor your journey, or are they ready to be redefined?

Labels can confine or liberate. The terms we use for family relationships carry weight and can influence how we perceive belonging and connection.

Mosaic Families reflect complexity. These families are formed from prior systems that bring together unique histories, relationships, and emotional textures. The Mosaic Family concept emphasizes honoring these distinct pieces rather than forcing uniformity.

Redefining family requires intentionality. Understanding the diverse forms of modern families, such as web families or mosaic families, allows us to foster and develop empathy, flexibility, and deeper connection.

Your family narrative is yours to name. Whether shaped by biological ties, chosen bonds, or blended histories, your family mosaic is a masterpiece that deserves language reflective of its richness.

Redefining the Words We Were Given

The Step-Family

"Step-family" is a word society gives us; a convenient label, easy to say, easy to categorize. For those who live inside these families, the world rarely feels as simple as it sounds.

It traces back centuries, with the *"step"* prefix denoting a relationship formed not by blood, rather by remarriage. It seems neutral enough, even clinical. Yet, the reality behind that word carries far more layers than it initially reveals. Anyone who has walked this path knows it; there is nothing neutral about blending two families, two histories, two sets of heartaches, joys, and expectations into one.

When I hear the word *"step,"* I hear a subtle yet persistent distance, as if one step removed, as if the connection is somehow lesser: a footnote to the original family story. How many of us have stood in that space, trying to love, trying to belong, while still feeling like we are hovering on the periphery?

Maybe you have felt it, too. Maybe you have wondered, quietly:

Does this label really capture who we are?

Or is it keeping us boxed in, defined by what we are not, rather than what we are building together?

For many people I have met, both in my research and in the therapy room, the term carries a weight they never expected or intended to take on. Popular culture has not helped much, either. Please consider how stepparents, especially stepmothers, are portrayed in the stories we grew up hearing: as villains, antagonists, and outsiders. These narratives shape us long before we are aware of them. They lay a foundation of suspicion, even resentment, before anyone can write their own family story. And for children in these families?

Imagine hearing yourself referred to as a *"stepchild"* over and over again. What does it feel like to be labeled by what you are not? To have your identity constantly framed by absence, by a role you did not choose, by a word that defines your place in someone else's story?

We do not grow up seeing ourselves this way. Children do not naturally think of themselves as "less than," or as an addition to someone else's family. They see themselves as sons, daughters, people. Yet labels like "stepchild" subtly reshape that self-image, turning connection into condition, and belonging into a question.

To constantly have your place qualified by something outside your control?

One client who, as an adult, beautifully expressed this tension: *"Every time someone called me a stepchild, it felt like they were reminding me that I did not really belong."* Another shared, *"I just wanted to be part of a family, not part of a category."*

These are not isolated sentiments. They reflect what so many of us feel but rarely say out loud: that language has power. The words we use to describe family can either build connection or create distance. Language is not merely a tool for communication; it is the architect of our reality. The words we choose can either build bridges of understanding or erect walls of division, shaping how we see ourselves, others, and the world around us.

Here, however, is the truth I have come to understand; no label, no term, can fully contain the richness, the messiness, the beauty of the relationships we are trying to create. Families, especially those that emerge from the broken pieces of previous ones, are not linear equations.

They are mosaics. And mosaics do not care if a piece comes from a first marriage, a second partnership, or an entirely different life chapter; they care that each piece is placed with care, intention, and love.

Maybe that is why the term *"stepfamily"* feels like it is missing, something vital. It freezes us in the past, reminding us of what came before, rather than honoring what is being crafted now.

So, what if we paused for a moment to rethink it?

What if we started with the lived experience instead of starting with labels?

What if we asked:

How do these relationships feel, beyond how they are defined?

What stories are we writing together, not because of the label, but despite it?

Can we release ourselves from terms that reduce us and instead embrace the intricate, evolving connections we are shaping?

Because at the end of the day, family, whether by birth, marriage, or choice, is not a static definition. It is an ongoing act of creation.

The Blended Family

The term *"blended family"* is often tossed around casually, evoking images of smooth transitions and perfect family dinners. For anyone who has lived it and stood in the middle of the merging process, it becomes clear how misleading that word can be. It suggests ease, like blending ingredients in a recipe, when the process is more like carefully fitting mismatched shards into a mosaic ... sharp edges and all.

The idea of a *"blended family"* gained traction in the 1980s and 1990s, as divorce and remarriage became more common. It sounds modern, even hopeful. Does it reflect the emotional reality families face when they come together after loss, divorce, or betrayal? My research and personal experience have consistently shown me that blending is rarely a smooth process. It is layered, complex, often messy, and always deeply human.

One participant in my study summed it up candidly:

"They called us a blended family, but nothing felt blended. It felt like oil and water at first."

Blending suggests smoothness, but families are not 'smoothies;' they are mosaics. Every shard, every history, every personality has its shape and color. The goal is not to dissolve into one another, but to be placed together with care and consideration. Their words lingered with me because they mirrored what many others had expressed: a constant tension between trying to form something whole and carrying the weight of past relationships, heartaches, and loyalty.

Oversimplification of Integration

The 'blender image' suggests that all the differences get mixed seamlessly. Real life is far more intricate. Every member, especially the children, brings history, grief, and hopes to the table. Some are holding broken pieces that they do not even know they have, nor how to share.

As previously shared:

"I carried so much baggage from my first marriage into my second."

Her honesty reveals a reality many feel yet few admit; the pieces from the past do not just dissolve. They show up at dinner tables, holidays, and school events, reminding us that we are not starting with a blank slate. We are arranging jagged, lived-in pieces, often while nursing wounds that are still healing.

It begs the question:

What if blending is not about dissolving differences, but learning how to hold them together gently?

Impact on Individual Identities

Labels like "blended" can unintentionally gloss over the rich, often fragile, identities each person brings into the family mosaic. When we use this word too casually, it risks silencing the distinct voices of children, stepparents, and extended family members. Each one has its unique narrative, joys, disappointments, and traumas, all layered beneath the surface.

One participant described this tension:

"I felt like I had to fold into the new family, but no one asked how I felt about it."

How many children, how many parents, have felt the same way, like they were expected to fit neatly without room to honor their own unique story?

So I ask:

In your own family, whose story might need 'space' to breathe?

Loyalty Conflicts

Perhaps the most heart-wrenching theme that emerged from my research and personal journey was loyalty conflict. Children, especially, are often caught in the crossfire, torn between honoring their biological parents and forming new bonds with stepparents or half-siblings. It is not a simple choice. It is a tightrope walk. It is why I fought for my children and won custody of them due to the parental alienation syndrome, but at what cost, as it put them in the middle of an adult conflict that should not have existed in the first place. I compelled their mother to believe that our differences have no place in the loyalty of our children's love for us.

One client in therapy shared,

"It felt as if I got too close to my stepdad, I was betraying my real dad."

Another confided,

"I never knew if loving my step-siblings meant I was leaving my old family behind."

These are not minor dilemmas. They will shape a child's views of love, loyalty, and belonging for years to come.

So I invite you to reflect:

Where might unspoken loyalty conflicts still live beneath the surface in your own family?

Romanticizing the Integration Process

Popular media often portrays blended families through a romanticized lens, a fresh start, a hopeful new chapter, and a picture-perfect second chance. This narrative, however, can create silent pressure to meet unrealistic expectations. Many participants, clients, and friends have described feeling as though they were failing when conflict arose, as if they had missed some secret formula for resolving it.

Joyce, for example, admitted, *"I thought we were supposed to just blend. No one told me how much grief and work came with it."*

It leads me to wonder:

How often do we burden ourselves and our families with a fairytale version of togetherness when real connection is forged in the messiness of day-to-day life, through conversations, and with patience?

The Bonus Family

On the surface, the term *"bonus family"* sounds inviting and even charming, as it is a bright, shiny label meant to soften the edges of remarriage and family blending. When you peel back the layers though, the word carries an air of simplicity that often fails to honor the lived experiences of those navigating these complex dynamics. The idea of a *"bonus"* may work well in a game show, but the stakes are much higher in real life, and the emotions far messier.

Calling it a bonus can skip over the grief that came before. A mosaic doesn't cover pain with polish. It honors it, frames it, and lets it become part of something meaningful.

It is easy to assume that adding new family members will naturally feel like a *"plus,"* as if more hands, more hearts, and more relationships can only be positive. If you talk to anyone who has walked the path of remarriage, raising stepchildren, or blending households, you will hear a much different story. It is not that there are no beautiful moments; there are plenty, but they are often hard-earned, built brick by brick, conversation by conversation, tear by tear.

In my research, participants echoed this reality. One child in my office, Fawn, put it plainly: *"At first, everyone told me how lucky I was. They said it was a blessing to have more family, but no one warned me about the loyalty conflicts or the nights I spent wondering if I really belonged."*

Her words reveal what so many feel yet hesitate to say. Being called a 'bonus' does not necessarily make you feel like one. In fact, it can sometimes gloss over the grief, adjustment, and identity struggles that swirl beneath the surface of blended family life.

Oversimplification of Experience

What happens when the *"bonus"* does not feel like a gift?

When children are mourning the loss of their intact family?

When parents are juggling co-parenting arrangements and legal battles?

The bonus label skips over these realities, presenting a highlight reel without acknowledging the behind-the-scenes labor. Many participants and clients have spoken candidly about the emotional hurdles they faced, learning how to trust again, managing divided loyalties, or dealing with the unspoken grief from their first families breaking apart.

Judy's story still stays with me. She shared: *"People kept calling my new marriage a bonus, but inside, I felt like I had lost so much. It wasn't until I addressed that loss that I could really appreciate what I was building."*

It makes me wonder:

How many of us have been given a label that seems bright on the outside but is hollow underneath?

Neglecting Individual Narratives

Everyone in a blended family comes with a story ... stories of past relationships, heartbreak, and childhood experiences that left tender scars. Yet when we slap on the term *"bonus,"* we risk compressing all those stories into something one-dimensional. For some children, especially those who have recently lost a parent or sibling, adjusting to a new parent or stepsibling does not feel like an added benefit; it feels like navigating unfamiliar terrain while still holding onto their sense of identity.

One child client in a therapeutic setting described it like this:

"It felt like I was supposed to fit into this new role overnight — as if being part of a bonus family meant I should forget how things were before."

Is it any wonder that many struggle when we fail to create space for those personal histories to breathe?

Romanticizing Unity

Cultures love a happy ending. The term *"bonus family"* feeds into that desire, suggesting that love will naturally flow, relationships will fall into place, and everyone will live harmoniously. The participants and clients that I spoke with told a different story. They discussed sibling rivalries, parenting disagreements, and moments when pulling away felt easier than leaning in. In my blended family, as a "stepfather," it was challenging to create harmony, especially when children are not fond of the non-biological parent.

Jake reflected on this: *"I had all these expectations that it would feel like one big happy family. But real connection took years, not months."*

So here is a question worth asking:

What happens when reality does not match the idealized picture? Are we permitting families to admit the struggle; to speak openly about the work it takes to build trust and connection?

Unrealistic Expectations

Words matter. When we call something a *"bonus,"* there is an implicit suggestion that it is easy or at least should feel positive from the start. What about the families who do not feel that way? Those still wrestling with tension, resistance, or sadness?

One client in my office described it this way:

"It felt like I was failing because it did not feel like a bonus. It did not feel easy. There was so much history between us all."

His words echo a common experience in Mosaic families — the struggle to reconcile the complexity of real-life relationships with the simplicity of idealized labels.

Blended families deserve the grace to be seen for what they truly are, not simplistic add-ons, but intricate ecosystems of history, emotion, and resilience.

Ignoring Emotional Pain and Conflicts

The word *"bonus"* leaves little room for pain, for conflict, for grief. For nearly every participant in my research, there were moments of deep struggle. They talked about loyalty bonds, where children felt torn between loving their biological parents and welcoming a stepparent. They shared stories of resentment that had been brewing silently beneath the surface, only emerging when families felt safe enough to be honest about the challenges.

These are not minor hurdles; they are defining moments. If we continue to negotiate terms that flatten these realities, we deny families the language they need to process, heal, and grow. James spoke of many experiences, yet few were discussed openly, exposing the heavy weight of repeated rejection. *"I never expected to feel this kind of rejection again. It hurt worse the second time."* His words pierce through the glossy veneer that the word *"bonus"* often suggests. For him and others, forming a new family was not about a fresh start; it was navigating love and trust through the rubble of past betrayals.

Participants like Sue described staying in marriages longer than they should have, which was driven by guilt and conflicts over loyalty. She confessed, *"I did not want my kids to suffer, so I stayed longer than I should have."* This reveals how the desire to maintain family harmony often silences personal needs, creating an emotional bond that complicates the process of blending families.

Joy candidly reflected, *"I learned by attending individual therapy that healing must happen before stepping into something new."* Her insight underscores that for many; the process of merging families is not merely additive; it requires excavation of the hurts that linger beneath the surface.

These voices remind us that when we frame family structures with terms like *"bonus,"* do we risk glossing over the jagged edges of grief, loyalty binds, or the emotional labor it takes to integrate?

How often do we pause to honor the unspoken struggles each person brings to the mosaic?

Embracing a Nuanced Understanding

The more I spoke with participants and reflected on my journey, the clearer it became that “bonus family” might sound cheerful, but it lacks the depth to honor what these families are building.

What if, instead, we shifted our language entirely?

What if we embraced the image of a mosaic — a design composed of distinct, often broken pieces, carefully arranged into something uniquely beautiful?

This concept allows space for grief, individuality, jagged edges, and smooth ones. It honors the stories, histories, and hard-earned connections that define real families, not despite their differences but because of them.

Are you ready to reconsider the language we use to describe families? To move beyond labels and lean into something richer, something that acknowledges the resilience, complexity, and beauty of lives woven together over time?

In the next section, we will explore exactly why *Mosaic Families* offers a deeper, more compassionate framework — one that celebrates the artistry and authenticity of bringing together fragmented yet meaningful lives.

A New Term for Two Families Merging: The Mosaic Family

Through my personal experience, education, clinical practice, and research, I have coined the term "Mosaic Family." In the intricate dance of life, when two nuclear families with a missing biological parent come together, they form a mosaic family. In this vibrant arrangement, each piece, distinct in color and shape, contributes to a collective beauty greater than the sum of its parts. Each family member's individuality is crucial, yet it thrives best within respectful boundaries. Just as individual shards of glass come together to form a stunning image, the blending of diverse backgrounds, experiences, and traditions shapes a richer family narrative, fostering resilience and love.

In this convergence, differences are not challenges to be overcome but are elements that enhance the picture of shared life. Boundaries serve as the framework that allows these differences to coexist harmoniously, teaching us that unity is found not in uniformity but in the celebration of our unique stories coming together into something beautifully complex. This mosaic of relationships cherishes the beauty of variety and complexity while acknowledging the importance of personal space and mutual respect.

We construct a new family and cultivate a nurturing environment where every piece, every story, is valued and essential. Respecting boundaries ensures that each member feels heard and seen, allowing for healthier interactions and deeper connections.

In our home, we had two children from my previous marriage and two from hers. At first, we were a house full of strangers bound by adult decisions. The kids did not choose this arrangement, yet they were the ones who had to navigate it every day. I remember sitting around the dinner table early on, watching as silence filled the space between us. Eye contact was scarce. Trust was thin. But then again, we kept showing up. We honored each child's rhythm. We did not force the unit; we built it slowly, with respect, boundaries, and a lot of grace. Over time, laughter returned. Little inside jokes were shared. And one day, without realizing it, we weren't just blending, we were mosaicking. We were building something new that honored our unique origins.

It is a reminder that the richness of family life is found in its diversity, and when viewed from a distance, the mosaic becomes an inspiring symbol of togetherness. It provides growth and the unbreakable bonds forged through shared experiences, all of which exist within the framework of kindness and understanding. I assert that the mosaic metaphor effectively encapsulates the journey of two broken homes coming together to form a new, cohesive unit.

Reflecting Diversity and Individuality

At the heart of a mosaic lies the idea of diverse, distinct, and varied pieces coming together to create a unified whole. This is particularly relevant in the context of mosaic families, which often consist of individuals from diverse backgrounds, experiences, and emotional histories. Each member of a mosaic family brings a unique narrative and identity shaped by their previous homes, just as each tile contributes its color, shape, and texture to the collective artwork. This diversity fosters a rich environment where individuals can celebrate their differences while forming meaningful connections.

Psychological research highlights the significance of acknowledging and respecting individual identities within a family structure, as outlined in the Bowen Family Systems Theory[1]. Studies in family dynamics show that when family members are encouraged to maintain their individuality while collaborating with others, overall family cohesion improves. The mosaic metaphor emphasizes this principle by honoring each person's unique background and contributions, thereby promoting a sense of belonging that is essential for emotional well-being.

1 https://www.thebowencenter.org/introduction-eight-concepts

Interconnected Relationships

In a mosaic, the individual pieces are interconnected, forming a complex design that reflects the relationships within a blended family. Each relationship may vary considerably in strength and harmony, mirroring the multifaceted nature of human interactions. Research in family studies shows that the success of these types of families often hinges on the quality of relationships between stepparents, stepsiblings, and biological parents. The mosaic model emphasizes that individuals can form new bonds that incorporate elements from their original family structures, even in the face of challenges.

When a second divorce occurs, however, the carefully placed pieces of this intricate mosaic risk becoming fragmented again. The emotional ties painstakingly built between stepparents and stepchildren, as well as between siblings who may have finally felt like family, are often strained or severed, leaving gaps where connection once flourished.

I felt this deeply during the unraveling of my own blended family. My wife at the time decided to move back, three states away, to help care for her aging parents. It was not a malicious choice; it was a family obligation. It marked the beginning of the fracture. At the same time, my parents, holding to a rigid Christian belief that I should not have remarried, grew emotionally distant. Layer that with the reality of parental alienation from my children's biological mother, and what was already fragile began to splinter. I had chosen to love and raise her child as my own, to forge something redemptive out of brokenness.

Looking back, I realize that the complexity of adult decisions had a profound impact on the children involved, my children, her child, and our whole household. These weren't simply logistical changes. They were emotional earthquakes, shaking the very bonds we'd worked so hard to form. I now understand how quickly a mosaic can feel like scattered shards again, not from a lack of love, but from the harsh demands of real life, aging parents, divided loyalties, and unresolved grief.

Many participants in my research spoke about this loss, describing the pain of being disconnected not only from a spouse, but also from children they had come to love deeply. I felt this when I went through the blended family divorce.

Jana shared her story poignantly, *"Losing the marriage was one thing, but losing the relationship with my stepchildren felt like losing a part of myself."*

Second divorces create a ripple effect, disturbing the cohesion of the mosaic and introducing feelings of rejection, abandonment, and confusion. For children, especially, the fracturing of yet another family structure can compound earlier wounds, reinforcing a sense of instability and making it harder to trust in future relationships.

Just as a mosaic's beauty lies in how each piece fits and supports the whole, so too do blended families depend on the delicate balance of their connections. When a second divorce occurs, it is not merely two individuals parting ways; it can shatter the fragile unity that the family had worked so hard to construct.

Resilience and Creativity

One of the most powerful aspects of a mosaic family is its inherent resilience. While a mosaic can be altered or repaired, it must navigate the inevitable challenges that arise when two distinct units combine. Research has shown that resilience in family structures often hinges on effective communication, mutual respect, and flexibility, traits that are vital for mosaic families as they strive to integrate their differing histories.

Creating a mosaic requires creativity, just as an artist must find innovative ways to arrange their pieces to form a cohesive and visually appealing image. Similarly, mosaic families must embrace creativity in developing new traditions, rituals, and shared experiences that celebrate the backgrounds of all members. This creative engagement fosters collaboration and a commitment to building a unique family identity while honoring previous familial legacies. Thus, the mosaic metaphor highlights the importance of adaptability and creativity, essential qualities in transitioning from two broken homes to a new, unified family.

Boundaries as the Grout

Another critical element of successful mosaic families, as reflected in the mosaic metaphor, is establishing boundaries. Within a mosaic, grout holds the individual pieces together while maintaining their distinct identities. Drawing on research in family therapy, we know that clear boundaries are crucial for healthy family functioning, especially in these families where loyalty conflicts may arise between biological parents and stepparents.

Mosaic families must communicate openly and foster understanding to define their boundaries. This process enables family members to coexist harmoniously while respecting each person's unique experiences and emotions. By focusing on this essential aspect of family dynamics, the mosaic model emphasizes the importance of creating a solid foundation for relationships that supports individual growth while striving for unity.

I remember a moment in our blended family when my wife came to me frustrated, asking why I seemed to correct her children more than my own. At first, I was defensive; I did not see it that way. My son, who was the oldest, had already developed routines: he brought down his laundry, washed his bedding, and did chores without being told. Her children were younger, less disciplined, and their biological father had even admitted it was hard to get them to follow through on tasks. I realized what she was really expressing wasn't just about chores, it was about fairness, perception, and the invisible lines we were crossing as we tried to parent together. I was in the middle of earning my master's in counseling at the time, and even then, I was beginning to understand the profound importance of boundaries in mosaic families.

One hard truth I have learned, both personally and professionally, is that discipline is one of the most emotionally charged roles in a blended family. I once had a friend whose marriage nearly collapsed after her child falsely accused her husband of inappropriate behavior. There was a full investigation. The children were removed from the home. She chose not to leave her husband. Two years later, her child confessed that she had fabricated the story out of anger after being punished. It devastated the entire family.

This woman later joined me on my podcast, *Coached Soul*, to share her story publicly. Her courage and insight have helped others facing similar trials. Stories like hers are sadly not uncommon. Over the years, I have observed similar dynamics unfolding in counseling rooms and headlines. My firm advice, forged from both pain and learning, is this: let the biological parent take the lead in discipline. The stepparent should partner through communication, alignment, and mutual presence, and avoid being the primary enforcer. This approach creates more precise boundaries, reduces resentment, and fosters unity rather than division. Grout holds pieces in place, but it doesn't reshape them; it simply supports them. That is what boundaries do in a mosaic family. They handle each part with care, respecting the origin of every piece.

Moving Beyond Simplification

While traditional terms like *"blended, step, or bonus family"* might suggest a simplistic merging of two households, the mosaic family framework challenges this assumption, presenting a more nuanced understanding of the complex realities involved in forming a new familial structure. Drawing on insights from family systems theory, we recognize that the pathways to integration require more than just logistical coordination; they necessitate emotional labor, ongoing dialogue, and a commitment to fostering a supportive atmosphere.

By framing two independent mosaic families with a missing biological parent, we highlight the intricate dynamics, the beauty of diversity, and the collective strength gained from overcoming challenges. This perspective enables families to view their journey as a creative and collaborative process, transforming potential fractures into opportunities for growth and connection.

In conclusion, the metaphor of the mosaic family emerges as a profound and relevant analogy for describing the complexities of combined households formed from broken homes. Emphasizing the importance of diversity, individuality, resilience, creativity, and the need for clear boundaries, the mosaic concept provides a rich framework that encompasses the nuanced realities of modern family life.

As both an author reflecting on personal experience and an academic engaged in research, I firmly believe that embracing the mosaic metaphor allows us to celebrate the multifaceted dynamics of mosaic families, fostering acceptance and collaboration. Through this unique lens, we recognize that achieving a supportive and loving family environment is a collaborative journey; one where each unique piece contributes to a harmonious and beautiful whole.

The term *"mosaic families"* captures the beauty and complexity of modern family life in a way that words like *"blended," "step,"* or *"bonus"* simply cannot. It reflects the intricate and sacred arrangement of relationships, each piece distinct, yet essential to the whole. This metaphor highlights the beauty of diversity, the significance of individuality, and the complexities inherent in merging different family backgrounds into a unified whole. By examining what a mosaic family embodies, we can gain a deeper appreciation for the intricate dynamics at play within these modern family structures.

As we delve deeper into the concept of mosaic families, it becomes evident that understanding these complex dynamics is crucial for fostering harmonious relationships and promoting growth within mosaic families. Not only does appreciating the beauty of diversity enhance our perspective, but it also allows us to recognize each individual's unique contributions to the family unit, ultimately enriching the collective experience. In this context, let us examine the challenges and opportunities that arise when creating a cohesive environment within a mosaic family.

As you embark on cultivating your unique mosaic family, remember that the beauty of this journey lies not just in overcoming challenges but in celebrating the distinct contributions of each member. Each shard, whether smooth or jagged, bright or subdued, holds significance.

Embrace the process, for every piece adds richness to the mosaic of your lives. You are not merely assembling fragments; you are co-creating a narrative of resilience, acceptance, and connection. Together, you are crafting a work of art, a harmonious and resilient family destined to thrive through love, patience, and understanding.

Breaking Down the Mosaic: Naming the Pieces That Hold Us

To fully embrace the mosaic metaphor, we must examine its components more closely. Just as an artist chooses each tile with intention, so too must we understand the roles, boundaries, and relationships that shape mosaic families. These pieces are not abstract; they are lived. Let us now examine the emotional, relational, and structural elements that form the heart of this family design.

Family Mosaic Pieces Explained

In every Mosaic Family, each member brings unique "pieces," individual histories, roles, values, and emotional experiences. A mosaic, however, is not just about the tiles; it also includes the grout, the binding elements that hold the entire picture together.

Without the grout, the individual pieces remain disconnected, fragile, and incomplete.

Assembling the Mosaic

While each shard of our individual story holds significance, true transformation occurs when we intentionally fit these fragments into the greater picture ... our family mosaic. No family is built from scratch; every member brings their unique piece, shaped by prior relationships, past wounds, cultural backgrounds, and personal identity.

The challenge lies in healing our personal fractures and understanding how these distinct pieces can fit together harmoniously. Like a mosaic artist carefully selecting and binding varied tiles, families must consciously decide how to honor each member's story, creating cohesion without erasing individuality.

The table below outlines some of the most common elements in Mosaic Families, and more importantly, the essential *"grout"* that binds them together. These are not rigid rules, but guiding principles that foster connection, respect, and stability as families assemble their mosaic.

Table 1 *Family pieces and what holds them together to create the "mosaic" (blended) family.*

Mosaic Piece (Unique Family Elements)	Grout (What Binds & Supports Each Piece)
Biological Parent	Respect for prior relationships & clear parental roles
Stepparent	Patience, acceptance, & gradual trust-building
Stepchildren	Open communication & emotional safety
Ex-Spouse	Healthy boundaries & co-parenting agreements
Siblings (Biological & Step)	Conflict resolution skills & shared experiences
Grandparents / Extended Family	Inclusive traditions & respect for diverse family ties
Cultural/Religious Backgrounds	Mutual respect & openness to learning each other's traditions
Past Traumas / Emotional Baggage	Therapy, self-reflection, and healing practices
Family Traditions from Previous Families	Blended new traditions honoring old, while creating shared meaning
Different Parenting Styles	Unified parenting strategies & consistent boundaries
Unresolved Loyalties or Conflicts	Transparent dialogue & space for children to express feelings freely
Individual Identity (for each family member)	Affirmation of uniqueness & encouragement of self-expression
Emotional Needs	Empathy, active listening, and emotional availability
New Family Milestones (marriages, births, moves)	Shared rituals and flexibility to adapt together

From Pieces to Pattern

What you just explored is more than a list — it is a lived reality for many families. These elements do not exist in isolation. They interact, overlap, and sometimes collide. And yet, held together by grace, structure, and intention, they form something sacred. The next step is not just naming the pieces; it is learning how they move together within a living system.

So, what now? We need a new metaphor. Mosaic Families honor jagged edges, celebrate uniqueness, and affirm that love and belonging are crafted intentionally. Every crack matters. Every story counts. And no matter how you entered your family story, by birth, by bond, by brokenness, you belong.

You are not a label.

You are a living piece of something beautiful in the making.

What if there were a way to understand mosaic families ... not just as a metaphor, but as a living system; a framework that gives language to the beauty, the boundaries, and the broken pieces? That is where we are headed next.

From Metaphor to Map

For years, I searched for a way to name what I had lived. The dinner-table tensions, the silences after custody swaps, the ache of trying to belong in more than one household, all of it required more than poetic language. It needed a framework. Mosaic Family Systems Theory (MFST) was born out of that need, not to explain families in cold categories, but to offer a living model that sees every shard, every shift, and every sacred fracture as part of the design.

Now that we have redefined the language of family, it is time to offer a model to hold those truths. Mosaic Family Systems Theory emerged from a need for something more honest, more human ... a way to hold the broken pieces together with structure and soul.

Mosaic Truth

Words build walls or they build windows.

The labels we inherit do not have to define the love we create.

You are not just a "step." You are not a "bonus." You are not a leftover.

You are a living piece in a story still being told.

Mosaic families are not named by convenience; they are crafted by intention.

Honor the names that honor your journey.

And when the language fails, write your own.

Reflective Questions

- ? How have the labels: steps, *blended,* and *bonus,* shaped your perception of family?
- ? Are there roles you have been assigned in your family that no longer fit your experience or identity?
- ? In what ways have you felt boxed in by the terminology others use to describe your family?
- ? How do the distinct pieces of your family's mosaic reflect unique stories, struggles, and strengths?

- ? What would it look like to let go of rigid labels and embrace a more flexible, compassionate language for your family's journey?
- ? How might shifting the language you use create more space for healing, belonging, and acceptance in your family?

Key Takeaways

- **Language has power.** The words we use to define our families shape how we experience connection, belonging, and our sense of identity.
- **Rigid labels often fall short.** Terms like "step-family," "blended family," or "bonus family" simplify complex emotional realities and can reinforce exclusion, unrealistic expectations, or loyalty conflicts.
- **Mosaic Families offer a richer framework.** This term honors the individuality, resilience, and varied histories each person brings, recognizing that unity does not require uniformity.
- **Relationships are crafted, not categorized.** Healthy, lasting family connections are built intentionally through empathy, flexibility, and acknowledgment of every member's unique journey.
- **Your family's narrative is yours to redefine.** Moving beyond limiting labels empowers you to create a more authentic, inclusive, and supportive family environment.

Chapter Five
The Grout Theory

Before we ever 'blended' a family, I searched for an existing framework that could help explain what I was living. Existing models offered language, but not the lived tension I felt at the dinner table or custody exchange. There was no framework or theory unique to this concept. Mosaic Family Systems Theory did not begin as a theory. It began as a means of survival, then evolved into a source of insight, and ultimately became a structure.

Some pieces must be turned toward the light before they find their place.

What if there were a way to make sense of the emotional chaos, the blurred roles, and the constant strain many families feel? What if there were a language, a framework for naming what hurts, what helps, and what heals in complex family systems?

That is the purpose of MFST. This chapter introduces the core structure that supports the rest of the book. MFST was born from years of personal experience, clinical work, and research with families who have lived through divorce, remarriage, blending, and rebuilding. If the *mosaic* is the metaphor, MFST is the map.

When the grout sets, so does the grace

Families today rarely fit the tidy molds of the past. At the same time, theories like Bowen's Family Systems Theory (BFST) have long served as valuable blueprints for understanding intergenerational patterns, emotional dynamics, and family functioning. They primarily emerged in an era where the nuclear family was considered the standard.

Traditional family systems theory, particularly as developed by Bowen, assumes a single-origin household and a clean generational structure. Yet mosaic families do not begin at the same starting point. They are assembled from fragments, prior marriages, blended siblings, custody exchanges, and step-relations. Bowen's model offers foundational tools, such as differentiation of self and emotional triangles. However, MFST expands that framework to meet the layered identities, role ambiguity, and loyalty binds unique to blended families.

What happens when families no longer start from a shared, intact origin?

What about families pieced together from distinct, sometimes fragmented histories?

Origins from Dissertation Research

My dissertation revealed a common thread: participants often felt the language and models available to them did not capture their lived realities. Terms like *"step-family"* and *"blended family"* lacked the depth to encompass loyalty conflicts, the pain of second divorces, and the emotional work of merging fractured systems. MFST emerged as an answer, one that frames blended families not as broken systems in need of repair, but as intricate mosaics that require artistry, patience, and respect.

Even the pieces you've tried to throw away still belong in the picture.

Participant Quotes Supporting MFST (Hudgins, 2025)

These voices articulate the very challenges that MFST seeks to address: stories of rejection, baggage, loyalty binds, and the delicate intricacies of forming meaningful relationships.

"Being called a 'stepmother' felt like I was always standing outside the circle, never fully accepted."

"They called us a blended family, but nothing felt blended. It felt like oil and water at first."

"Losing the marriage was one thing, but losing the relationship with my stepchildren felt like losing a part of myself."

"I carried so much baggage from my first marriage into my second."

"I thought we were supposed to just blend. No one told me how much grief and work came with it."

Why These Quotes Matter. These participant quotes became the cornerstone of MFST because they reflect lived, emotional truths that traditional models, like BFST, overlook. Their stories highlighted the need for a model that addresses feelings of exclusion, the invisible weight of past baggage, loyalty binds, and blurred roles. These candid reflections illuminated gaps in existing frameworks, guiding me to construct MFST with emphasis on individuality, boundary setting, and intentional relational crafting.

The Purpose of MFST is to provide both clinicians and families with a model that:

- Honors the individuality of each member.
- Recognizes and addresses the emotional labor of merging families.
- Encourages flexibility, empathy, and resilience.
- Offers clear clinical steps that prioritize emotional safety and intentional family building.

Unlike the family's traditional genogram, the MFST version highlights shifting roles, prior family attachments, boundary clarity, and emotional loyalty tensions.

Why Create a New Model?

Traditional family systems theories, particularly as developed by Bowen, emphasize key concepts such as emotional triangles, self-differentiation, and multigenerational patterns (Hudgins, 2025). These are powerful tools, but they assume that the family begins with a shared, intact origin. They rely on clean generational roles: parent, child, and grandparent; however, in mosaic families, those lines are rarely straight.

I know this firsthand. I was a stepfather navigating unspoken rules in someone else's parenting story. I was a biological father, carrying the weight of past wounds and present hope. I was an ex-husband, learning to co-parent through pain. I was a husband again, trying to hold a new love without erasing the old. At one point, I was all of those at once. Bowen did not quite have a category for that. The roles overlapped. The loyalties conflicted. And yet, it was still a family.

My children lived in the storm of those overlaps. They did not experience our family as a clean generational map; they experienced it as an emotional maze. One week, they were in one home, with one set of rules and one culture. The following week, a different house, a different parent, a different rhythm. They weren't misbehaving; they were mourning. Acting out wasn't always defiance. Sometimes it was grief wearing a mask.

Bowen's idea of self-differentiation is powerful, yet what happens when a child's very identity is split across households? Does their sense of safety shift every Sunday night? Mosaic Family Systems Theory helps us recognize that what appears to be Oppositional Defiant Disorder (ODD) may be unresolved loyalty binds, boundary confusion, or emotional displacement. It gives us a lens to ask not just, "What's wrong with this child?" — instead, "What has this child been asked to carry?"

This is where MFST begins, not with a clean slate, but with real lives, layered stories, and the raw tension of making meaning in the midst of it all.

Mosaic families don't start with a blank canvas. They begin with pieces, where some are vibrant, some are jagged, and all are meaningful. We come with past attachments, roles we did not choose, grief we haven't fully named, and traditions that sometimes clash. As a therapist, professor, researcher, and someone who has lived through it, I know this is not just theory; it is Tuesday night dinners, exchange weekends, quiet car rides full of emotion that no one knows how to name.

MFST names this reality. These aren't broken families. They are human ones; built with intention, shaped by loss, and held together with grace. Not seamless, but sacred. Not blended, but beautifully pieced together. MFST helps us stop asking, *"Why can't this feel normal?"* and start asking, *"In what ways do we make this work in a way that honors every piece?"*

Each person brings prior attachments, griefs, loyalties, cultures, and roles that often do not fit into clean categories. As a therapist, professor, researcher, and someone who has lived it, I know this is not just theory; it is real life. It is Friday evening custody swaps, Friday night dinner tension, and the quiet ache of trying to belong in more than one place.

The Mosaic Pieces & The Grout: How Families Hold Together

To truly understand the MFST framework, imagine a mosaic artwork. Each tile, different in size, color, and texture, represents a family member and their lived history. A mosaic does not hold without grout, the binding material that connects, protects, and gives the design its strength.

MFST identifies both the individual pieces and the emotional grout. It teaches us that healthy mosaic families require attention to both individuality and connection.

"The strength of this family lies not in seamlessness, but in the intentional placement and respect of every piece."

Introducing the Mosaic Compass: A Visual Framework for MFST

To visually anchor the core concepts of MFST, the *Mosaic Compass* offers a one-page framework with four guiding quadrants: **Identity**, **Boundaries**, **Loyalty**, and **Adaptability**. These principles form the foundation for understanding how the mosaic family functions, grows, and heals. Each quadrant represents a vital domain of relational health: *Identity* honors each family member's unique story and role; *Boundaries* serve as the emotional grout that holds distinct pieces together;

Loyalty names the hidden tensions that often go unspoken and deeply felt; and *Adaptability* reflects the sacred skill of navigating change with resilience. Like a compass, this tool is not meant to provide exact answers, but to offer orientation, guiding families, clinicians, and readers through the emotional terrain of mosaic life. Refer to the visual diagram on the next page as a quick-reference map for MFST in action.

A visual guide to navigating Mosaic Family Systems Theory

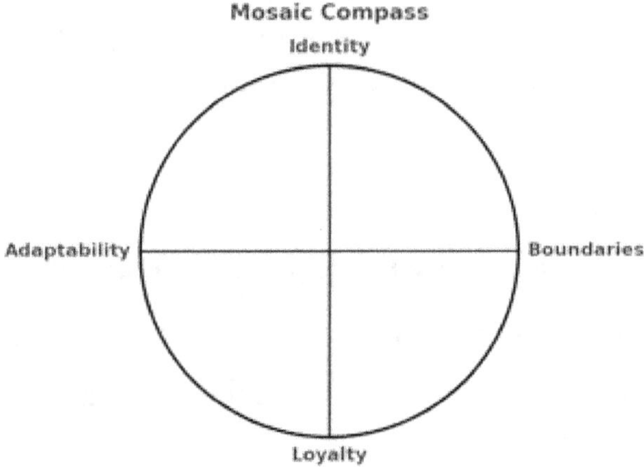

Center: Graceful Intention

This is the emotional and spiritual *core* of the compass — what binds all quadrants together.

- Purpose: Reminds us that mosaic families are not assembled by accident but through conscious, compassionate, and patient choices.
- Example keywords: grace, presence, trust, repair, honoring the story.

"Grace is the invisible grout. Without it, identity hardens, boundaries fracture, loyalty binds, and adaptability becomes resistance."

Quadrant 1: Identity

Who am I in this family — and how is my story honored?

- Focus: Core self, past roles, unique emotional histories.
- Keywords: role clarity, story ownership, core self, differentiation, naming pain.
- Clinical example: A stepchild feels invisible in one home and over-involved in another — MFST names both realities.

Quadrant 2: Boundaries

What holds us together without erasing who we are?

- Focus: Emotional space, physical limits, parenting roles
- Keywords: clarity, consistency, respect, role safety, shared expectations
- Clinical example: A stepparent disciplines without the biological parent's support, creating confusion—MFST repositions boundary roles.

Quadrant 3: Loyalty

Where does my heart feel pulled, and how do I navigate divided love?

- Focus: Loyalty binds, grief for first families, guilt, triangulation.
- Keywords: emotional ambivalence, neutrality, safe expression, validation.

- Clinical example: A child shuts down after transition weekends — MFST recognizes this as a loyalty conflict, not defiance.

Quadrant 4: Adaptability

How do we evolve, hold space, and respond to change with grace?

- *Focus: Flexibility, growth mindset, trauma-informed pace*
- *Keywords: resilience, patience, repair, emotional elasticity, transition tools*
- *Clinical example: A family struggles during the holidays due to different traditions — MFST encourages co-creating new rituals that honor the old.*

Just as the **Mosaic Compass** helps us orient ourselves emotionally within the landscape of a mosaic family, the following framework brings that orientation into action. Where the Compass names the heart of the work, identity, boundaries, loyalty, and adaptability, the **Mosaic Systems Framework** outlines how these forces interact in daily life.

Think of it as the blueprint that guides the placement of each piece. The table below breaks down the individual "tiles" each family member brings and identifies the "grout" needed to hold those pieces together with care, safety, and intention. Together, the Compass and the Framework equip both families and clinicians to move from emotional confusion toward relational clarity.

Table 2 — *Mosaic Family Systems Framework*

Mosaic Piece (Individual Tile)	Grout (Binding Element)
Core Identity (each family member's unique story)	Acceptance & Validation
Prior Attachments & Losses	Grief Acknowledgment & Processing
Emotional Boundaries	Clear Communication
Parenting Roles	Role Clarification & Agreements
Loyalty Conflicts	Safe Emotional Space & Neutrality
Cultural & Family Traditions	Mutual Respect & Integration
New Shared Experiences	Creativity & Flexibility
Conflict & Disagreements	Conflict Resolution Skills
Healing & Growth	Individual & Family Therapy

These elements are not theoretical; they are lived. Every piece and every binding element in the table reflects what mosaic families experience in real time. When families come together with distinct roles, histories, and hurts, it is not enough to coexist. They need language, structure, and shared understanding. This is where MFST brings in both heart and strategy. And it all starts with the most important piece: the individual.

Zooming In: The Power of Identity in the Mosaic

Systems are made up of people, and every piece in the mosaic starts with one question: Who am I in this story? Before we explore the clinical implications of MFST, we must return to the heart of every mosaic ... identity. This is not theory alone. This is lived. It is the child caught between households. The parent is still grieving a prior marriage. The stepparent is trying to find their place. MFST begins here because, without honoring each piece, the design will not hold.

Why Start with Core Identity?

A mosaic begins with choosing the first tile. In MFST, that starting point is always the core identity, which each family member is part of, shaped by their past, attachments, and personal values.

Traditional theories often categorize family members under broad generational labels. Bowen's model, for instance, refers to "parents" and "children" without distinguishing between biological, step, or half-sibling roles.

Mosaic families aren't that simple. A child may be a stepchild in one household, a half-sibling in another, and a biological child elsewhere, all at the same time.

Each of these roles carries emotional weight: loyalty binds, attachment ruptures, and identity confusion. MFST helps us to pause, name these distinctions, and resist asking individuals to collapse their story into a single, tidy label. Their unique identities must be acknowledged and validated before asking them to integrate into a new family structure.

Where Bowen focuses on generational hierarchy and emotional triangles, the MFST framework focuses on personal narratives, fractured attachments, and the emotional reality of merging lives with unfinished stories.

Think of a mosaic:

Each tile holds its color, history, and shape. What binds them together is not uniformity, but intentional placement and flexible, compassionate 'grout.'

MFST identifies both the pieces and the emotional elements needed to hold the family together in a way that honors individuality while building connection.

Before we can explore how mosaic families grow strong, we must revisit one of the most foundational ideas in family theory: self-differentiation. Bowen described it as the ability to maintain a strong sense of self while staying connected to others, yet mosaic families challenge that definition.

When roles are layered, loyalties are divided, and identity is shared across multiple homes, self-differentiation looks and feels very different. MFST doesn't discard Bowen's insight; it expands it to match the lived experience of today's complex families.

Self-Differentiation Reimagined: MFST Expanded BFST

One of the most enduring concepts in family theory is Bowen's concept of self-differentiation, which refers to the ability to remain connected to one's family while maintaining one's individuality within it. For clinicians, this often rings familiar: the well-differentiated person can honor their thoughts and emotions, even under pressure, without becoming distant or enmeshed.

It is a powerful idea. What happens when the "family" is not one intact unit, but a mosaic of step-relations, half-siblings, rotating households, and emotional history? That's the reality many families face today. In mosaic systems, self-differentiation is not just about knowing who you are; it is about knowing which version of you is being asked to show up, because boundaries often become blurred, and this is the reason blended family concepts do not work in this context. It is identity work that must be navigated.

- Divided loyalties between biological and step-relationships.
- Competing attachments across multiple households.
- Ambiguous roles like step-sibling, half-sibling, or "bonus" parent.

Bowen's original model did not account for that complexity. MFST expands it, not to discard Bowen's wisdom, but rather, to deepen it. Differentiation in a mosaic family means holding space for each role without erasing the others. It's not about detaching from pressure; it's about knowing who you are when pressure comes from five different directions at once.

The comparison below outlines how MFST reimagines differentiation for mosaic families, building on Bowen's framework while honoring the emotional nuance of blended systems.

Table 3 ***How MFST Expands Bowen's Concept of Differentiation.***

Bowen's Differentiation of Self	Mosaic Family Systems Theory (MFST)
Focuses on balancing individuality and connection universally.	Recognizes the added complexity of blended family roles (stepchild, half-sibling, etc.).
Views "children" and family members by generational position (parent, child).	Highlights the unique emotional dynamics of each relational role in mosaic families.
Encourages emotional boundaries and self-identity.	Extends differentiation to include role-specific identity work, loyalty tensions, and fractured belonging.
Applies broadly to any family type.	Specifically tailored to blended, mosaic families with layered relationships.

Understanding the theory is only the beginning. The real power of MFST becomes evident when we apply it to everyday life, in kitchens, courtrooms, during bedtime routines, and during difficult conversations. In this next section, we'll shift from concept to practice. These teaching moments are where MFST becomes more than a framework — it becomes the tools for clarity, healing, and connection in real families, just like yours.

Teaching Moment: How MFST Applies Practically

I recall a time when one of my children sat quietly in the back seat, refusing to speak after a weekend transition. It wasn't defiance, it was disorientation. One home had one set of rules, one rhythm. The other had a different set entirely. Somewhere between pickup and drop-off, they lost their sense of place.

In that moment, I did not need a theory; I needed a lens. Bowen's idea of self-differentiation helped me stay relevant to the present, yet it did not help me understand the fractured roles my child was carrying. That's what MFST offers: a way to see the emotional weight behind the silence. A way to ask, *"What role is this child being asked to play, and who are they allowed to be in that role?"*

This next section serves as a teaching moment, not just for clinicians, but also for parents, stepparents, caregivers, and anyone living within the complexity of a mosaic family. It is where MFST becomes practical, personal, and deeply relevant. To illustrate how MFST works, the following is a real-life family situation involving Ethan.

In a recent session, a 12-year-old boy named Ethan struggled to articulate why he was withdrawing from his new stepfather. On the surface, it appeared to be a case of disrespect or typical adolescent behavior. Applying my theory of MFST principles allowed a deeper story to emerge.

Ethan loved his biological dad but only saw him on weekends. Showing affection to his stepdad felt like betrayal. The problem wasn't attitude; it was divided loyalty and emotional confusion. Through open conversation, both parents began affirming Ethan's connection to his biological dad, which freed him to build trust with his stepdad without guilt. MFST provided the space to untangle the roles and affirm Ethan's emotional reality, without rushing to fix or blend too quickly.

Reflection Pause
Take a moment to consider:

- Which "tiles" in your family or in the families you serve are being forced to fit, rather than honored as they are?
- Are there loyalty bonds, fractured roles, or unspoken attachments that need intentional space to be acknowledged?
- What kind of 'grout' is missing: communication, emotional safety, or boundary clarity, to help hold the family together without glossing over the cracks?

Why MFST Matters

Families today are no longer shaped by a single narrative. Whether you're a teacher trying to support a child who switches households every week, a lawyer navigating high-conflict custody cases, a counselor walking through grief with a teenager, or a parent trying to love across emotional distance, you've seen the complexity of mosaic families.

MFST provides us with language and the tools that traditional models often overlook. It does not aim to blend or simplify. Instead, it helps us honor each person's past, pain, and position, while still working toward connection. And it matters because when complexity is ignored, families suffer.

One example is Parental Alienation Syndrome (PAS), where a child becomes estranged from one parent due to the manipulation of the other. As a parent who lived through this, I know the heartbreak firsthand. Fighting for custody of my children was one of the hardest things I have ever done. Winning custody did not feel like a victory; it stirred the hornet's nest.

For decades, countless children have become silent casualties of courtroom battles, their voices lost beneath the weight of flawed theories. Parental Alienation Syndrome (PAS), introduced in the 1980s by Richard Gardner, claimed to explain why children rejected one parent during high-conflict custody disputes.

However, the promise of PAS was hollow. It has always been deeply flawed, lacking empirical validity, riddled with gender bias, and dangerously easy to weaponize in courts. Instead of uncovering the truth, PAS pathologizes children, turning their pain into a diagnosis rather than revealing the systemic dysfunction, coercion, and psychological manipulation at play.

I once stood before a judge because the children's mother accused me of being a danger to our daughter, all over a martial arts conversation. What I said was: *"If you don't do your homework or pay attention in class, you could get hurt."* I wasn't threatening; I was trying to parent through caution and teach the value of discipline and follow-through. Nevertheless, what I meant and what was heard were two very different things. That moment taught me how fragile communication can be when trust has already been broken.

Thankfully, a well-informed judge saw through the distortion. He warned the mother that if she interfered again, he would hold her in contempt of court and affirmed that my parental rights must be respected. He also ordered that therapy continue, due to the emotional toll PAS had already taken on our children.

The DSM rejected PAS due to the lack of sufficient peer-reviewed research, thereby leaving it without clinical credibility. Courts, therapists, and parents have paid the price for relying on an invalid framework that offers no tools for healing.

Therefore, through research and more to come, I have coined a new term called: *Disruptive Parental Attachment* (DPA©), which helps support MFST and the trauma-informed framework for reframing parental alienation:

The court's reliance on unsubstantiated allegations, often made by the more persuasive or manipulative parent, can result in the irreversible rupture of a child's attachment to a once-loved parent. In these scenarios, love becomes weaponized, and the child becomes a casualty of emotional warfare. The outdated framework of PAS failed to protect families in such circumstances.

What I needed, what we all need, is not just a legal win, but a relational path forward. MFST and DPA offer that path. It helps families establish clear emotional boundaries, validate fractured roles, and rebuild trust without forcing premature "blending."

MFST does not erase pain; it helps us name it, hold it, and begin placing the pieces with intention. It provides parents, educators, and clinicians with the tools to view the entire system, rather than just the symptoms. This theory matters because families matter. Moreover, too many are navigating chaos without a compass. MFST offers a way to build forward, not perfectly, but honestly, and with care.

Experiences like these don't just shape a parent; they shape our entire perspective on families. I began to realize that the real challenge wasn't just managing conflict, but understanding the roles, expectations, and emotional weight each person carried. That's why MFST is not just a concept; it is a call to approach families with more care, more clarity, and more courage.

So, how do we take this forward? How do we move from theory and courtroom battles to real moments around the dinner table, on the couch, or in a counseling session? That's where we turn next: to the work of assembling the mosaic with intentionality, insight, and hope.

What's Next: Assembling the Mosaic

So, how do we put this into practice?

- How do you, as a parent, stepparent, counselor, or friend, help arrange the pieces intentionally?
- How do you foster unity while still honoring individuality?
- And how do you create something vibrant, resilient, and authentic, not by blending, but rather by crafting a mosaic with care?

As a clinician, biological father, and former stepfather, I have witnessed firsthand the complexity of this issue. Early in my practice, I treated children as a group; just "kids." I did not stop to ask if they were biological, step, or half-siblings. From the therapist's chair, it was easy to overlook how deeply a child's role affects their emotional life.

Then came my own home. One of my children once asked me, softly, not in rebellion but in heartbreak, *"Do I have to love everyone the same?"* That one question opened the floodgates.

Behind many so-called "behavior problems" was something else entirely: confusion about roles.

Am I the stepchild today or the biological one?

What if I'm closer to one parent but don't want to hurt the other?

What does it mean to belong when I belong in more than one place?

This internal tug-of-war doesn't always manifest as language; it often manifests as anger, withdrawal, silence, or shutdown. Beneath it all is a loyalty bind, a fractured identity, a child trying not to disappoint anyone.

Treating all children the same is not the goal. In mosaic families, they don't need uniformity; they need understanding. Their emotional lives are shaped by the specific piece they hold in the family's design. That deserves intentional care.

MFST is not just a theory; it is a lens. These stories are not case studies; they are lived experiences, messy, sacred, painful, and real. MFST comes alive not in the abstract, but in the ache of a child, the silence between co-parents, and the confusion of finding your place in a family for which you didn't ask. What follows is not data, it's mosaic life in motion. To illustrate how MFST can guide real-life family situations, let's examine an example of Lucy.

MFST in Action: A Story of "Lucy"

Lucy (not her real name) was nine when her parents divorced and twelve when her mother got remarried. She lived week-to-week between households and had just begun calling her stepdad "Dad" when her biological father reentered the picture after two years away. In therapy, Lucy grew quiet and withdrawn. At home, she started lashing out, refusing to speak to either of her father figures.

Her behavior was misread as defiance; however, MFST gave me a better lens: Lucy wasn't oppositional; she was torn. She felt guilty for loving both men. She felt like she had to take a side. No one had named her loyalty conflict, and so she carried it alone.

Using MFST principles, her parents learned to validate Lucy's feelings without forcing a false choice. Her biological dad gave her permission to love her stepdad. Her stepdad stepped back, making space for Lucy to decide how close she wanted to be. With clear boundaries, honest language, and family sessions focused on role clarity, Lucy started to relax. She laughed more. She spoke without fear.

This is the power of MFST: not to fix people, but to free them to be themselves in their family.

When a family is empowered to acknowledge the truth of who they are, where they have come from, and what each person carries, they stop pretending and start healing. This is what MFST makes possible; not a perfect picture, but certainly an honest one.

Another Family. Another Fracture. Another Chance to Heal.

The mosaic doesn't form only once. It forms again and again, with every complicated conversation, every unseen grief, every moment a child chooses silence over confusion. Ethan's story is not unlike Lucy's, yet it reveals a different tile in the mosaic: the quiet, conflicted heart of a boy caught between loyalty and belonging. This next moment is for the clinicians, the stepparents, the teachers, and anyone wondering why connection sometimes stalls. MFST helps us see beneath the silence.

Now, let's explore how this framework translates into fundamental strategies for real families, helping us move beyond survival and into intentional connection. Here's how MFST helps resolve these challenges:

1. **Identifying** the emotional pressures linked to each person's role (e.g., stepchild, half-sibling, stepparent).
2. **Creating space** for honest conversations about loyalty conflicts, identity confusion, and feelings of belonging.
3. **Establishing emotional boundaries** based on clarity and communication, not assumptions or inherited roles.
4. **Honoring each story**, allowing members to define their place rather than being forced into a prefabricated mold.

MFST Process Model for Therapists and Family Coaches

It is essential to identify the first marriage and subsequent marriages or partnerships with children from prior relationships. How do we approach grief and child behavior in broken families? Families exhibiting loyalty binds, unclear roles, or difficulty integrating histories. How does integration affect the children? Clients who express feelings like an "outsider" in their family roles (stepparents, stepchildren). Is there isolation within the family?

Use the following six-phase approach when working with mosaic families:

1. Mapping the Mosaic (Assessment)

Create a visual or narrative family map. Identify roles, relational fractures, cultural traditions, previous family systems, and unspoken expectations.

2. Validating Individual Stories

Let each member tell their story without judgment or urgency to "blend." This builds emotional safety and trust.

3. Clarifying Roles & Boundaries

Support the family in naming roles (e.g., "bonus parent," "step-sibling") and defining household expectations. Avoid forcing uniform roles where nuance is needed.

4. Navigating Conflict & Loyalty Binds

Normalize the emotional tension between biological and blended ties. Facilitate a neutral ground for addressing unspoken pressures and teach relational repair strategies.

5. Designing Shared Experiences

Help the family create new rituals that don't erase the past, but build toward a connected future, family nights, shared meals, and co-created traditions.

6. Evolving the Mosaic (Integration)

Encourage flexibility and patience as the family continues to evolve. Integration is not a one-time goal. It is a living, ongoing process.

From Metaphor to Movement

Mosaic families are not built in a moment; they are assembled with intention, story by story, piece by piece. As we have seen, the goal is not to force sameness, but to honor differences. Naming the mosaic is only the beginning. Living it, tile by tile, boundary by boundary, is where families begin to heal. The fundamental transformation occurs when insight becomes action, and when a story becomes a shared space. In this next section, we move from the concept of the mosaic to how it forms in real life. MFST reminds us that what binds families together is not perfection, but presence. Not uniform roles; respectful clarity. Not the absence of conflict; the courage to stay connected in the middle of it.

From Insight to Integration

However, what does it actually look like to live that truth? To move from theoretical understanding to relational embodiment? Mosaic families are not just systems — they are stories, identities, and sacred negotiations in motion. This chapter explores what it means to honor differences, navigate conflicts, and co-create a sense of belonging in the day-to-day rhythms of real life. The theory gives us the lens. But the integration? That's where the mosaic breathes.

Whether you're navigating this as a parent, a professional, or someone who grew up in this kind of home, know this: your mosaic matters. Furthermore, it can be whole, even if it is not seamless. This chapter introduces a new perspective on mosaic families, not as puzzles to solve, but rather as living systems to be honored. In the next chapter, we move from theory to embodiment: what does it truly mean to embrace your family's mosaic?

We will delve deeper into MFST, examining the key dynamics, relational tensions, and role patterns that shape Mosaic families. You will see yourself, your clients, or your loved ones more clearly and, I hope, more compassionately.

Pause and consider: Which "tiles" in your family have never been honored? What kind of emotional grout is needed now to hold your family mosaic together?

Mosaic Truth

True family systems do not emerge from shared origin; they are shaped by shared intention.

Mosaic families are not built from scratch; they are assembled from brokenness, boundaries, and brave new bonds.

What holds them together is not perfection, but presence.

Reflective Questions

- ? What relational roles within your family or clients' families might be forced to fit in, rather than honored individually?
- ? How might loyalty binds or unresolved attachments be impacting a family member's sense of belonging or identity?

- ? What communication patterns, boundary work, or therapeutic support could serve as the grout to hold each family member's individuality without glossing over emotional cracks?
- ? How often do we unintentionally expect children, stepparents, or siblings in blended families to conform to labels that don't fit their lived experiences?
- ? Where can we offer space for grief, prior attachments, or role ambiguity to be processed rather than ignored?

Key Takeaways

- Mosaic Family Systems Theory (MFST) recognizes that blended families do not start with a shared origin, but are intentionally assembled from individual histories, identities, and roles.
- MFST emphasizes that honoring each member's core identity is essential before expecting family unity. Unlike traditional models, MFST accounts for loyalty conflicts, role ambiguities, and divided attachments that blended families face.
- Differentiation of self in mosaic families involves role-specific identity work, requiring space for each family member's unique position to be validated.
- MFST offers a flexible, practical framework prioritizing emotional safety, boundary clarity, and the intentional crafting of new family narratives. Real voices from blended families illustrate the emotional labor, grief, and resilience inherent in mosaic family life.

- MFST equips both clinicians and families to build cohesive, resilient family systems without erasing individuality.

Chapter Six

Embracing the blended Mosaic Family

The beauty of a mosaic family is not found in perfection; instead, in the way each distinct piece, shaped by loss, history, and hope, comes together to form something significant. Shared bloodlines do not define these families, shared courage does: the daily work of showing up, honoring each other's story, and choosing connection despite the fractures. As we navigate the spaces between us with patience, grace, and resilience, we begin to see that family is less about what fits easily and more about what is intentionally placed. MFST gave us the map; this chapter brings us into the living room, the kitchen, the car rides, the quiet grief, and the earned laughter. Here we learn not just how to name the mosaic, but how to live it.

I recall a moment early in my mosaic journey that still resides in my heart. My stepson was about seven at the time, and we had just moved into a new home. The boxes were everywhere. The routines were undone. And so were the emotions.

One night, I noticed he was unusually quiet at dinner. Afterward, he sat on the steps, fidgeting with the laces on his sneakers. I sat down beside him, not to fix anything, but just to be near. After a long silence, he said, "I miss the old house. And I miss my other room. ***And I don't know where I fit here yet."***

That sentence, *"I don't know where I fit yet,"* struck me because I felt it too. We were all figuring out how to fit, how to share space, how to make love louder than the confusion. I looked at him and said, "You don't have to fit perfectly yet. You have to be here. That's your piece."

In that moment, I realized that building a mosaic family is not about snapping into place like a puzzle. It is about showing up as you are, even when the edges are jagged. It is about building something beautiful, not because it is perfect, but because it is real.

According to my dissertation research (Hudgins, 2025), nearly 40% of families in the United States are now considered "blended," and that number continues to rise. Behind the statistics are real people: stepparents, half-siblings, grandparents by love, not blood; each navigating the beautiful, yet complicated, terrain of becoming a family.

These aren't just numbers on a page. They represent living mosaics; homes held together by second chances, grace, and the courage to try again.

My research not only confirmed this rise. It also revealed something deeper. Mosaic families are not broken by default; they are often forged with a deeper intention. As societal norms shift and remarriage, cohabitation, and step-relationships become more prevalent, we're witnessing a transformation in how family is defined and lived.

This chapter is written for families like these. For the ones still learning how to fit, forgive, and form something whole from pieces they never expected to hold.

Sarah's Mosaic: Holding It Together Until It Broke

Take Sarah, for example. A mother of three, she did not just inherit a blended family; she built one, raised one, carried one. Her second marriage began with love and effort, yet also with weight: two stepchildren under the age of six, her children later born into the mix, and a husband whose addiction quietly unraveled their home from the inside out.

Sarah wasn't just trying to stay married. She was trying to hold everyone together, feeding five mouths, homeschooling, paying bills, working two jobs, absorbing lies, and fielding bill collectors. Her husband would bring home just twenty-five dollars after making eight hundred. The rest? Lost to gambling. But she stayed. She prayed. She tried to love him 'out of his addiction.' Until even her children said, "We can't live like this anymore."

And when she finally asked him to leave, something miraculous happened:

"The moment the door shut behind him, my neck released. I hadn't been able to turn my head in six months from the stress. But that day, I could finally move again."

Her body had been carrying what her voice wasn't ready to name. Sarah's story is not about giving up. It is about finally making space to breathe. Her mosaic family did not fall apart — it re-formed. Slowly. Painfully. Authentically.

She still believes in marriage. She still believes in commitment. But she's learned this:

"You can't love someone out of their issues. Their issues are their issues. If both people aren't equally committed, it is not a

marriage — it is a hostage situation dressed up as hope." Sarah (Hudgins, 2025).

There is a sobering kind of wisdom that only rises from the ashes of something once sacred. Sarah's voice speaks not just of heartbreak, but of hard-earned clarity, the realization that no amount of love can heal what someone refuses to confront. Her words echo what so many silently endure: the slow unraveling of a family that once held such promise.

Yet, this is not the end of the story. It is where the mosaic begins.

Across the country, sociologists and family studies experts are noticing a shift, not only in structure, but also in meaning. Mosaic families, once seen as fragmented or unconventional, whispered about or misunderstood, are now recognized as a vital part of the modern relational framework, helping to redefine what family truly means in everyday life.

As cultural norms evolve and the visibility of diverse family structures grows, the mosaic emerges not as an outlier, but as a reflection of real life; layered, lived-in, imperfect, and sacred.

While the precise shape of families continues to evolve, one truth remains constant: the need for intentionality. Mosaic families are not born, they are crafted. Piece by piece. Story by story. Person by person.

Like a specialty coffee blend, each member arrives with a distinct flavor, boldness, bitterness, sweetness, and subtlety, all shaped by past experiences and relational scars. The goal is not to make each taste the same; it is to blend them in a way that honors every origin while creating something richer as a whole.

The barista doesn't erase the bean's identity. They elevate it through intentional harmony.

The same is true for mosaic families. They do not thrive by forcing sameness. They thrive by honoring differences. By making space for every jagged piece. By building trust slowly, through shared rituals, emotional safety, and mutual respect.

This truth has echoed throughout my clinical work and research. One participant told me, *"It felt like I was bringing my own story into a family that already had its narrative. I did not know how to fit, but I knew I wanted to." Another shared, "Each of us had our baggage. It wasn't until we actually talked about it that we stopped tripping over each other's pain."*

These reflections aren't just anecdotes; they are insights. Reminders. They teach us that mosaic families are not built on perfection, but on permission ... permission to be whole, to be healing, and to be human.

The Mantra of Adaptability

I grew up with the military mantra: *"Adapt and overcome."* It was drilled into us, expected of us, especially when survival depended on it. No one warned me how much harder that mantra would be to live inside a family. Yet, having served in the military myself, the mantra stayed with me. I had expected to transition from enlisted to officer, what we call going from *green to gold*, transitioning from enlisted to officer, after earning my college degree.

Adaptability in mosaic families is not just a mindset ... because it is a lifeline when we fail to adjust to the unpredictable, emotional fractures form. Bonds that once felt promising become fragile. And the very foundation of what we're building starts to crack beneath our feet.

When my marriage to my children's mother ended, it broke something deep inside me, not just as a husband, but as a father. At the time, I did not fully understand how my attachment wounds influenced my love, my reactions, and my interpretation of conflict. I will discuss this further later in the book. But for now, what you need to know is this: both of us came into the marriage carrying unhealed pain. And the moment we began parenting together, that pain did not disappear; it multiplied.

She carried wounds from her childhood, scars left by her parents' divorce and custody battle. That pain took shape in our home through Parental Alienation Syndrome (PAS), a heartbreaking and complex dynamic where one parent subtly turns the child against the other. In our case, I watched my relationship with my children start to erode, not because I was absent or unsafe, but because I was redefined.

Let me be clear. I have never abused my children. I have never struggled with substance issues and paid child support. I did not walk away from them. But I did have to fight for them. I fought in court not just for custody, but for connection. For the right to love them fully and be present in their lives. No parent should have to prove their worth to stay in their child's world; many fathers do. I did.

In many divorces, especially when one partner has a personality disorder, it becomes a toxic cycle: criticism, gaslighting, manipulation, and emotional withdrawal. The father, already stretched thin, reacts with frustration or despair. And suddenly, he becomes the villain. Her narrative becomes the truth. And the truth gets rewritten.

I have seen this play out too many times, both in my own story and in the lives of the men I counsel. It is a pattern. She provokes. He reacts. She positions herself as the calm, protective parent. And he is painted as unstable, angry, and unfit. The manipulation does not stop with the marriage. It reaches into the children's minds, reshaping their sense of safety and memory. Alienation is not just a legal outcome; it is a slow emotional unraveling.

When you add features of Borderline Personality traits, emotional chaos, boundary violations, idealization, and rejection, the volatility only escalates. The children get pulled into a loyalty war they never asked to fight. Fathers become ghosts in their own homes. And families suffer wounds that last for generations.

In my case, the root of the alienation ran deeper than our relationship. Her mother had alienated her from her father years before. Trauma rarely begins with us; it is passed down, silent and unresolved. It manifests later in our choices, fears, and parenting.

One participant in my research, Jennifer, described this kind of unexpected grief:

"The divorce did not just affect me and my spouse — it fractured my connection with my stepchildren. I wasn't prepared for how quickly you could lose relationships that you worked so hard to build."

I understood what she meant. After that chapter closed, I remarried. I called it a fresh start. A chance to rebuild something from the broken pieces. A new mosaic.

But even that came with its surprises.

I met my wife through a Christian dating app, and I fell fast and hard. We both brought children into the marriage; she had a beautiful four-year-old daughter, and I brought my two children, ages seven and four. On the surface, it seemed like a perfect fit, a hopeful beginning. Yet inside, my anxious attachment style was still driving the ship. I craved connection so deeply that I tried to force it too quickly. I wanted us to become a family overnight. I wanted love to glue us together.

Mosaic families are not puzzles. They do not snap into place. They must be assembled gently and thoughtfully over time.

That journey ... our journey, is still unfolding. And I would not trade it for anything. It has required me to stretch. To slow down. To ask better questions. To revisit pain I thought I had buried. To revisit pain I thought I had buried. To unlearn what strength was not and learn what it truly is. To love more honestly. To love more honestly.

This chapter, and this book, are not written from a pedestal. They come from a place of experience, both personal and professional. As a licensed therapist, a doctoral researcher, and a Christian man who has known failure, redemption, and everything in between, I invite you to walk with me.

Because in mosaic families, adaptability is not optional. It is sacred. It is how we learn to stay when everything in us wants to flee. It is how we become softer without breaking. It is how we turn the shattered pieces into something beautiful and whole.

Turning shattered pieces into something beautiful and whole is not just an act of survival; it is an act of sacred creativity. Nevertheless, knowing *why* we must adapt is only the beginning. The real challenge is in learning *how* to do it, day by day, piece by piece. Because mosaic families are not built all at once, they are assembled over time, through everyday decisions, awkward moments, small breakthroughs, and deep internal work.

It is in the ordinary and often messy details of life, school pickups, birthdays, discipline disagreements, holidays, and shared custody schedules, that the mosaic truly begins to take shape. This next section will walk us into that lived reality.

Navigating Life's Pieces of the Mosaic Picture

Mosaic families are not assembled in silence. They are constructed in the noise of change, grief, hope, and sometimes a profound personal reckoning. The journey of a mosaic family reminds me of crafting a piece of intricate stained glass; each shard is distinct; each cut made from a different story. Together, they do not erase what came before; they illuminate it.

Transitions through marriage, divorce, remarriage, and the fragile attempts to rebuild ask us not to forget the past, but to carry it differently.

When I remarried, I had no idea how much of my own story I was still dragging with me. I brought not only my children into the marriage, but also the unspoken fractures I had never fully faced. I entered our new family like a man trying to serve coffee in a teacup; eager, idealistic, and underestimating the pressure required to pour into something so delicate.

I used to think blending a family was like brewing a simple pot of coffee, strong, predictable, dependable. I quickly realized it is more like crafting a hand-pulled espresso with carefully steamed milk and perfectly layered foam—every ingredient matters. Every layer requires intention. And if you rush it, you ruin it.

Each member of a mosaic family brings their temperature, flavor, and timing. And if one element overwhelms the others, or if someone is left out entirely, the result is not connection, but chaos. I have been the over-pourer. I have tried too hard. I have mistaken intensity for intimacy. I have longed for a quick belonging when what my family needed was slow trust. In doing so, I hurt others. And I hurt myself. Nevertheless, healing began the moment I stopped trying to fix the mosaic and instead began to honor each piece.

Boundaries became sacred. Listening became an act of love. I started noticing when to press in and when to let go. When to stir gently and when to let things settle. This is not just theory. It is lived practice. It is sacred failure turned into sacred formation.

One participant in my research shared, *"We were expected to blend immediately, but no one talked about how hard it is to feel like you belong when you already have parents, siblings, and loyalties elsewhere" (Hudgins, 2025).*

Another echoed, *"The pieces did not fit perfectly. Some days felt like we were pretending to be a family, but we started finding our rhythm over time."*

I have lived those words. And I have watched those rhythms form slowly through awkward meals, mismatched holidays, custody handoffs, missed calls, and moments of surprising grace.

Biological families often have shared traditions and rhythms that feel like a part of one's muscle memory. However, when the structure breaks down due to divorce, loss, or betrayal, everyone has left holding pieces of a story that no longer makes sense. Grandparents, kids, exes, even friends; each one becomes a shard of something unfinished. We scramble to make sense of our place in the new picture.

Sarah's teenage children once begged her to leave their father:

"We can't live like this anymore."

She left, and that did not end the pain. Her daughter stopped seeing him for months. Even doing the right thing came with unbearable grief.

Vicki described how she lost not just a marriage, but her identity:

"I had nothing but my clothes."

Her words haunt me because so many walk away from a marriage only to realize they are also walking away from routines, communities, in-laws, and even faith traditions.

James captured what happens when history starts pulling us apart:

"We gradually drifted. Friends, their pull, different pieces of our past — we lost what we had built together before we knew it."

And the children? They are often the **quietest casualties**, caught between loyalty and longing, between love and confusion. *They are asked to choose when they never wanted to pick sides.* Their silence often hides the heaviest ache.

And we, the parents, are left navigating roles we never trained for: mediator, step-parent, co-parent, part-time dad, and full-time burden carrier. We juggle discipline styles, bedtimes, and birthdays, all while trying to stitch together a sense of home that feels like it belongs to everyone.

Nevertheless, here's the hard-won truth:
The pieces are not supposed to fit perfectly.
That is not a flaw. That is the design.

A mosaic is not made by sanding down the edges to make everything match. It is made by honoring every crack, every odd angle, every color that does not quite blend. What makes a mosaic beautiful is not its perfection, but its imperfection.

So here is the question I now ask myself, and I offer it to you:

Can I begin to see each person in my family, my children, my partner, my ex, even myself, as a piece that belongs, even if it does not match?

Because when we stop forcing things to fit and start honoring them for what they are, something sacred begins to take shape. And that is where the mosaic begins, not with control, but with compassion.

Creating the Mosaic

If navigating the pieces is about surviving the tension, then creating the mosaic is about choosing what to do with what remains.

This is the part no one tells you about: when the dust settles, the court orders are finalized, the friends have taken sides, and the house feels quieter than it should. This is when the real work begins. Not the work of managing others, but the humbling, holy work of facing yourself.

Building a mosaic is not just about reconstructing a family; it is about reclaiming one's identity.

It is the slow, sometimes painful process of holding up each shard and asking, *"What does this piece mean now?"*

Not every fragment will return to its original location. Not every relationship will return. Some parts must be let go, not out of bitterness, but out of wisdom. Others must be mended; carefully, prayerfully, one boundary at a time.

This is where healing becomes intentional, where forgiveness stops being a vague spiritual idea and becomes a practiced discipline.

Vicki shared how the very pain that once nearly 'undid her' eventually became the catalyst for her restoration:

"The second time, I was prepared. I did a lot of dealing with myself, leaning on God, and healing during the last three years of the marriage. When it ended, I was stronger, more grounded. It taught me who I was."

That is what healing looks like. Not a return to what was, but a clear-eyed move into what can be.

James reflected on his own story, not with regret, but with perspective:

"We had a pretty good setup. We had known each other since high school, had a child together, and I raised her other children. Everything went well for a long time. We had faith, went to church, built a life. Looking back, we had a lot going for us."

And sometimes, even when the foundation is strong and the intentions are good, life breaks down anyway.

Here is the thing about mosaics: they are not made from whole tiles.

They are made from the broken ones.

And what determines the beauty of the mosaic is not how few cracks it contains; it's how lovingly each piece is placed.

Fitting the Pieces

Matching a mosaic family is not about finding perfect fits. It is about finding faithful ones. It is the sacred task of discovering how vastly different lives, shaped by loss, love, loyalty, and longing, can be placed side by side and still tell one shared story. Matching in this sense does not mean uniformity. It means choosing to *belong together anyway.*

At first, I assumed love would be the adhesive. If I gave enough, tried hard enough, and showed up consistently, we'd all snap into place. Mosaic families are not puzzles with a clear box-top image. They are living, breathing works of art that are formed slowly, with grace and grit.

And every person must find their place in the pattern.

Joy captured this beautifully when she reflected on how parenting continued even after divorce:

"We adopted two girls together. Even after the divorce, we still had to talk and parent together. That bond stayed. It wasn't all bad — it shaped who I am as a mother."

This is the complexity of mosaic life. Even broken relationships leave behind pieces that still matter. Pieces that still match.

Integration of Individual Pieces

Matching does not mean forcing things together. It means learning what each piece carries and honoring it. In mosaic families, people arrive with pain from previous relationships, fears about new roles, and hopes they barely dare to name. Accurate matching means asking deeper questions:

Where does your story hurt?
How can I help you feel safe?
What do you need to know about me?

It is not just emotional work; it is a sacred art form.

Creating New Patterns

Over time, new patterns emerge. Not because we erase the past, it's because we weave something new through it. Maybe it is weekly movie nights. A shared grace at the table. A child calling a stepdad "coach" before ever calling him "dad." These small moments are brushstrokes. They have not forced matches but chosen ones. They mark the slow forming of a family rhythm that feels honest and earned.

Adaptability and Resilience

Matching pieces doesn't always go smoothly. Some will slide into place. Others will resist. You'll face misunderstandings, discipline differences, hurt feelings, and awkward silences. If you're willing to show up with humility — to apologize, to listen longer than is comfortable, to try again — you'll discover something remarkable:

It is not about how fast the mosaic comes together.
It is about how deeply you're willing to care for each piece.

Acknowledging the Gaps

Not everything will match. Some edges will remain rough. Some stories will not fully intertwine. There will be gaps between what a child remembers and what a stepparent hopes for ... between who we wanted to be and who we've become. Gaps do not mean failure. Gaps mean we are still growing. When we name the places that hurt or don't yet connect, we invite compassion into the cracks. And sometimes, it is the light that shines through those very spaces that makes the mosaic unforgettable.

Ultimately, what makes a mosaic powerful is not perfection.

It is that everything placed within it *matters.*

Finding Harmony in the Mosaic

The true beauty of a mosaic family is not found in the absence of conflict. It is found in the willingness to keep showing up after it. Harmony is not born from perfection. It is forged through the sacred struggle to understand one another, again and again.

Every person in a mosaic family carries their rhythm. Their color. Their own story. Harmony is not creating those rhythms in the same way. It is about learning how to live beside one another without canceling each other out.

For a long time, I thought peace would come from alignment — if we could get on the same page, share the same parenting style, respond the same way to conflict, things would settle. Absolute harmony came when I stopped trying to make us sound alike and started listening for the beauty in our differences.

I remember a night when all our kids, hers and mine, were scattered across the house after a long and tension-filled day. There had been tears, raised voices, and hurt feelings. I felt like a failure. I sat on the edge of the bed, head in hands, wondering if we would ever feel like a real family.

And then, my stepson walked in, not to apologize, to ask if I wanted to play a video game. Just a moment of shared time, nothing big. It *was* big. Because in that simple, quiet invitation, I saw the mosaic forming, not in forced unity, but in small moments of connection that did not require me to be perfect, only present.

Mosaic families are not built all at once. They are composed of moments like that, a board game invitation, an unexpected hug, a child laughing at a joke you thought they ignored. The harmony comes in the accumulation of ordinary grace.

Yes, there will be friction. There will be loyalty conflicts, misunderstandings, and days when it feels easier to pull away than to press in. But each decision to stay, to communicate, to learn creates something extraordinary. This mosaic sings, not because every note is the same, but because together they tell a deeper, more profound story.

As we continue this journey together, I invite you to stop striving for flawless structure. Instead, lean into the *formational beauty of imperfection*. Let the jagged edges have a place. **Let the silence between you be filled with patience.** Let your differences become your design.

Harmony in mosaic families does not happen when we get everything right.

It happens when we keep loving, especially when it would be easier to leave.

Mosaic Truth

Healing in mosaic families begins not with fixing the pieces, but with honoring them.

Belonging is not born from blending; it is earned through patience, grace, and the daily choice to stay, even when the edges do not match.

Reflective Questions

? How does each family member's history shape their role in the mosaic family?

? What loyalty conflicts or unresolved attachments might exist that need to be addressed openly?

? What part of your story still feels out of place? Can you give that piece a purpose, even if it doesn't "fit" yet?

? In what ways can clear communication and intentional boundary-setting strengthen your mosaic family's connections?

? How can embracing imperfections and acknowledging emotional gaps foster deeper connection and trust in your family?

Key Takeaways

- Mosaic families are not born by default; they are intentionally created, with each person bringing their history, pain, hopes, and identity to the table.
- Challenges like loyalty conflicts, unclear roles, and fragile emotional boundaries are real, but they do not have to break the family. With care, patience, and grace, they can become entry points for healing.
- Adaptability is not just a survival skill. It is a form of love. Harmony grows when we stop forcing people to fit in and start honoring who they already are.
- Like a well-crafted latte, mosaic families thrive when each person's individuality is respected and integrated thoughtfully, not blended into sameness but layered with intention.

Reader's Window

When the mosaic breaks again; there is a moment after divorce that no one prepares you for.
Not the court date.
Not the paperwork.
But the quiet.

I remember sitting alone in a house that once rang with my children's laughter. The walls still carried their handprints. The couch cushions remembered where we used to read stories. Now it only echoed.

And I asked God, What now?

That ache, the one between what was and what will be, is where many mosaic families live for a while — within the ruins.

Jana told me, *"It wasn't just the betrayal. It was losing the person I built a life with ... and the family we had created. It felt like everything I hoped for was suddenly gone."*

Vicki shared, *"The second time, I was stronger. But it still hurt. I knew I wasn't walking away from just a man — I was walking away from years of trying to make something sacred out of something broken."*

In the next chapter, we will go there.

Not to romanticize the pain. Not to offer quick fixes. But to walk through what happens when the mosaic crumbles again, and how some of the most sacred designs are born from what we never expected could be rebuilt.

Because redemption doesn't always start with answers.

Sometimes, it begins in the rubble, with nothing but your breath, your faith, and the stubborn belief that beauty might rise again.

"Sometimes the most sacred rebuilding begins with nothing but your breath, your brokenness, and the belief that even ruins can hold the blueprint for beauty." *—Dr. Steve Hudgins*

Chapter Seven

Ruins to Renewal

There are storms we see coming, and then there are storms that leave us standing in the wreckage, wondering what just happened.

Divorce is one of those storms.

It does not just tear at the surface. It rips up the roots. It shakes the foundation of identity, security, faith, and belonging. For many, it leaves behind more than broken vows. It scatters dreams, disrupts rhythms, and redefines what it means to be family.

Buried beneath the debris is something we rarely expect ... the possibility of renewal.

Finding time to flourish after divorce is not just an act of survival. It is a conscious, sacred choice to nurture the seeds of hope that remain, sometimes fragile, sometimes faint — yet still there. Healing is not about rushing to rebuild. It is about letting your soul bloom in the light of new beginnings, even while the ground still feels unsteady.

Jana described her second divorce as *"devastating."*

"It wasn't just the betrayal. It was losing the person I built a life with — and the family we had created. It felt like everything I had hoped for was suddenly gone, leaving me to rebuild from scratch."

Her words echo a reality many of us have lived: that divorce is more than the loss of a partner. It is the shattering of who we thought we were, and who we would become.

When the Church Adds Shame Instead of Grace

For me, as a Christian, the devastation carried spiritual weight. I did not just lose a marriage; I lost a piece of identity tied to what I believed marriage was supposed to mean. I grew up seeing it as sacred, as a covenant.

Divorce felt like disobedience. Like failure. Like shame wrapped in Scripture.

Like a shattered stained-glass window, my life cracked under the weight of what I thought could never be redeemed. Stained glass is not discarded when it breaks; it is reframed, relighted, and re-leaded with new light. The same is true for mosaic tiles. Even fractured, they are used again. Loss does not erase beauty; it reframes it. In those broken places, I began to glimpse the possibility of redemption. And yet, I had not chosen it. I did not want it. Still, there I was ... separated, aching, resentful, and suddenly unmoored.

What grieved me more than the divorce itself was the response of some in the faith community, the whispered judgment, the polite distancing, the unspoken assumption that I had somehow disqualified myself from belonging, even from my parents.

And I want to say this plainly:

It is time for the Church to stop wounding the already broken!

Too often, churches shun the divorced with silence or shame. They preach grace until it comes to marriage, and then suddenly, grace becomes conditional. But have we forgotten?

David was both an adulterer and a murderer and was still called a man after God's own heart.

Saul persecuted the Church, yet he became Paul, the voice of the New Testament, who contributed to increasing the number of believers through his own experience.

Elijah was so depressed that he asked God to take his life.
That Thomas doubted.
That Jonah ran.
Peter denied Christ.

Still, they were *used*. Not despite their failures, but often *through* them.

I recall stopping going to church or worship due to this feeling., I was, however, baptized in 2013 and renewed myself according to The Way.

My life is now faith-based, rather than religious.

There is no judgment of others, and this is often mentioned in my online reviews.

Is it not time we stop discarding the divorced and remarried as damaged goods and start *reclaiming* them as vessels of wisdom, compassion, and redemption? The Church should be the first place people run after their ruin, not the last. Because the gospel is not about pretending brokenness never happened; it is about bringing brokenness to the only One who makes all things new.

Yes, I have been judged.
Yes, I have been blamed.
I have also *owned my story*.

That's why I'm writing this book: not to glorify pain, but to preserve purpose. Not to revisit the wreckage, but to help others find their way through it without losing their soul.

Like a shattered stained-glass window, the structure of my life had broken. Yet stained glass is not thrown out when cracked — it is re-leaded, re-framed, and lit from behind with new light. Mosaic tiles are the same. Even fractured, they are used again. Loss does not erase beauty; it shapes it. And it was in those broken places that I began to glimpse the possibility of redemption.

This is not just about avoiding divorce.

It is about awakening the Church to be a place of healing again.

It is time for ruins to become renewal.

It is time for the broken to be seen, not as burdens, but as builders of something sacred.

Let me be clear — this is not a condemnation of the Church.

It is not a call to walk away from worship.

It is a plea to return to it rightly.

Because for me, worship is not a performance. It is not about appearing whole.

It is an *honor* — a sacred offering born from the ashes of what God has rebuilt in me.

I stand and serve because I know redemption. I sing because I have been forgiven. And I continue this work, not because I am perfect; because I know what it feels like to be shattered and still chosen.

Maybe I needed a moment here, a kind of commercial break, for anyone who calls themselves a Christian to pause and look inward. Not to point fingers. Not to place blame. It is worth remembering that the world is already burdened *with guilt.* What it needs is grace.

Jesus once said, *"I desire mercy, not sacrifice."*

We have made the church about sacrifices. What we need now is mercy.

My rant is over; however, my passion remains because I believe in the healing power of nature. Not the kind that pretends it did not hurt, but the kind that dares to hope again.

When Jesus approached the man who had been lame for thirty-eight years, He did not start with theology or rebuke.

He asked one question: *"Do you want to be healed?"*

So I will ask it here — gently, boldly, honestly:

Do you want to be healed?

Because if so, we must first stop reaching for what feels good ... and begin reaching for what restores.

The Pull Toward Quick Comfort: Why It Fails

If you're standing in the wake of divorce, craving the warmth of a new relationship, I see you. I know that ache, that hollow emptiness that screams to be filled. I remember the pull to escape the silence, to prove I was still lovable, still worthy, still whole.

It is so tempting to look outward when something inside feels shattered. You convince yourself that the next person will mend what the last one broke. That maybe love, the second time around, will make the ache go away.

What if, instead of reaching for someone new ... you reached for stillness?

What if, instead of chasing comfort, you brewed a quiet, rich cup of coffee, sat with the heat, and let the solitude speak?

Vicki understood this waiting. She shared:

"I spent three years emotionally preparing before leaving. I leaned on God, but I also leaned on learning to rediscover who I was. I refused to bring old baggage into something new."

James echoed that wisdom:

"I knew I had to step back and figure out where I went wrong before jumping into anything else. It gave me time to think about what I needed — and who I wanted to be."

Carly admitted:

"I realized I needed to understand what went wrong the first time and who I wanted to be before I brought someone else into my life again."

Their stories resonate because they reveal a truth many overlook:

Healing cannot be rushed.

The desire to connect is real, and so is the danger of repeating the past if we skip the pause. It is like taking a sip of fresh coffee too soon, hot, promising, and instantly painful. The flavor was there ... but the timing was off.

Rushing into a new relationship without grieving the old one often leads to 'old wounds dressed in new clothes.' When that happens, we confuse companionship with completion and wonder why we still feel lost with someone lying beside us.

Emotional healing invites stillness. Not isolation. Not punishment. But stillness.

The kind of stillness that allows you to taste both the bitter and the sweet. To discover your flavor before blending it with someone else's. The kind that says: *before I know whom I want, I must remember who I am.*

The Identity Crisis Beneath the Surface

When my marriage ended, I did not just lose a relationship; I lost a mirror. The roles I had known as husband, father, protector, and provider had once provided me with a sense of grounding. They told me who I was. And when those roles were stripped away, I found myself staring into a fog I could not name. A fog filled with grief, anger, shame, and guilt, swirling together like a storm that wouldn't lift.

Who am I now?
Who am I when no one else is naming me?
That question haunted me.

This is where many divorcees linger, caught not just in heartbreak, but in the fracturing of their selves. Divorce is not just the end of a partnership. It is the shattering of identities. You are not just left with silence; you are left with the echo of who you used to be, and no one to affirm that you still matter.

For someone like me, with an anxious attachment style, the disorientation was profound. I had spent years reaching for reassurance outside myself; anchoring my worth in connection, hoping that being needed would mean being loved. When the connection was severed, however, I was left flailing. And worse, blaming myself for everything that was broken.

Even now, remembering the past remarriages, that undertow tries to pull me back. Mosaic family life is full of triggers. It is easy to fall into shame when others accuse, yet they do not always understand the internal chaos of attachment, a topic I will explore more deeply later in this book. Just know this for now: if you feel like you're spinning, it doesn't mean you're broken. It means your nervous system is trying to protect you. You are not crazy. You are carrying pain that needs tending, not judgment.

You are not alone in this.

Joy told me her second relationship forced her to examine the story she had been living unconsciously. She realized she had been shaped more by patterns than by purpose. She said, *"I had to figure out what I was reacting to — and stop letting old pain write my future."*

Sarah echoed that wisdom:

"I had to learn to value myself outside of expectations. My second marriage taught me that rushing did not serve me."

That's what identity work looks like; not standing taller but sitting deeper. Peeling back the roles, the reactions, the guilt, and asking:

Who am I when no one else defines me?

And better yet... *Can I love that person enough to stop running from them?*

The Importance of Taking a Sabbatical After a Divorce

Many people jump into new relationships to fill a void. I did too. It comes from my heart, not from someone who's got it all right; it comes from someone who *got real.* Someone who stood in the rubble, wept in the silence, made choices they had to wrestle with, and still said: *"There is something worth building here."*

Looking back, I can now name it clearly: anxious attachment, shaped by childhood wounds, unmet emotional needs, and the quiet desperation to prove I wasn't broken.

Dating, even during the divorce process, gave me a temporary high; an illusion of being seen, needed, and worthy. I have been where you are. And I'm still learning too.

I remember one relationship in particular. She lived three hours away. She had five children. And I would drive to visit her on the weekends opposite those when I had my kids. What was I thinking? I'm thankful to have a job that covers my living expenses, allows me to travel, and enables me to give, while also covering child support. At the time, it felt noble. It felt good to serve, to show up, to help someone else. Underneath that service was a silent question echoing inside me:

Will this make me enough?
And then came the sting.

One evening, I noticed her laptop was open. An email caught my eye. I shouldn't have read it, but I did. And there it was: a message to another man, full of warmth, affection, and things she never said to me.

It crushed me.
Am I just a provider?
Am I just *a placeholder?*

I did not wait for an explanation. I did not say goodbye. I walked out.

Call that harsh. Maybe it was.

It was, however, also the moment I hit rock bottom emotionally.

That experience drove me to do the hardest thing I had avoided: look inward. I began personal therapy, not just to process the hurt, but to understand myself finally. To explore the patterns that kept leading me into pain. And it was from that deep dive, one marked by tears, humility, and deep emotional work, that I eventually found not only healing, but also purpose.

That was the beginning of my journey toward becoming a licensed therapist. It started not in a classroom, but in the wreckage of my own reflection.

This is the space where healing begins, not when we move forward, but when we finally turn inward.

Which leads to the deeper question we all must wrestle with:

Understanding Identity Crisis

As I navigated the complexities of my divorce, I found myself grappling with a harrowing identity crisis. My marriage had shaped my self-perception and played a significant role in my life story. When that relationship fell apart, I was left with haunting questions: "*Who am I without my partner?*" This disorientation was unsettling, throwing me into a whirlwind of confusion and vulnerability.

The sense of self I once held firmly felt frayed and uncertain. It was as if the foundation of who I was had crumbled beneath me, forcing me to confront a reality I had never expected. On top of this emotional upheaval, I was also dealing with the shadows of my childhood trauma and my struggles with anxious attachment disorder.

Having an anxious attachment style intensified everything I experienced during this tumultuous time. My need for connection and reassurance made separating my identity from my partner's incredibly challenging. The fear of abandonment, rooted in past experiences, loomed large in my mind. It often felt like I was losing not just a partner and my children but also the part of myself that was so closely tied to them.

As I faced this identity crisis, I realized that my anxious attachment made it difficult for me to trust in my own worth and independence. I struggled with feelings of inadequacy and an overwhelming desire to hold on to what once was, making it hard to accept the opportunity for renewal and self-discovery. Yet, as painful as this journey was, it also pushed me toward a transformative process of rediscovery that, while challenging, holds the promise of growth and healing.

I did not know how to heal through therapy at the time; it felt overwhelming and out of reach. Instead, I thought the only way to feel worthy again was to pick myself up and find another relationship. I believed that my value depended on someone else's recognition of me. It was a misguided way to seek validation, rooted in my struggles with anxious attachment.

In my search for worthiness, I often jumped into new relationships too quickly, hoping they would fill the void left by my marriage. I thought that being with someone new would help me reaffirm my identity and prove to myself that I was worthy of love. However, this approach only added to my confusion and vulnerability. Each new connection brought its challenges and left me feeling more lost, as I was still grappling with my sense of self.

Looking back, I realize the healing journey was much more profound than finding another partner. It required me to confront my past, explore my identity, and learn to love and accept myself first.

Joy shared a similar experience: how, after her divorce, even though she continued to co-parent alongside her ex-husband, she had to redefine herself, finding strength in that journey. She reflected, "I had to figure out who I was without the marriage title, and it was hard. But raising our daughters together even after the divorce showed me that my strength was not tied to being someone's wife, it was about who I was becoming."

James also reflected on the importance of pausing after his divorce, sharing, *"I knew I had to step back and figure out where*

I went wrong before jumping into anything else. It gave me time to think about what I needed and who I wanted to be."

While it has been a difficult path, I need to understand that someone else does not define my worth. True healing comes from within, and I am learning to build a solid foundation of self-acceptance and resilience that does not depend on the presence of someone else in my life.

"I realized I needed to understand what went wrong the first time and who I wanted to be before I brought someone else into my life again." (Carly's quote, Hudgins, 2025).

Interruption of Insight: What If My Story Disqualifies Me?

Let me pause here. Because maybe you're wondering...

How can a man who is a licensed therapist, a professor, a faith-based leader, a father, and a doctor still find himself in this kind of pain?

Does it make me less credible? Less trustworthy? Less worthy of guiding others? I have asked myself those very questions — *more than once.*

And here's what I have come to believe: what qualifies me is not my perfection — it is my perseverance.

It is the willingness to stand in front of others and say, *"I have failed, I have learned, I have lost, and I'm still here. Still believing in healing. Still reaching for grace. Still choosing love."*

This book is not my defense.

It is my offering.

It is not written to erase the past, but to redeem it.

Not to say, "look how strong I am," but to say, "here's where God met me when I was at my weakest."

And I cannot ignore the cost.

It did not just hurt me; it hurt my children.

When I remarried and later divorced again, I watched the ripple effects land in the hearts of the people I loved most. Each new connection brought its own set of challenges. Every shift in the family system added confusion, hope, disappointment, and pain. I thought I was building stability, but inside, I was still grappling with my sense of self.

Looking back, I realize now that healing is not something you can skip and expect others not to bleed.

My children did not need a perfect father. They needed a healing one. A present one. And I have become that man.

If you've ever been judged, misunderstood, or silenced, especially by people who claim to know your heart, please know this: you're not alone.

You're not disqualified.
You're not broken beyond repair.
You're in the right place.
And maybe, just maybe … this chapter was written for you.

Learned Advice, I give ….

If I could sit across from you, coffee in hand, and offer one thing from all I have lived, it would be this:

Do not rush to rebuild what broke you until you've sat long enough to understand how you got there.

Divorce doesn't just end a relationship; it exposes everything that was under the surface. Your fears. Your patterns. Your blind spots. It forces you to look at yourself, not through the eyes of judgment, but through the lens of grace and truth. It asks you to grow. Slowly. Intentionally.

Many of the participants in my dissertation shared this kind of hard-won wisdom; truth forged through lived experience in the complexities of mosaic family life.

Jana emphasized the **importance of self-awareness** and healing before even considering remarriage:

"I think that I would say, take your time and make sure you're out of that limerence phase. Know yourself, know what you want, and make sure you've done your own healing before you bring someone else into your life."

Carly spoke about **boundaries and emotional safety**:

"Slow down, really understand who you're choosing, and put yourself first with what you need and with healing. Learn to trust yourself again."

Vicki reminded others to **listen to what their gut**, and their circle, might be saying:

"If there were somebody in a similar situation, I would remind them to trust their instincts. Believe the people around you, because they are seeing things you may be glossing over. Take time to heal first."

Sue reflected on the importance of **clear communication and planning**:

"We should have talked about it, and we did not. We both came into the second marriage with our own ideas on parenting, and

they clashed. Better boundaries and pre-marital conversations would have helped."

And Sarah brought it all home with a truth that speaks volumes:

"You could be happy if you are a healthy individual, and you marry a healthy individual, and you're both committed to making a healthy relationship together. But you both have to be equally committed, and if you aren't, it is never going to work."

These are not just quotes.

They are warnings wrapped in love and wisdom born from pain. They speak to every man and woman standing in the in-between, wondering whether to move on or move inward first.

Because the truth is, you cannot build something new if the foundation is still cracked from before.

Which brings us to what most people never prepare for:

The Emotional Whirlwind: Navigating the Roller Coaster

No one tells you that after divorce, your emotions will ambush you in the grocery store aisle, in a song on the radio, in the quiet of your car after dropping off your child.

Another You may expect grief, although you don't expect it to be this *chaotic.*

You don't expect to feel *relief and rage in the same breath.*

You don't expect to miss someone who hurt you. Alternatively, to feel guilty for wanting space. Or to question your sanity when you cry in the morning and feel free by nightfall.

Divorce rarely offers a clean break.
Love tangles with resentment.
Relief collides with guilt.
Sadness competes with flickers of hope.
And the highs and lows feel relentless.

Many people, desperate to feel anything other than this whiplash, go numb. They bury themselves in busyness. They distract themselves. They date. They scroll endlessly or pretend they are fine. Avoidance is not healing. It is surviving.

And survival is not the same as restoration.

Mark described this emotional unraveling with brutal honesty:

"When they left, the house felt empty. My child was gone. It was devastating. I poured everything into my son, and then suddenly, I was alone."

That loneliness is not just about physical absence. It is about the internal collapse of a structure you thought would hold.

The fear that follows can be suffocating.
Financial instability.
Single parenting.
New living arrangements.
Courtrooms and custody calendars.

The sheer weight of the unknown can paralyze even the strongest.

And here's the truth that most people don't say out loud: Sometimes the most challenging part is not just losing your spouse, it is losing the rhythm of the life you built together.

The house feels unfamiliar.

The meals feel forced.

And the silence? It echoes deeper than you expected.

And right about here, maybe you're asking the same question I once asked:

"Will I ever get through this?"

"Can I ever get off this roller coaster?"

Yes.

You can.

But not by rushing to numb it. Not by pretending it never happened.

You get through it by slowing down long enough to feel it.

To grieve.

To rage.

To rest.

To find your feet again, not in who you were with someone else, but in who you're learning to become now.

Healing is not a straight line. And it is not fast.

Yet it is possible.

And even now, in the chaos, something in you knows it.

That's why you're still here.

Still turning pages.

Still searching.

So, take heart — this storm will not define you.

It will refine you.

Social Dynamics: Who Stays, Who Goes

It is one thing to lose your partner.

It is another thing entirely to lose your place in the world around them.

Divorce doesn't just sever romantic ties; it *reshuffles your entire social landscape.* The dinner invitations stop. The texts go unanswered. The people who once said, "We love you both," now slip quietly into silence or "choose a side."

And suddenly, you're grieving more than a marriage.

You're grieving *community.*

Betrayal doesn't always come from the person you divorced.

Sometimes it comes from the people who disappear.

From the in-laws who now treat you like a stranger.

From friends who avoid your calls because they do not know how to hold your pain, or worse, because your truth challenges their comfort.

Vicki described this fracture plainly:

"It is the little things. Friends, in-laws — you're no longer part of those circles. It hits in places you don't expect."

And she's right. It is not always the big moments.

It is the unfollowing — the quiet exit, the digital silence that reminds you that you are no longer included.

Sometimes all a metaphor needs is one extra breath, just enough context to transform a modern phrase into a universally understood emotional gut-punch.

The birthday party you hear about afterward.

The church row that no longer saves you a seat.

It is being erased quietly, without conversation, without closure.

And sometimes, there's betrayal layered beneath the silence.

I remember when she left. She said that my being in the hospital scared her. I realized that her girls needed her more than I did. And she walked away.

Something in my gut said this wasn't the whole story.

I called a friend and asked, "*Do you think she's talking to another man*?"

They did not just doubt me — they questioned my integrity.

But I was right.

Within six months, she remarried after the divorce.

And as for Me?

I was facing the darkest season of my life — a medical diagnosis with a 34% chance of survival. I was not only alone emotionally — I was battling for my life physically. And still, I kept quiet.

Because I'm private.

Because I did not want to poison the water.

Because even in my pain, I was trying to protect her reputation more than my own heartbreak.

Divorce is a cruel sword.

And often, what it cuts away is not what you intend.

Sometimes the death is not just to the marriage, but to friendships, circles, and even parts of yourself you did not know could bleed.

And I'll admit this:

I did not tell the whole story to my friends. I withheld things because I feared how it might reflect on both of us.

But I speak now — because **silence turns pain into shame**.

And I am not here to shame. I am here to learn, to heal, and to teach others how not to drown silently in what they think they must suffer alone. Through healing, I found a voice.

Not a perfect one.

But an honest one.

And this is where the loss becomes even more personal — not just who left your life, but what disappeared from it.

I stayed quiet because I believed speaking would cost me more.

But what I did not realize then ... was that silence was costing me my healing.

And yet, in hindsight, the pieces started to surface.

I remember one evening after a basketball game, nothing big, just another busy night of kids and transitions.

She leaned toward her daughter and said, *"He's here. Say goodbye. We'll see him later."*

I did not think much of it at the time. I assumed it was just a friend. Maybe someone from her side of the team, and now, looking back, I realize **that was 'him**.'

A man whose daughter also played basketball.

A man who lived two hours away.

The one she married six months later.

And me? I was still fighting for breath.

It wasn't just the betrayal that stung.

It was the realization that I had been erased while still standing in the room. That even as I tried to hold space for her healing, mine was quietly unraveling.

Why I Speak Now

So why do I speak now?

Not to blame.

Not to shame.

Nevertheless, because the truth unspoken turns inward.

And I will no longer carry that weight.

I used to believe silence was noble.

That protecting others from my truth was an act of love. I thought that telling my side of the story would only make things worse, stir up more pain, and make me look bitter or broken.

So, I said nothing.

Even when I was misjudged.

Even when others twisted the narrative.

Even when people who had never lived in my skin told my story for me.

I stayed quiet because I believed speaking would cost me more. What I did not realize then ... was that silence was costing me my healing.

I don't speak now to clear my name.

I speak to ***claim my voice.***

I speak because truth, when held in humility, is not vindictive — it is liberating.

I speak because shame thrives in secrecy. And because someone reading this needs to know that you are also allowed to speak.

Not to defend yourself.

Not to retaliate.

But to heal.

This is not about blame.

It is about becoming.

What We Lose Beyond Marriage

Divorce doesn't just break your heart — it breaks your calendar.

It breaks your bank account.

It breaks your sense of rhythm, predictability, and peace.

Suddenly, the most minor parts of your day, school drop-offs, shared meals, weekend plans, even the sound of the front door opening, shift into unfamiliar territory.

Routines once taken for granted are replaced with legal documents, custody exchanges, and moments that feel more like negotiations than parenting.

It is not just emotional pain. It is logistical chaos.
Managing child support.
Navigating courtrooms.
Tracking parenting schedules.
Paying bills on a single income.
Filling a fridge that used to be shared.
Sleeping alone in a house that still holds their toothbrush.

You are not alone, as some have shared in my research (Hudgins, 2025):

"After the divorce, I had to start from scratch. I did not realize how financially dependent I was until I was completely on my own."—Joy.

"The legal fees alone drained my savings, and I was left struggling just to cover my basic needs."—Lena.

This is the part few people talk about — the daily implosion. The countless tasks once handled together now fall squarely on your shoulders.

"I moved out and lived in my sister's front office room on a futon for six months. I literally had to start over."—Vicki.

I lived this. Fighting for the right to see my children was a battle I never imagined I would have to face, not because I was unfit, but because the system too often assumes a narrative before hearing the heart.

Balancing court dates, client sessions, visitation weekends, and raw emotional upheaval felt like walking a tightrope in a thunderstorm, every step uncertain, every moment demanding more than I had to give.

"When they left, the house felt empty. My child was gone. It was devastating. I poured everything into my son, and then suddenly, I was alone." —Mark.

And yet ... something surprising began to grow in that chaos:

Resilience.

Not the kind that looks polished.

The kind that shows up in wrinkled shirts and tired eyes.

The kind that says, *I'll keep showing up for my children, even if the system makes me prove I deserve to.*

Because here's the truth: when everything familiar falls apart, what is left behind is the chance to rebuild with intention.

And that's where we go next.

The Invitation to Heal: Slow, Intentional, Lasting

Healing doesn't knock. It whispers.

Usually, when the noise has died down, when the chaos of court dates, moving trucks, and changed passwords has finally settled, it comes not as an event, but as an *invitation* — an invitation to sit with yourself.

To stop sprinting.

To stop fixing.

And to finally feel.

Here is the truth you need to hear: healing is not a race. It is a slow brew — a process of grounding yourself, cup by cup.

Shock and numbness may come first. But over time, the storm settles.

And then?

You begin to feel.

You begin to confront.

You begin to reclaim.

Many of the participants in my study did not find healing in grand gestures, but in quiet choices.

Joy said:

"After my divorce, I took time to heal before even considering another relationship. That changed everything for me."

James shared:

"Healing wasn't immediate, but over time, I realized that I deserved a relationship where I felt valued and respected."

Tiffany admitted: *"I did not allow time for healing because three months later, I remarried a second time."*

That reflection, filled with hindsight and remorse, reminds us that fast love can't fix deep wounds.

For me, healing looked like therapy — two years of it. It looked like journaling. Like pulling back every layer of grief, childhood trauma, military pain, and anxious attachment. It looked like sitting still long enough to let God meet me there, not with answers, with presence.

Tori's insight mirrors that truth:

"It took me years to realize I needed to redefine what love and respect meant to me."

And Sarah reframed her entire journey with one bold sentence:

"Divorce wasn't the end of my story. It was the beginning of me choosing myself for the first time."

These voices, and mine, stand as proof:

You cannot heal by rushing to erase the past.

You heal by learning to sit with it.

To understand it.

To bless the ashes ... and then build something new.

And once the invitation to heal is accepted, the next step becomes clear — you must not do it alone.

Do Not Isolate: Step Into Life Again

When the heart breaks, the soul's first instinct is often to hide.

To pull back.

To disappear.

To protect what is left.

And after divorce, isolation doesn't knock loudly; it creeps in quietly.

It tells you it is just for a while. That no one will understand. It is your fault. That you're better off alone until you've figured it all out.

But here's the truth: isolation feels safe, but it slowly becomes a cage.

Withdrawal feeds the lie that you're too broken to belong, that your pain is too much. That your failure disqualifies you from joy. And I get it. I have watched it in others. One of my clients, at sixty-eight, endured a brutal divorce. For two years, he withdrew from everyone. No church. No friends. No hobbies. Just silence. One day, after gentle encouragement and time, he booked a solo cruise, his first bold step back into life. A man who once felt discarded rediscovered laughter, conversation, and the sacred act of living again.

And I have lived it, too.

In 2023, I took my first cruise — just me. Not as a romantic escape, but as an act of defiance against the dull ache that said, "Stay small. Stay safe." I met new people. I laughed. I sipped coffee on the deck and remembered that *life can still be good.* That I was still allowed to enjoy it.

I haven't remarried since my divorce in 2017. But I have chosen to engage intentionally, bravely, and imperfectly.

And that's what I offer to you: choose something.
Join the hiking group.
Start volunteering.
Take a painting class.
Sit at the café instead of having your coffee to go.
Say yes to that invitation you usually decline.
Move toward life. Even if your hands still shake.
Participant voices echoed this journey:

Joy said she withdrew after her divorce, pouring everything into co-parenting. Eventually, however, she realized that stepping into life outside her children brought back the confidence she hadn't felt in years.

Sue confessed that isolation only made her depression worse. Slowly, church and hobbies helped her reconnect with the community and with herself.

Sarah admitted, *"People I thought would support me just faded away, and I felt completely alone."* That fading silence becomes a weight all its own.

Carley confessed, *"I wanted to reach out for help, but I did not even know where to start."* And Joy put it: *"I lost my entire social circle when my marriage ended."*

So, here's the key: take time to heal, but don't use isolation as your permanent address.

Let stillness restore you, and don't let silence imprison you.

Yes, resist dating if your divorce is still fresh, especially if it has been less than two years. Don't wait to start living. Build a life worth sharing, whether someone joins you or not. Because the world still holds places that can make you feel whole again.

And you still belong to them.

Reclaiming Joy: Building Your Circle, Slowly

What if joy is not waiting at the end of your healing?

What if it is hidden right here beneath the ashes, within the quiet, between the ache and the choosing?

As you stand at this crossroads, divorced, healing, maybe wondering when or if love will find you again, know this:

This season is not barren.

It is fertile ground.

It is brimming with the possibility to redefine, rediscover, and reclaim joy in its most authentic form.

Your next relationship will only be as strong as the foundation you build on your own.

It will only be as fulfilling as the confidence and wholeness you nurture within yourself.

Yes, the temptation to fill the void quickly is real. Yet true healing, like brewing the perfect cup of coffee, cannot be rushed.

The flavors deepen in stillness. The aroma lingers longer when savored slowly.

Start small.

Begin by reestablishing your social circle. Engage in activities that ignite your passions. Surround yourself with friends who uplift you, who see you beyond your relationship status, and who speak to the deepest version of who you're becoming.

Sarah shared,

"It took me years to stop seeing myself through the lens of my marriage and instead focus on who I was becoming."

Carly echoed this truth:

"I needed to step back and understand what went wrong first. I did not want to carry old pain into something new."

This invitation is not to wait.

It is to cultivate actively.

Explore new hobbies. Pour yourself into creative projects. Reconnect with your values. Rebuild the rituals of your daily life, one intentional act at a time. Hold off on dating, not as punishment, but as *preparation* for something deeper and more enduring.

Embrace this sacred pause. It is not a setback. It is the soil in which the next version of you takes root.

Healing is not a race.

It is not a straight line.

It is a winding, sometimes messy, beautiful human process.

The harshest storms in the garden of life often prepare the ground for the most breathtaking blooms. Embrace the rain. Let it wash away the past. Nurture your roots with care. Because soon, you will rise anew.

Stronger.
Wiser.
Ready.

The garden metaphor reminds us: just as gardens require time, attention, and the right conditions to flourish, so does your inner world. Divorce is not the end. It is the turning point. Every storm and heartache enriches the soil, giving life to resilience, wisdom, and joy.

And here is the call to action I want to leave with you:
Do not wait for joy to knock at your door.
Go plant it. Water it. Tend to it.
It will grow. So will you.

Because when love comes again, and it will, it will not find someone desperate to be saved.

It will find someone who has already been resurrected.

So, breathe deep.

You've survived the storm.

Now it is time to cultivate what the storm revealed.

This is your moment to choose connection, not as escape, but as intention. To connect with your values. Your children. Your friends. Your faith. Yourself. And eventually ... someone new. Not however, from desperation. From rootedness.

Because the greatest gift you can offer another soul is not a patched-up version of who you used to be.

It is a secure, self-knowing, grace-anchored you.

And just as we reclaim joy one careful breath at a time, we must also learn how to 'brew' connection from the ground up, not just with others, but also with the fractured child within. That's where we turn next.

Mosaic Truth

Redemption is not the absence of brokenness; it is the bold reimagining of what love can become.

Even shattered stained glass catches the light when grace reframes it.

Reflective Questions

- ? How can you intentionally create space to reconnect with yourself before seeking another relationship?
- ? Which roles have defined you, and which no longer serve who you are becoming?
- ? Are you willing to sit in discomfort, trusting that healing happens in the pause?
- ? Which participant voices — Jana, Vicki, James, Joy, Sarah, Carly, Mark—resonate with your experience?

Key Takeaways

- Healing after divorce is not a waiting game. It is an intentional, nurturing process.
- Rebuilding your life requires patience, reflection, and surrounding yourself with supportive people.
- Participant experiences highlight the importance of self-awareness, emotional healing, clear boundaries, and trusting your instincts before entering new relationships.
- True resilience and fulfillment are cultivated when you focus on rediscovering your identity and nurturing your personal growth.
- Like a well-tended garden, your life blossoms when you give yourself time, care, and grace.

Chapter Eight

The Art of Brewing: Attachment and Identity

Connection is not automatic. It is brewed slowly, carefully, with intention and heat. We all long to feel known, to feel chosen, to be safe in the arms of someone who sees beyond our past. For many of us, especially those shaped by rejection, trauma, or emotional instability, connection doesn't come naturally.

It comes with confusion. With fear. With longing that doesn't always land in healthy places.

We crave closeness yet fear abandonment.

We seek intimacy but flinch at vulnerability.

We chase love, and often in patterns that leave us exhausted, overlooked, or misunderstood.

This is not weakness.

It is often the residue of attachment wounds, wounds that did not begin in your marriage, but were *revealed* by it.

And even more often, they were brewed in childhood.

This chapter is about more than healing — it is about understanding.

Understanding why we attach to the people we do.

Why do we repeat specific patterns?

Why some relationships feel like home, even when home wasn't safe.

And how our identity, often shaped before we even had language for it, determines how we show up in love, conflict, and connection.

When we were young, we learned what love meant by how it was given or withheld.

We learned if we were safe by how consistently someone showed up.

We learned if we were lovable by how they reacted when we needed them most.

And those early brews? They became the flavor of our attachment style. This chapter is an invitation to trace those threads between your past and your present, your story and your patterns. To brew a connection not from default, but from *deliberate healing*. Because a connection that lasts is not based solely on chemistry, it is not built on chaos, rescuing, or clinging.

It is brewed from something more rooted:

- Connection that is not codependence.
- Love that is not based on obligation.
- Presence that is not performance.

It begins not with finding the right person.

It begins with becoming the 'right self.'

When the Mirror Lies Back

What if the person staring back at you in the mirror doesn't feel familiar anymore? What if your reflection feels fractured, blurred by questions you can't quite name — like Who am I now? Who have I been? And why do I keep attaching to people who do not stay?

This is not just confusion. It is what happens when attachment collides with identity. After divorce, especially within the complexities of a mosaic family, the roles that once defined us fall apart. The emotional mirrors we used to measure our worth crack. Suddenly, we're left trying to make sense of who we are without someone else's eyes reflecting to us.

This section is about that moment. About why we love the way we do. About how our earliest bonds shape the people we choose and why we sometimes choose pain in the name of love. Human attachment is not just a psychological term; it is the invisible blueprint that guides how we relate, trust, reach out, and retreat. It is the way we brew connection ... or fear it. Moreover, most of it began long before our first marriage.

As you continue reading, you may find pieces of your past childhood wounds, family patterns, and relationship cycles surfacing with new clarity.

That is not shameful.

That is healing, beginning to speak.

Before we can change how we connect, we must understand why we connect the way we do.

From here, you can continue with:

"What if, sometimes, when we look in the mirror, the reflection staring back seems fractured, distorted ..."

... and flows into the original body of your writing, with all its depth and precision.

Preface: When Attachment Wounds Run Deeper

Attachment styles influence how we love, trust, and connect with others. Sometimes, the story goes deeper. When emotional needs are consistently unmet in childhood, when love is given and taken away unpredictably, when safety is fragile or shame is used to control ... those early experiences leave more than emotional scars; they shape the blueprint of our identity, relationships, and coping mechanisms.

In many cases, these wounds manifest as anxious, avoidant, or disorganized attachment styles. With support and reflection, many individuals go on to form meaningful, lasting, and connected relationships, even after a difficult start. Many who commit to healing eventually shift toward what is known as secure attachment, a process I have experienced personally and will unpack later in this chapter.

When attachment injuries are compounded by trauma, neglect, or chronic invalidation, the patterns can deepen. What began as an emotional adaptation can evolve into more complex relational challenges, sometimes even traits associated with personality disorders.

Let me be clear:

Not everyone with insecure attachment develops a personality disorder.

Most do not.

For some, the pain goes underground, mutating into patterns of distrust, emotional instability, identity confusion, or chronic conflict in relationships. These are not character flaws. They are survival strategies, adaptive and protective responses to environments that once felt unsafe, chaotic, or neglectful.

Over time, these protective walls can harden into rigid ways of thinking, reacting, and attaching that cause pain not only to the individual but also to those who love them. Even then, however, healing is possible. With therapeutic support, self-awareness, and compassionate accountability, many people develop what is known as 'earned secure attachment,' a new relational foundation built not on fear but on trust.

And before we move on, we must also name something that masquerades as love: trauma bonding.

Trauma bonding is not a real connection; it is a survival-based attachment formed through repeated cycles of abuse, inconsistency, and intense emotional highs and lows. It often feels powerful. Familiar. Even intoxicating.

It is not healthy love.
It is a bond rooted in fear, not freedom.
In obligation, not safety.

Often, those with unresolved attachment wounds mistake the intensity of trauma bonding for intimacy.

Understanding the difference between healthy attachment and trauma-fueled entanglement is key to rewriting our relational story.

As we now explore the relationship between attachment and personality, I invite you to approach this next section with curiosity and compassion. You may see reflections of yourself. You may see someone you love.

Either way, remember:

These patterns are not life sentences.

They are invitations: To heal. To grow. To become.

Are Any Personality Disorders Associated with Secure Attachment?

Short answer: No.

Secure attachment is rarely associated with the development of personality disorders.

Let's unpack why that matters.

Why Not?

Secure attachment forms when a child grows up knowing they are safe, seen, soothed, and supported. It is not about perfect parenting; it is about *consistent enough caregiving*. Children who experience emotional safety, appropriate boundaries, and reliable love grow up with something many people spend decades trying to earn: a stable sense of self.

They learn to trust others.

To regulate their emotions.

To believe they are worthy of love without having to perform for it or chase it.

So, when those children become adults, they are better equipped to form relationships that are mutual, respectful, and stable. They can set boundaries without guilt. They don't fall apart when conflict arises. They recover after rupture. They can be alone without being abandoned, and together without being smothered.

Personality disorders, on the other hand, often emerge from the *opposite foundation*:

Chronic emotional neglect.

Unpredictable or unsafe caregivers.

Trauma that goes unacknowledged.

Love that feels like a trap instead of a shelter.

When the emotional ground is shaky from the start, identity gets built on survival, not security. And over time, that survival strategy can harden into deeply ingrained relational patterns — ones that affect how a person sees themselves and how they connect with others.

That's why secure attachment and personality disorders rarely overlap.

Can Someone with a Personality Disorder Ever Develop Secure Attachment?

Yes.

Absolutely.

Secure attachment is not just something you inherit. It is something you can *earn*. With enough self-awareness, reflection, and consistent relational healing, many people with insecure or even disorganized attachment styles can move toward a secure base. It takes work. It takes time. Nevertheless, it is absolutely possible. This kind of healing often begins with one safe relationship.

A therapist.

A mentor.

A spouse who shows up differently than anyone ever has before.

Over time, with trust and truth, the nervous system begins to rewrite the story:

"I am not abandoned."

"I am not too much."

"I am safe to be loved."

So now, let's look at what this healthiest form of connection actually looks like — not in theory, but in practice. When you know what secure attachment looks like, you can then begin to recognize it in others, and most importantly, begin to nurture it within yourself.

Let's start there.

Why This Chapter Matters in Mosaic Relationships

So why is this chapter even here? Why are we talking about attachment in a book about mosaic families and remarriage? Because attachment explains why we marry the way we do, and why some of us remarry in ways that repeat the same pain.

Your first marriage may have failed, not because you lacked effort or love, but because unhealed attachment wounds were driving the connection. And when those wounds go unrecognized, they often choose again for us in our second marriage, sometimes louder, sometimes faster, sometimes more painfully.

Understanding your attachment style helps you stop asking, *"Why do I always end up here?"* And start asking, *"What am I really reaching for?"*

This chapter is here to show you that connection is not just about chemistry; it is about your story. Who you attach to, how you attach, and whether that attachment brings healing or harm, is often rooted in what you learned long before you said, 'I do.' And until you understand that you risk repeating the same pattern with a new partner and expecting a new outcome.

This, however, is not about shame. It is about clarity. Because clarity brings choice. Even better, choice brings healing. This is where we begin to rebuild. If insecure attachment explains why we fall into familiar patterns that hurt us, then secure attachment shows us what it means to form a connection that heals us.

Secure attachment is not a fantasy. It is not perfect. And it is not limited to people who had perfect childhoods. It is the lived experience of safety, trust, and emotional balance. It is the kind of connection that feels steady, even when life is not. This section will help you recognize what secure attachment looks like — not just in others, but in yourself.

Because once you can name it, you can begin to nurture it.

Secure Attachment: A Model Worth Brewing

What, then, does a healthy connection look like? In a world of blended stories, broken trust, and relational instability, secure attachment is not just a theory; it is a lived reality for those who were given (or learned to build) safety, connection, and emotional consistency.

If you've ever wondered what it looks like to love without panic, to connect without losing yourself, or to belong without needing to prove your worth, this is it.

Secure attachment is not perfection.

It is presence.

It is boundaries with warmth.

It is communication that seeks understanding, not control.

And even if you did not experience it growing up, it is something you can learn to build now, in your parenting, your marriage, and your mosaic family.

Let's start by understanding what secure attachment really looks like, from childhood to adulthood, and why it is the foundation of every healthy relationship you long for. Let me put it this way: Secure attachment occurs when a child knows deep down that their caregiver will consistently show up for them, both emotionally and physically. It is that inner sense of safety that says, "I can count on you. You've got me." When a child feels consistently seen, soothed, and safe, they build confidence to explore the world, make mistakes, and seek comfort without fear of being rejected or shamed. What does this look like as we age?

As a Child

Securely attached children feel safe and secure in their caregivers' care. They explore the world confidently but seek comfort from their caregivers when they feel scared or anxious. They demonstrate distress when separated but are easily comforted upon reunion.

As an Adult

Adults with secure attachment tend to have healthy, balanced relationships. They are comfortable with intimacy and independence, can communicate needs effectively, and manage conflict constructively.

Imagine a child who, with a beaming smile, confidently explores a playground, climbing to new heights on the jungle gym and making new friends with ease. This child, having developed a secure attachment, feels a deep sense of safety and protection from their caregivers. Even when a sudden scare occurs, a loud noise, or an unexpected fall, they know they can turn to their loving parents for comfort. While they may show signs of distress during separations, their trust in the reliability of their caregivers means they are quickly soothed upon reunion.

Fast forward to adulthood, and this securely attached child grows into an individual who thrives in relationships. They approach intimacy with confidence, striking a balance between their need for closeness and independence. Communication flows naturally for them; they express their thoughts and feelings openly, which allows them to navigate conflicts constructively and healthily. This sense of security fosters stable and nurturing relationships, reflecting the solid foundations laid during their early years. If you relate to this experience, cherish the understanding of how that safe base can shape positive relationships in your life.

How Secure Attachment Shows Up in a Mosaic Family

Grounded in their experiences within a mosaic family, securely attached individuals appreciate the many forms of love and support in their lives, leveraging these insights to cultivate positive, lasting relationships that reflect the diverse connections they have known.

To establish secure attachments, caregivers in a mosaic family can:

Be Consistent and Present: Show up emotionally and physically for the child, providing stability and reassurance.

Promote Open Communication: Encourage children to express their feelings and thoughts about their family dynamics without fear of judgment.

Celebrate Each Relationship: Recognize the significance of each caregiver in the child's life and cultivate positive interactions among them.

Model Healthy Relationships: Demonstrate respectful and supportive interactions, which teach children how to build their own relationships.

John, one of my clients, shared his approach to creating safety and consistency in his mosaic family after his divorce: *"I did not want my kids to feel like everything was being ripped apart, so I made sure they knew I was still their dad — always. Even when I moved into a new house, I tried to maintain the same routines: Sunday breakfasts and bedtime check-ins. It gave us something to hold onto, and eventually, that built trust again — not just with them, but with myself as well."*

As an Adult in a Mosaic Family:

For adults, particularly stepparents or individuals with children from previous relationships, secure attachment facilitates healthier relationships and fosters a sense of stability within the mosaic family. These adults approach their roles with confidence and a positive mindset.

Behavior Examples

Open Communication: An adult with a secure attachment style actively encourages and participates in open dialogue within the family. They are comfortable discussing feelings, expectations, and conflicts, which helps to create a family climate of trust and understanding.

Supportive Relationships with Stepchildren: They build meaningful connections with their partner's children, treating them with care and establishing boundaries while fostering a supportive environment. A securely attached adult can foster feelings of belonging and safety among all children.

Effective Conflict Resolution: When conflicts arise, these adults approach problems calmly and constructively, encouraging problem-solving discussions that focus on collaboration rather than confrontation. They model healthy emotional regulation for the entire family.

What would healthy communication be like in a secure attachment?

Stepchild:

"I don't want to go to that dinner. It is uncomfortable for me. I feel like I don't belong."

Stepparent (calm, validating):

"I really appreciate you sharing how you feel. That takes courage. You do belong, even when it feels messy or confusing. Can you help me understand what feels uncomfortable about it?"

Stepchild:

"I don't know... It just feels fake. Like everyone's pretending."

Stepparent (non-defensive, open):

"Thank you for being honest. I know this family has gone through a lot of change, and it is okay if it doesn't feel real yet. I don't expect you to pretend; just be yourself. What would help you feel more comfortable, even if we go for a little while?

Core Characteristics of Securely Attached Conversations:

- **Validation over fixing:** Emotions are acknowledged without rushing to "solve" them.
- **Curiosity over control:** Asking questions, instead of assuming, fosters openness.
- **Regulated tone:** Even when emotions rise, the secure person stays calm and grounded.
- **Boundaries with warmth:** Respecting individual needs while maintaining emotional presence.

Impact on the Mosaic Family

The presence of secure attachment styles among both children and adults can create a positive and cohesive mosaic family dynamic. Family members feel comfortable relying on one another for emotional support, which leads to stronger bonds and a more intimate sense of belonging.

In one instance, Carly expressed that her second marriage worked, not because things were easy, but because emotional openness became a shared value. *"We agreed to do things differently this time, more talking, more checking in, more listening. Even when the kids struggled, we stayed present. That's what saved us,"* she said.

To nurture this secure environment, it is essential to maintain open lines of communication and establish consistent routines that create predictability and stability. Regular family check-ins or shared activities can reinforce familial connections and keep relationships strong. By modeling healthy relational behaviors, securely attached family members help foster an atmosphere of love, acceptance, and understanding, ultimately benefiting the entire mosaic family unit.

In such an environment, all family members, regardless of their attachment styles, can feel supported and encouraged to grow and connect with one another. This leads to a thriving mosaic family dynamic characterized by resilience, love, and emotional well-being.

It is essential to remember that secure attachment is not a guarantee; rather, it is a possibility shaped by the environment, consistency, and emotional availability. Not everyone had the gift of feeling safe and seen in childhood. For many, early relationships were inconsistent, unpredictable, or emotionally distant. These early experiences can plant seeds of anxiety and fear that follow us into adulthood, quietly shaping how we give and receive love.

I did not always know what a secure connection looks like. For years, I equated love with fixing. I believed that if I could just be stable enough, strong enough, and have enough, then I would be loved. However, over time, through therapy, reflection, and the quiet moments of rebuilding with my children, I began to understand that security is not something I can force. It is something I choose to model. Now, when my children reach out to me, not because I have fixed everything, but because I'm present; that's when secure attachment takes root.

Not just in them.

In me.

In the mosaic family system, where relationships are layered and often carry remnants of past losses, these attachment wounds can surface with surprising intensity. Understanding anxious attachment is key to recognizing why some individuals feel a desperate need for closeness while simultaneously fearing the very abandonment they try to prevent.

Not everyone grew up with consistency. Some of us learned love through tension. We became hyper-attuned to others' moods, felt responsible for everyone's peace, and learned to chase closeness to avoid feeling abandoned.

This is where anxious attachment begins.

Anxious Attachment

(or Preoccupied Attachment)

Not everyone grew up knowing love was safe. Some of us learned that love could disappear without warning. That closeness had to be earned. If we did not try hard enough, please deeply enough, or give constantly, we might be left behind. This is the root of anxious attachment.

It is not about being needy. It is about being wired to survive uncertainty. **Anxiously attached individuals don't fear love; they fear losing it.** And often, they chase it with everything they have, even if it means losing themselves in the process.

Anxious attachment, when left unrecognized or unhealed, can deepen over time, especially if reinforced by relational trauma, abandonment, or chronic invalidation. In some individuals, this attachment style becomes more than a pattern; it becomes a lens through which they see themselves and others, often with overwhelming emotional intensity. When early attachment wounds combine with environmental instability or trauma, they can lay the foundation for more complex struggles, including personality disorders.

Three different personality disorders are associated with anxious or disorganized attachment. One of the most associated conditions is borderline personality disorder. A diagnosis is often misunderstood, yet deeply rooted in emotional pain, longing, and the fear of being unloved.

Borderline Personality Disorder (BPD)

Often, it may sound like this, as I have heard it in my practice: *"I know I can be too much, but I just need to know you're not going to leave me. One minute, I feel like you love me, and the next, I feel invisible. I hate that I get so emotional, but when I care, I really care, and when I feel ignored, it feels like I'm dying inside. Please don't give up on me."*

People with BPD often struggle with intense fear of abandonment, emotional highs and lows, and unstable relationships. These patterns usually stem from early experiences where love and safety were inconsistent or unpredictable. As children, they may have experienced caregivers who were both comforting and frightening, leaving them emotionally confused and insecure.

Those with BPD typically did not experience consistent emotional safety growing up.

Can this be treated or managed?

BPD is highly treatable. With long-term therapy, especially approaches such as Dialectical Behavior Therapy (DBT), individuals can learn to manage their emotions, build stable relationships, and develop an earned secure attachment style. Healing is possible.

Another typical style associated with anxious attachment is the

Histrionic Personality Disorder (HPD)

HPD is often linked to anxious attachment because it involves an intense need for approval, attention, and reassurance from others. People with this pattern may have grown up feeling that love was only given when they were "on," charming, entertaining, or emotionally expressive. If caregivers were inconsistent — alternating between being attentive and emotionally unavailable — the child may have learned to earn connection through performance, drama, or heightened emotional expression.

'Do you even notice me anymore? I feel like no one cares unless I'm making people laugh or telling a story. I walk into a room and I try to light it up, but when the spotlight fades, I feel ... empty. I don't mean to be dramatic; I don't want to be forgotten.'

This often leads to adults who feel deeply insecure underneath their outward charisma. They may struggle with a fear of being unseen, unimportant, or abandoned, even in the presence of close relationships.

Can this be treated or managed?

Yes. With consistent therapy, especially approaches that focus on building a stronger sense of self-worth and emotional regulation, individuals with histrionic traits can develop more authentic and stable relationships. Healing involves learning that you do not need to perform or exaggerate to be loved.

Another common style associated with anxious attachment is the

Dependent Personality Disorder (Codependent)

This disorder often forms when a child learns that their needs will only be met if they stay close, compliant, or emotionally fused with the caregiver. As adults, they struggle with making decisions, fear abandonment, and rely heavily on others for reassurance and guidance.

Can this be treated or managed?

Yes. Through therapy, individuals can develop confidence in their voice, establish healthy boundaries, and learn to rely on others without compromising their autonomy. Healing means discovering that you are allowed to stand on your own and still be loved. Often, clients have shared in my practice both inpatient and outpatient:

"I just want to keep the peace — I don't want to upset anyone. If they are okay, then I'm okay."

"I know I'm exhausted, but they need me. If I don't help, who will?"

"I don't even know what I want anymore. I'm just so used to putting everyone else first."

"I feel guilty saying no. What if they get mad? What if they leave?"

These voices reflect someone who is deeply afraid of being rejected, emotionally abandoned, or seen as selfish for having their own needs. Codependent people often equate love with self-sacrifice and struggle to recognize where others end and they begin.

Would you like to explore how codependency might show up in mosaic families, like a stepparent over-functioning for a child, or a biological parent caught between loyalty binds?

The Voice of Codependency — In My Own Story

Looking back, I can see how the seeds of my codependency were planted early. I did not date much in high school, not because I did not want to, more because I lived on a military base overseas. I felt isolated, out of place, and often unsure of my place. During my spring semester, when we relocated to Oklahoma, I began dating someone, a kind, and beautiful soul. However, before anything could really unfold between us, she was tragically killed in a head-on collision. I was on my way to pick her up from her house when it happened, unaware that she had died an hour earlier. We did not have cell phones in the mid-80s. There was no warning. No goodbye. Just silence.

Such a loss has a profound impact on you. It leaves a crack in the foundation, one that makes me question whether love will always be taken away just when it arrives.

In college, I began dating more frequently, and I recall feeling insecure. One moment still lingers in my mind. I received a phone call from someone I had a crush on back in high school, someone from that time when I lived abroad. I asked her, *"If I had asked you out in high school, would you have said yes?"* She paused, then answered, "Yes. Why didn't you?"

And I remember replying, *"Because I was afraid that I wasn't good enough. I was afraid you'd say no."*

That fear of not being enough, of being rejected, of love slipping through my fingers, became a quiet undertone in my relationships. I learned to please, to perform, to pour myself out for others, hoping it would make me worthy of staying. I did not realize then that this was codependency. I just thought I was being loving, loyal, and dependable. Nevertheless, underneath, I was terrified of abandonment.

My Attachment Style is Anxious

Allow me to pause here and say this clearly: ***"I love both of my parents."***

Please understand me as I continue to write the following because anxious attachment was my disorder, prior to me becoming a doctor and therapist. The purpose of this book is to share my journey and to raise awareness, encouraging the necessary changes going forward.

I am not trying to paint the worst picture of my parents, nor am I denying all that they did right. This is my inner child speaking, giving voice to the unspoken memories that shaped my emotional wiring. And while there were wounds, there were also gifts. In therapy, it is essential to allow this inner child to emerge and be acknowledged, so that they can feel safe and heard.

Finding Myself in the Mirror of Attachment

If I'm being honest, I didn't always feel confident in myself. My journey into understanding attachment did not begin in a textbook; it began in the quiet ache of childhood. I had comfort, yes. I had relatives who loved me, who listened, who made the effort to show up. Despite this, I often found myself craving touch and closeness. A hand on my back. A hug that lasted just long enough to say, *"you matter."*

My father served in the Air Force. When I was just a year and a half old, barely able to walk, he was deployed to Thailand. Later, around the age of seven, he was sent to Korea. These were not just geographic separations. They were emotional ones. Not having that consistent father-child bond during those crucial developmental years deepened the roots of my anxious attachment. I grew up learning how to reach for someone who was often just out of reach.

And then there was my mother.

As a child, I did not have the words to describe what I was experiencing; I only knew that something always felt ... off.

Years later, through therapy and deep reflection, I gained a deeper understanding. My mother had a full hysterectomy early in life, and the unresolved grief, loss, and trauma from that experience may have shaped her emotional availability. I also came to realize that some mothers struggle to bond with children born with medical differences. I was born with a cleft palate. That kind of vulnerability, mine and perhaps hers, was never talked about. It was tucked behind layers of perfectionism.

Every summer, we would visit the Lackland Air Force Base hospital, known as Wilford Hall, and attend a camp for children with cleft palates. I was the first patient to undergo a unique surgery performed by Dr. Gruber, which changed my life. It was an all-day, grueling experience of X-rays, hearing tests, and longitudinal studies on people with cleft palates. Imagine these surgeries and separations impacting me as a baby.

My mother was deeply concerned with appearances. Everything had to be flawless, herself, our family, even the house. I still remember people coming over, friends, relatives, and neighbors, commenting on how cold our home felt. Not cold in temperature, but in spirit. It felt like a museum. Pristine. Untouched. Carefully curated. Anything that could not be neatly placed or controlled, such as emotions, needs, or flaws, was often dismissed or ignored.

"You are backtalking." – Got soap, hot sauce, or a backhanded comment.

"Go to your room, I don't want to hear it." – I often spent alone time here.

"If you only had stood still, you wouldn't have gotten hit as badly." – spanked out of anger that resulted in welts and bruises, and she denied it when I confronted her, but my grandparents, cousins, and a special aunt that I was close to know the tragic events I went through.

Perfectionism was not just about maintaining a good family image. It became deeply personal.

I felt it in the most minor details. I was not allowed to wear jeans with holes in them, even if they were trendy. And I will never forget being thirteen, lying on the floor, begging her to stop, as she held me down, picking at the pimples on my face.

"Please stop," I cried. *"They are already making fun of me at school."*

She could not bring herself to stop hurting me. She never did this to my sister. Because in her world, flaws were not allowed. I understand now that she likely meant well. In her own way, she was trying to help me fit in, to look better, to avoid rejection. Back then, it made me feel like I was the imperfection she needed to fix. Unfortunately, because I write about my past and the changes I have made in my life to become a healthier person, she has cut me out of her life and has denied me the chance to see my father. As I write this, he is in hospice care.

That emotional climate taught me that messiness, especially emotional messiness, was unsafe. If I wanted to be accepted, I needed to be polished. Pleasing. And sometimes invisible. And yet, the child in me still longed for something softer. For warmth. For permission to just be.

Still, I hold the whole picture.

I remember the good, too: my father teaching me how to work on cars, taking me hunting, and sharing his love for the outdoors. My mother passed on valuable skills, such as how to cook, clean, wash laundry, and decorate with intention and beauty. Both tried to instill values, morals, and a sense of right and wrong.

One of the greatest gifts they gave me was their belief in God. We attended church on Sundays and Wednesdays, and those early moments helped shape my understanding of faith. That foundation would grow deeper later in life; the seeds were planted in those sacred, simple routines. Still, the longing remained. That need for consistency. For closeness. For emotional presence.

It followed me into adulthood. It crept into my relationships. It echoed in the silence, in the space between messages, in the fear that love might vanish if I did not hold onto it tightly enough. I remember sitting in therapy, slowly connecting the dots between my childhood and what I would later learn was called anxious attachment. It was a hard truth to swallow at first, realizing that somewhere deep down, I had believed love had to be earned. That I had to chase it. Prove myself worthy of it.

But it was also freeing. Because naming it gave me power. And with time, grace, and a lot of self-reflection, I began to heal. I started to trust myself. I learned to rebuild a new, more secure foundation. It did not happen overnight. It took years. And ultimately, it led me into the very work I do now. Becoming a therapist was not just a profession; it was also a part of my own healing. And the more I studied, the more I healed. The more I heal, the more I can guide others through their healing process. During my time of cancer and facing death, I did reach out to those whom I hurt and did not realize the pain I was causing due to my insecurities of attachment disorder.

So, what does anxious attachment look like?

As a Child

Anxiously attached children may have caregivers who are inconsistent in their responses. These children might become overly clingy, excessively seek reassurance, and exhibit anxiety or distress when separated from their caregivers.

As an Adult

Adults with this attachment style often crave closeness and fear abandonment. They may become preoccupied with their partner's availability and exhibit jealousy or insecurity in relationships.

Imagine a child who yearns to be close to their caregiver yet remains uncertain whether that comfort will be consistently offered. Sometimes their parents are warm and attentive, while at other times they are distracted or emotionally unavailable. The child, desperate for safety, becomes hyperaware, clinging, scanning for signs of disconnection, and internalizing fear that love might be withdrawn at any moment.

As this child grows into adulthood, those patterns do not simply disappear. They often continue to crave deep connection while fearing they are too much or not enough. Relationships may feel like emotional tightropes, deeply desired, yet always under threat. The adult may constantly question their partner's commitment, interpret minor shifts in tone or behavior as signs of rejection, and cycle between intense need and emotional overwhelm.

Jana, one of the women I interviewed, described the emotional chaos she felt after her second divorce. *"I thought if I could just love enough, give enough, prove myself, it would be okay. But when he left, it felt like a replay of everything I feared deep down. I was never sure he was in it. And honestly, I was never really sure I was enough."* Her experience reflects the heart of anxious attachment — the hunger for security paired with the lingering belief that love must be earned, rather than received.

How Anxious Attachment Looks in a Mosaic Family

In a mosaic family, anxious attachment can manifest in various ways, particularly among children who may feel uncertain about their place within the new family dynamic.

Child Behaviors

Clinginess: A child may become overly attached to one parent or caregiver, fearing separation or abandonment.

Fear of Rejection: They may worry about being liked or accepted by step-siblings or stepparents.

Emotional Ups and Downs: These children may experience emotional swings between happiness and distress, especially when they sense any emotional distance.

Overanalyzing Interactions: Even slight changes in attention or tone can trigger fear or excessive worry.

Difficulty with Transitions: Moving between homes or adjusting to new family members may provoke heightened anxiety.

Constant Reassurance-Seeking: Questions like, *"Do you still love me?"* or *"Will you always be my parent?"* are common.

Jealousy or Rivalry: Insecurity may lead to competition with step-siblings for affection.

Distrust of Stability: Even in loving environments, these children may struggle to believe it will last.

One client in a session mentioned how her stepson would always hover near her, even after a full day together, stating, *"At bedtime, he would ask repeatedly if I'd still be here in the morning. It broke my heart. I realized he wasn't trying to manipulate — he was scared. His world had already changed once. He needed to know I wasn't going to vanish, too."*

Anxious Attachment in Adults in Mosaic Families

For adults, especially stepparents or those bringing children from previous relationships, anxious attachment can complicate emotional roles and expectations.

Adult Behaviors

Need for Constant Reassurance: They may frequently ask their partner for validation or confirmation of love.

Overreacting to Conflict: Even small disagreements can feel threatening, triggering fear of loss or rejection.

Difficulty Balancing Relationships: They may feel insecure if their partner shows attention to biological children, interpreting it as a loss of connection.

Hypervigilance: They may monitor every interaction, fearing subtle signs of abandonment.

Jana admitted that during family transitions, she often questioned her place in the family. *"When my husband would spend time with his daughter, I knew it made sense, but I still felt pushed aside. I did not say anything at first, but it started to eat at me. I would question everything, his tone, his silence, even how long he hugged her."*

What would healthy communication look like in the context of anxious attachment?

Context: A teenage stepchild with anxious attachment feels left out after a biological parent and stepparent go to a movie with the stepparent's biological child.

Stepchild (hurt, reactive):

"I guess you guys just forgot about me again. Whatever. I don't even matter."

Stepparent (initially unsure, then attempts to engage):

"Whoa, slow down. That's not true. We did not forget about you. It just happened last minute."

Stepchild (escalating):

"You always say that. You just don't want me around. You never include me in anything!"

Stepparent (trying to soothe):

"I am really sorry it felt that way. That was never my intention. I can see this really hurt you, and I want to make it right. Can we talk about what would help you feel more included next time?"

Core Characteristics of Anxiously Attached Conversations:

Emotional intensity: The person often reacts strongly, even to minor situations, because they trigger deeper fears of rejection or abandonment.

Testing or protest behaviors: Phrases like "I guess you don't care" are not just anger — they are bids for connection.

Fear of being left out or forgotten: Even small shifts in attention or inclusion can feel deeply threatening.

Reassurance-seeking: They may need repeated affirmations of love, belonging, or importance.

Therapeutic Insight:

For caregivers or stepparents, the key is to **stay calm, attuned, and present**. Avoid dismissing their emotions and offer gentle truth with empathy. Instead of defending, try reflecting on the fear that lies beneath the words. Secure bonds are built by showing that **their intensity will not drive you away**.

Impact on the Mosaic Family

The presence of anxious attachment in adults and children can lead to emotional strain within the family system. Constant reassurance-seeking may exhaust other family members. Misinterpretations can create tension, misunderstandings, and emotional distance.

Emotional volatility can disrupt routines, stability, and connection. To mitigate these challenges, families must cultivate open communication, emotional consistency, and safe spaces for vulnerability. Reassurance must be genuine and paired with clear boundaries. Caregivers can help children and adults with anxious attachment build trust through predictable routines, affirming words, and physical presence.

Family therapy, narrative healing, and guided check-ins can serve as tools for deepening trust. Just as children with anxious attachment may struggle to feel secure in a shifting family landscape, adults with this style often wrestle with their own fears of abandonment, especially when roles and relationships are fluid.

While those with anxious attachment tend to reach out, sometimes desperately, for closeness and reassurance, others learn to do the opposite. Some children, when met with emotional distance or rejection, begin to turn inward. Instead of chasing connection, they learn to suppress their needs altogether. This brings us to another common pattern of avoidant attachment disorder.

Before I begin, there are several personality disorders that derive from this and often form the magnet for codependents. It is rather difficult for the codependent and narcissistic person to pull away from each other, and they are always in a state of conflict.

Narcissistic Personality Disorder (NPD)

Narcissistic traits often emerge when a child learns that approval and love are tied to achievement, image, or control, rather than to who they truly are on the inside. If emotional needs were ignored, criticized, or viewed as weaknesses, the child may have developed a grandiose image of themselves to survive and cope with hidden feelings of unworthiness.

Can this be treated or managed?

While narcissistic personality disorder is more resistant to change, it is manageable with therapy, especially when the individual is willing to look inward and do the work. Over time, it is possible to build healthier relationships and develop emotional insight, though this journey is gradual.

Often, people misuse this term, but let's clarify the voice. The voice of narcissism sounds like:

"I do a lot around here, and I never hear a 'thank you.' You act like I'm the bad guy just because I don't fall apart emotionally like you do. Not everything has to be a deep conversation. I'm doing my best — but perhaps your standards are too high."

This voice often sounds confident, even cold, yet beneath it lies a fear of vulnerability. The narcissistic partner learned early on to protect themselves by staying emotionally distant, relying on control, self-sufficiency, and image. Intimacy feels threatening, not comforting.

Often, if you are married and you are codependent, that response would look like: *"All I want is to feel close to you. I try so hard to make this work. I support you, I take care of everything, and still, I feel like I'm not enough. I'm not trying to overwhelm you ... I need to know that I matter."*

This voice is tender but tired. It comes from someone who learned that love must be earned through selflessness and sacrifice. They are not needy, they are afraid. And underneath their giving is a hope that someone will finally choose to stay and see them.

Let's take it a step further to see what this looks like in a relationship or marriage. Why? Because this is often what I encounter in my practice:

The Codependent–Narcissistic Cycle: A Common Fight

Codependent Partner:

"Why do you act like my feelings are a burden? I try to talk to you, but you always shut down or make me feel stupid for caring."

Narcissistic Partner:

"Here we go again. You're always upset about something. Maybe if you stopped overreacting, we could actually enjoy our time together."

Codependent Partner:

"I'm not overreacting. I want to feel like I matter to you, that I'm not the only one holding this relationship together."

Narcissistic Partner:

"You're so dramatic. Nothing I do is ever enough for you. Honestly, I'm starting to feel smothered."

Codependent Partner:

"And I'm starting to feel abandoned again."

This is the emotional seesaw: one reaches in, the other pulls away. The more the codependent partner tries to connect, the more the narcissistic partner detaches or deflects. It is not a calculated plan but a protective reflex. Both are reacting from deeply ingrained survival strategies.

In mosaic families, where past wounds and relational histories are already layered, this cycle can play out even more intensely. Stepparents may feel unappreciated. Partners may misinterpret needs as demands. What begins as a cry for connection turns into a clash of defense.

Here's the hope: when both partners recognize the dance, they can begin to change the rhythm. **Healing starts when we stop fighting to win and start listening to understand.** For some, listening, especially to emotions, feels dangerous. Vulnerability feels like weakness.

Dependence feels like a trap.

These are often the voices shaped not by indifference, but by avoidant attachment; not because they do not care, but because caring has always felt risky. When love has been inconsistent or when emotional needs are met with silence, judgment, or withdrawal, some people learn to survive by turning inward.

Where the anxiously attached chase closeness, the avoidantly attached protect themselves by avoiding it; both are seeking safety, just in different ways. Let's look at what this protective pattern looks like and why it often gets misunderstood as apathy when it is a deeply ingrained strategy to prevent pain.

Avoidant Attachment (or Dismissive Attachment)

Not everyone reaches for love with open arms. Some of us learned early that emotions were messy, unsafe, or unwelcome. So, we did the only thing that felt safe — we shut them down. For people with avoidant attachment, independence is not just a value. It is armor. Where others chase connection, they keep their distance. Not because they do not care, but because caring has always felt like a risk they couldn't afford to take.

Avoidant attachment often forms when a child experiences emotional distance, repeated rejection, or a caregiver who discourages expressions of need or vulnerability. These individuals learn to suppress their emotions to avoid disappointment or shame, thereby becoming self-reliant as a survival mechanism.

They may think or behave in ways like:
"I am safer alone."
"If I depend on someone, they will let me down."
"Needing others is a weakness."

As a Child

Avoidantly attached children often experience caregivers who are emotionally unavailable or dismissive. These children learn to suppress their feelings and may appear independent, and they may struggle with intimacy.

As an Adult

Adults with avoidant attachment tend to value independence highly and can be uncomfortable with closeness. They may have difficulty opening up, sharing their feelings, and may struggle to maintain long-term relationships.

Imagine a child who approaches their caregiver after a difficult day, only to be met with indifference, distraction, or criticism. Over time, the child learns to hide their feelings and stop seeking comfort. Instead of crying or asking for help, they retreat inward. They may appear strong or self-sufficient, then underneath lies a belief that emotional needs are unsafe or unwelcome.

As they grow into adulthood, this same pattern of emotional withdrawal continues. They may maintain relationships at a surface level, avoid conflict by shutting down, and interpret others' emotional needs as overwhelming or intrusive. When relationships begin to deepen, individuals may instinctively create distance, retreating into independence to avoid the perceived risks of rejection or dependence.

Carly, one of the participants in my research, expressed this internal tension well. *"I did not even realize I was keeping people at arm's length. I told myself I was just tired, or busy, or that I did not need anything. But the truth was, I did not know how to ask for closeness without feeling exposed. I had to unlearn the idea that needing someone was weakness."*

Her story reflects the core of avoidant attachment, emotional self-protection disguised as independence, often hiding deep fears of vulnerability and rejection.

What would healthy communication look like in the context of avoidant attachment?

Context: A teenage stepchild with avoidant attachment has been distant lately, skipping meals with the family and staying in their room. The stepparent gently initiates a check-in.

Stepparent (gently, without pressure):

"Hey, I noticed you've been keeping to yourself a lot lately. I just wanted to check in and see how you're doing."

Stepchild (flat tone, minimal eye contact):

"I'm fine. Just tired."

Stepparent (respectful, non-intrusive):

"Okay. I get that. If you ever want to talk or hang out, I'm here. No pressure."

Stepchild (shrugging):

"Yeah. Thanks, I guess."

Stepparent (affirming without forcing connection):

"I know things have changed a lot around here. I'm not trying to take up your space, just want you to know that you matter. I'll be downstairs if you feel like joining."

Core Characteristics of Avoidantly Attached Conversations

Minimal emotional expression: They often give short, neutral answers and may appear detached.

Desire for space: Connection can feel overwhelming or threatening, especially if they've been let down in the past.

Guardedness: Vulnerability is avoided because it has not felt safe or reciprocated before.

Pulling away when others get close: They may perceive attempts at connection as intrusive or controlling.

Therapeutic Insight

Avoidantly attached individuals do not lack emotional depth — they've learned to **protect themselves by disconnecting**. In mosaic families, where emotional expectations can be high, they may withdraw to maintain control and reduce anxiety.

Caregivers should offer a **consistent presence without pressure**, affirming availability while honoring the child's autonomy. Over time, this creates the safety needed for them to **approach instead of avoid**.

How Avoidant Attachment Looks in a Mosaic Family

A child with an avoidant attachment style in a mosaic family may respond to the increased complexity of their household by further suppressing their emotions. For instance, after parents have separated and new partners have entered the picture, this child might feel a sense of instability. The presence of stepparents and half-siblings can add layers of confusion and uncertainty regarding their place in the new family structure.

Behavior Examples

Emotional Distance: The child may withdraw emotionally, avoiding deep connections with stepparents or stepsiblings. They might avoid sharing their feelings about the changes in their family, believing that being independent and self-reliant is safer.

Self-Sufficiency: They may pride themselves on being "fine" and not needing help from anyone, reinforcing a belief that dependence on others is risky.

Reluctance to Communicate: When family discussions arise about feelings, conflicts, or the need for closeness, the avoidantly attached child might shut down or change the subject, feeling overwhelmed by the emotional intensity of these conversations.

As an Adult in a Mosaic Family:

For adults, particularly stepparents or individuals who have children from previous relationships, avoidant attachment can complicate both romantic and parental relationships in a mosaic family. Their need for independence and discomfort with intimacy can create barriers to forming strong bonds with their partner's children or with their own stepchildren.

Behavior Examples

Strained Relationships: An adult with an avoidant attachment style may hesitate to engage fully with their partner's children, feeling uncomfortable in the role of a stepparent. They may want to maintain emotional distance, believing this will protect them from potential rejection or emotional pain.

Conflict Avoidance: In family meetings where important issues arise, such as discussing household rules or resolving conflicts among children, this adult might withdraw or avoid participating, preferring to "stay out of it" rather than engage in potentially challenging emotional conversations.

Struggle to Connect: This individual may also struggle to navigate their partner's emotional needs, leading to frustration for the partner, who may seek more emotional support and intimacy. The inability to engage deeply in the relationship can lead to feelings of isolation within the mosaic family.

Impact on the Mosaic Family:

The presence of avoidant attachment styles in both children and adults can lead to a mosaic family experience where emotional connections may be superficial or strained. Family members might miss opportunities to create a sense of unity or belonging, leading to dynamics where some individuals feel alone, even in the presence of others.

To counteract these challenges, the family needs to foster open communication and create a safe environment where feelings can be expressed without fear of judgment. Recognizing and addressing the patterns associated with avoidant attachment can foster deeper connections and help everyone feel more secure within the family structure, promoting a sense of togetherness and understanding. Workshops, family therapy, or open conversations about emotions and family roles can provide opportunities for growth and healing within a mosaic family framework.

Avoidant attachment is not about a lack of care; it is about a fear of closeness; fear of closeness, of disappointment, of being seen too clearly. Fear can, however, be softened by consistency, patience, and the quiet reassurance that love does not always have to be earned through perfection or performance.

For some, the fear runs even deeper, as connection can feel like both a lifeline and a threat. They long for closeness and run from it. They crave love and fear it will destroy them. Their attachment style is not only anxious or avoidant; it is a combination of both.

This is the paradox at the heart of Disorganized Attachment.

Disorganized Attachment

Disorganized attachment is often the result of early relational trauma, abuse, neglect, or chronic unpredictability, especially when the caregiver is both the source of comfort and the source of fear. Children with this pattern face an impossible dilemma: *"I want to be close, but closeness does not feel safe."*

Child

Disorganized attachment often results from chaotic or traumatic environments. Children may exhibit a mix of behaviors, appearing confused or apprehensive about their caregivers, which can result in significant distress.

Adult

Adults with a disorganized attachment style can struggle with a profound fear of abandonment and difficulty forming healthy relationships. They may have unpredictable emotions and behaviors, often driven by past traumas.

Imagine a child named Adam, who lives in a mosaic family where the caregivers have inconsistent parenting styles. One moment, Adam's parents might be nurturing and loving, and the next, they could become emotionally distant, angry, or even frightening due to their unresolved issues.

When Adam reaches out for comfort or support, they might receive a confusing response that creates uncertainty, leaving Adam unsure of whether they will be met with affection or fear. In situations where Adam seeks comfort, they may appear confused, hesitating to approach their caregiver. When they do, they might exhibit anxiety and distress, displaying behaviors like freezing, crying, or suddenly withdrawing. This inconsistency fosters a sense of chaos, making it hard for Adam to feel secure or understand how to behave around their caregiver.

Now, imagine Adam as an adult. Despite his best efforts to form relationships, he often feels a profound fear of abandonment. When in a romantic relationship, Adam might swing from intense emotional closeness to pushing their partner away, fearing that vulnerability will lead to rejection.

For example, during a disagreement, Adam might suddenly lash out at his partner, feeling overwhelmed by memories of past neglect, only to feel deep regret and sadness afterward. He struggles with unpredictable emotions, often feeling both love and fear toward their partner, simultaneously. This inner turmoil complicates their ability to maintain healthy, stable relationships, as their partner may find Adam's behavior erratic and difficult to understand, leaving both parties feeling unsettled. The unresolved traumas from childhood echo through Adam's adult life, making it hard to find peace and security in his connections with others.

How Disorganized Attachment Looks in a Mosaic Family

A child with a disorganized attachment style in a mosaic family may respond to the complexity of their household with confusion and emotional chaos. Following the separation of parents and the introduction of new partners and siblings, this child might feel a sense of instability and uncertainty. The presence of stepparents and half-siblings can exacerbate their feelings of insecurity, leading to conflicting emotions about their place in the family.

Behavior Examples

Conflicted Responses: The child may show ambivalence in their interactions, alternating between seeking comfort from a caregiver and displaying fear or withdrawal. For example, they may want to hug a stepparent yet suddenly pull away, unsure of what they truly want.

Emotional Dysregulation: They might have explosive emotional outbursts, such as crying or aggressive behavior, often triggered by seemingly minor events. This intense emotional reaction can stem from their internal struggle with fear and confusion about relationships.

Role Confusion: The child may assume caregiving roles for younger siblings to seek a sense of control in a chaotic environment, which can lead to increased stress and anxiety as they feel burdened by responsibilities that should not be theirs.

Difficulty with Trust: The child may exhibit fearfulness around adults, often questioning their intentions or feeling threatened by unforeseen changes, such as a new partner or family rule, leading to withdrawal or hesitation in forming relationships.

As an Adult in a Mosaic Family

For adults, particularly stepparents or individuals with children from previous relationships, disorganized attachment can significantly complicate both romantic and parental relationships. Their unpredictable emotional responses and underlying feelings of inadequacy can create barriers to forming strong bonds with their partner's children or with their own stepchildren.

Behavior Examples

Fear of Intimacy: An adult with disorganized attachment may desire closeness but simultaneously fear the vulnerability that comes with it. They might oscillate between being overly accommodating to a partner's children and then withdrawing completely, leading to confusion for both the adult and the children involved.

Conflict-Driven Withdrawal: During family discussions about emotions, conflicts, or family dynamics, this adult might become overwhelmed and disengage. They may avoid discussions that require vulnerability, opting instead to "check out" during emotionally charged moments.

Inconsistent Engagement: This individual may exhibit fluctuating levels of interest or involvement in family activities, resulting in unpredictable relationships. At times, they may appear very invested, while at other times, they may withdraw, leaving family members unclear about their feelings or commitment.

Impact on the Mosaic Family

The presence of disorganized attachment styles in both children and adults can lead to a mosaic family experience characterized by emotional turbulence and misunderstanding. Instead of fostering strong familial connections, family members may experience confusion, fear, and isolation.

What Disorganized Communication Might Sound Like in a Mosaic Family

Context: A child with disorganized attachment is often triggered by a change in routine, such as being picked up unexpectedly by their stepparent instead of their biological parent.

Child (angry and confused):

"You did not even tell me she was coming! I thought you were going to pick me up. I hate this family."

Stepparent (taken aback, then grounding):

"I'm sorry for the surprise. I know changes like this can be hard. I did not mean to scare or upset you."

Child (teary, pulling away):

"I just never know what's going to happen anymore."

Stepparent (calm and warm):

"You're right. Things have been changing a lot, and that's really hard. But I promise — I'm here, and I'll always let you know next time. You don't have to go through this alone."

Core Characteristics of Disorganized Attachment

- **Push-pull behavior:** Alternates between seeking connection and rejecting it.

- **Emotional confusion:** Experiences both fear and longing in close relationships.
- **Unpredictable reactions:** May overreact to small changes or perceived threats.
- **Mistrust of others:** Struggles to believe caregivers or partners will stay consistent.
- **Fear of vulnerability:** Connection feels both desirable and dangerous.

To counteract these challenges, the family needs to establish a safe and stable environment conducive to open communication. Recognizing and addressing the patterns associated with disorganized attachment can promote deeper connections and a sense of security within the family structure.

Family therapy or counseling can be instrumental in equipping family members with the tools to understand each other's emotional landscapes and facilitate meaningful conversations about feelings, roles, and boundaries. Engaging in activities that promote trust and safety — such as family bonding exercises or workshops — can also help create a foundation of support and understanding, ultimately leading to healthier, more secure relationships in the mosaic family.

Disorganized attachment may feel like chaos, but it is not permanent. These patterns were born out of survival, not brokenness. And while they may have shaped your past, they do not have to define your future. Healing begins the moment we choose to understand our story, rather than be ruled by it. Whether your pattern is anxious, avoidant, disorganized, or some mix of all three, attachment is not fixed. It can be rewritten. It can be healed. And that is where we go next.

Attachment Disorders Can Change

Today, I stand in quiet gratitude for the journey I have walked—a path that transformed me from someone governed by anxious attachment into a man anchored in secure connection. This shift did not happen by accident. It emerged from the sacred intersection of personal therapy, academic pursuit, clinical work, and life's most brutal battles: surviving cancer, enduring the pain of divorce, and navigating the heartbreak of parental alienation.

Therapy became the mirror I had long avoided.

It helped me face emotions I'd buried beneath performance, productivity, and perfectionism. It taught me to sit with sorrow, to name what hurt, and to rewrite the scripts I'd been handed. Through this work, I discovered that attachment is not a life sentence. It is a learned pattern — and anything learned can be rewritten.

My studies in psychology gave me the language to describe what I had experienced.

As I learned about attachment theory, trauma recovery, and emotional regulation, I began applying those truths to myself. And what once felt like a tangled web of fear and striving slowly became a roadmap toward healing and authenticity.

My work with clients showed me this truth: healing is possible for everyone.

No matter how chaotic the past. No matter how disorganized, withdrawn, or anxious the patterns are. When we name our pain, honor our story, and intentionally build new patterns, healing takes root. This journey changed my life, and it gave birth to my purpose.

As a university professor, I can now empower the next generation of therapists.

As an author, I write to the wounded places I once carried in silence.

As the host of the Coached Soul podcast, I create a space for honest conversations about growth, identity, faith, and secure connection.

As a veteran, I have lived adversity.

As a Christian, I have wrestled with shame, sought redemption, and now choose to advocate for grace over judgment.

Through my ministry, *Faith Forward*, I share a God who sees, stays, and heals, not one who condemns those who struggle to love rightly.

And as a man, I speak to other men — especially fathers, stepfathers, and husbands, calling them to lead with vulnerability, tenderness, and strength rooted not in control, but in compassion.

Secure attachment is not just a clinical term. It is a lived possibility. It is the foundation for every redemptive relationship we hope to build. Together, we can raise families that feel safe.

We can create marriages that breathe. We can teach our children that love is not something to be earned or feared, but something we can give and receive with joy. Let this be your reminder: attachment disorders can heal. And so can you.

Your past may explain your patterns, yet it does not have to define your future. You are not broken beyond repair. You are not too late to change.

Every small act of healing you choose, every honest conversation, every boundary you set, every moment of presence you offer, is a piece of the mosaic being restored. Divorce may scatter the pieces of our lives, but with truth, time, and healthy boundaries, each fragment can be restored. And when love becomes intentional, even the most broken family can become a beautiful mosaic, one formed not from perfection, but from resilience, grace, and the sacred courage to begin again.

Mosaic Truth

Attachment is not about perfection; it is about presence.

In mosaic families, trust is built not by fixing every crack, but by staying near when others are tempted to run.

Reflective Questions

- ? Which parts of your attachment story are still influencing how you love, connect, or protect yourself?
- ? Can you recognize the voice of anxious, avoidant, or disorganized patterns in your past or present relationships?
- ? What would it look like for you to begin nurturing secure attachment within yourself, without waiting for someone else to offer it first?
- ? How do the stories of others — Carly, Jana, John, or the child with disorganized attachment — mirror parts of your own experience?
- ? Are you willing to look at the mirror not with shame, but with curiosity and courage?

Key Takeaways

- Insecure attachment styles (anxious, avoidant, disorganized) are not flaws, but survival strategies that can be understood, softened, and changed.
- Secure attachment is not a gift reserved for the few — it can be *earned*, nurtured, and lived out in daily choices, especially within mosaic families.
- When we understand our attachment patterns, we can interrupt harmful cycles and begin forming relationships rooted in trust, clarity, and emotional presence.
- True healing begins not when we find the "right person," but when we become rooted in the truth that we are already worthy of love, safety, and belonging.

PART THREE

BONDING THE MOSAIC

"Wounded hands still create beauty. Each shard matters."

Just as a mosaic's beauty emerges from the careful placement of imperfect shards, the foundation of our lives is constructed from our trials and tribulations. Though flawed, each experience contributes to a more extraordinary design, reminding us that strength and beauty are often found in fragments that seem disjointed at first glance. Just as no two pieces in a mosaic are identical, our journeys, marked by heartache and joy, create a rich mosaic that tells a unique story. These experiences, while imperfect, interweave to form a narrative that is both resilient and dynamic. In embracing our flaws and allowing them to shape us, we cultivate empathy and understanding for ourselves and others. Within this intricate design of life, where every challenge and triumph play a role, we discover the true essence of community and connection. Ultimately, we learn that the beauty of our lives lies not in perfection but in the authenticity of our shared humanity, a mosaic of love, growth, and transformation.

Chapter Nine

When Families Form Fast:

Lessons from the Front Lines of Love

No one tells you that becoming an instant family can feel like free-falling into someone else's unfinished story. One minute, you are in love, hopeful, maybe even healing from a past rupture, and the next, you are standing in a living room full of people who did not choose each other, trying to decide where your toothbrush belongs. You are not just joining a life; you are inheriting a history. A rhythm. A hierarchy. A set of unspoken rules you were never taught.

I remember walking through the front door that first week as a newly married man in a mosaic home. The air was thick with politeness, but no one knew where to sit. The table was set, yet emotionally, the silverware was still sharp. I had hoped love would be enough. But Mosaic families do not run on hope alone. They run on grace, clarity, patience, and the kind of love that shows up even when it is not returned.

This chapter is about what I wish I had known sooner. The hard-won lessons that do not show up in wedding vows or courtship conversations. What it means to become a stepparent without losing your identity. What happens when love is real, but the bonds take time? And how sometimes, the most sacred family connections are not inherited, they are built, brick by brick, on trust, truth, and time.

There is no manual for starting again. After divorce, what once felt known becomes unfamiliar: your name, your reflection, your role in the world. For those of us entering new love with children watching, there is no time to pause. We rebuild as we walk. We parent while we heal. We attach while we grieve. That was my reality, learning to date again, not just as a man, but as a father. I was no longer choosing a partner. I was choosing a future that would shape my children's hearts. In this chapter, I offer not theories, but lived truths about forming a family quickly, and imperfectly, while still believing in love.

There is a sacred tension in starting over, where healing meets rebuilding, where broken pieces do not just get discarded; they are chosen again, placed again, and honored again. This is the work of bonding a mosaic, not through force or fantasy, through faith, time, and intentional presence. Here, we move beyond surviving the fracture into living the reformation.

While traditional families are built over time with the careful layering of patience and understanding, instant families form like mosaics, gathering diverse pieces into one beautiful whole. They remind us that love can emerge swiftly from the cracks, creating a new masterpiece that celebrates both the history of its fragments and the unity of its newfound purpose.

Instant Doesn't Mean Easy: Parenting While Rebuilding Love

In the depths of vulnerability, we unearth the strength to reshape not just our identities but the very fabric of our families. Imagine waking up one day and finding yourself standing on the edge of a cliff, staring into the vast unknown after a significant life change. The winds of uncertainty whip around you, echoing with the fading sounds of shared laughter and the comforting presence of companionship that now feel like distant memories. Your identity has shifted, your household has scattered, and what was once solid ground has given way to emotional vertigo.

Now, you are not just reinventing yourself; you are entrusted with the tender hearts of your children, who look up to you in a world that no longer feels safe. That was my reality after divorce. My journey began cloaked in loneliness and permeated by a frantic search for belonging in a family landscape now cracked and uneven.

I took those hesitant first steps into the realm of dating as a single parent, and I discovered something unexpected: within vulnerability lives a raw power, a sacred potential to not only rebuild my life but to reimagine love, stability, and identity in ways I had never experienced before. Through intentional presence, relational wisdom, and a deepened sense of responsibility, I began to piece together a new kind of family. Not perfect, not linear, but beautiful in its design. A Mosaic.

This path is not easy. It is filled with unspoken rules, anxious transitions, the weight of unseen grief, and the invisible calculations every parent must make when love re-enters the room. Still, there is sacred work in this rebuilding, when we choose again, with eyes wide open, which means to love, to lead, and to create safety for the people we call family.

"I was pretty devastated because he had two kids that I raised with him ... and we had two kids together, one that passed away. So yeah, I was devastated." —Jana.

Jana's words mirror what many feel and do not speak: that even in choosing a new relationship, our hearts remain entangled in the invisible threads of previous connections, especially when children are involved. When love breaks down again in a mosaic family, it is not just a couple unraveling; it is a web, a rhythm, a home that splinters.

In this chapter, I share what I have learned, not from a clinical manual, but from the front lines of parenting while grieving, dating while protecting, and rebuilding while still bleeding. These are the lived truths of instant families: messy, brave, mosaic.

What no one prepared me for was the invisible weight of rebuilding while still bleeding. We are told that love can start again, yet rarely are we told what it costs to open your heart while holding your child's pain, or what it feels like to sit across from someone new at dinner while your identity is still unraveling. Instant families may sound like fairy tales, but they begin in the wreckage. Before we build what we have, we must first face what we have lost.

The Past

The past is not a place we leave; it is a place we carry. After divorce, the quiet moments are the loudest. The echo of a toothbrush no longer beside yours. The sound of cartoons from the next room while you sit alone in silence. Life after divorce is not just a logistical shift, it is a spiritual rupture. You wake up and everything familiar is gone, yet your calendar still demands meals, pick-ups, bedtime prayers, and strength you are not sure you possess.

I know this space intimately. It is a landscape marked by grief, yes, and also by courage. By the sacred work of redefinition. Parenting while heartbroken. Dating while disoriented. Hoping while still hurting. In the chapters ahead, I will share what this journey has taught me, not just as a therapist, but as a father, a man, and a believer in love that rebuilds from ruins.

This is The Past, not just mine, but maybe yours too. And from this honest place, we begin.

"I missed the companionship, the laughter, and even the routines ... but what broke me was when my child looked at me like I could fix it — and I couldn't." —Sarah.

When I went through my divorce, I found myself engulfed in a profound sense of loneliness that set in almost immediately. Transitioning from married life, filled with shared experiences and daily interactions, to the solitude of single parenthood was not just a shift in relationship status; it was a complete redefinition of my identity. With two children to raise, the journey into a single life proved both challenging and unexpectedly redemptive.

The initial loneliness was overwhelming. I missed the sound of footsteps in the hall, the murmur of evening conversation, the laughter tucked into shared dinners. I missed the mundane, the stuff that makes life feel whole. However, as I re-entered the world of dating, I quickly realized that the emotional terrain of single parenthood was equally complex. This was not just about moving on; it was about moving forward while carrying others with me.

"Coming home to an empty house after my internship was ... it crushed me. My son was gone. The dog was gone. Even the furniture was gone. I never knew you could grieve that hard and still have to go to work the next day." —Mark.

Dating as a single parent brings its own set of challenges that hold a different kind of weight than those faced in a first marriage. One of the most significant hurdles is learning to consider not only my own emotions, but also the well-being of my children. Every relational step felt like a ripple, one that could shift their sense of stability and safety. Introducing someone new did not just affect me; it reshaped their world.

Unlike my first marriage, where I had the luxury of building a connection over time, new relationships now came with more complex responsibilities and shorter timelines. It was not just two adults coming together; it was the merging of two families, each carrying its own rhythms, rules, wounds, and expectations.

"You don't just blend people. You blend pain. You blend loyalty. And sometimes, that mix explodes." —Vicki.

Children bring with them the emotional weight of past transitions. Some are eager to accept new beginnings. Others resist. Their resistance is not rejection; it is a form of protection. Adjusting to a new family structure is not only a logistical endeavor, but also an emotional reckoning. They are not just adapting to a new dinner table; they are grieving the old one.

And then there is the internal weight: the pressure to get it right this time, the fear of another fracture, the constant second-guessing. I often found myself consumed by questions:

How will my children react?
What if my new partner's kids clash with mine?
Am I repeating old mistakes under a new name?

These questions became a low hum of anxiety beneath every milestone. Even moments of joy felt tentative, as if I were waiting for the other shoe to drop.

Communication became the anchor in this storm. It meant listening, not just to my partner, and to my children. It meant giving them a voice, even when I wanted to shield them from hard conversations. It meant acknowledging their grief without minimizing my own.

"I was raising five kids. And he was bringing home twenty-five dollars a week. I was breaking inside, trying to be strong outside, because I still believed family could work." —Sarah.

Despite the difficulty, there were moments of light, glimpses of connection, hope, and new traditions. Shared laughter. A slow, tentative rebuilding of trust. When approached with honesty and time, a mosaic family can become something not just functional, but beautifully bonded.

In summary, the transition from being married to dating as a single parent is a landscape filled with emotional complexities. The blend of loneliness, the challenge of building new relationships, and the responsibility of caring for children creates a volatile, tender, and sacred mix. Through thoughtful navigation, by listening, by pacing, and by healing, we begin to experience something new: a happiness that is earned, not assumed. One that makes room for both brokenness and beauty.

"Take your time and make sure you're out of that limerence phase. Know yourself, know what you want, and ensure you've done your own healing before bringing someone else into your life." —Jana.

Embracing the opportunity to create a mosaic family allows for healing, growth, and a redefinition of what family means, one that honors the past while daring to build a future marked by grace, resilience, and shared intention.

The past provides us with context, yet it does not dictate instructions. As I stepped forward, no longer a husband but still very much a father, I realized I was not alone. What I was experiencing, trying to date while raising children, forming bonds across broken timelines, and rebuilding from relational ashes, was not unique to me. It was the emerging norm for millions of people.

We live in a world where second marriages, co-parenting dynamics, and stepparenting realities are reshaping what it means to be a family. These are not "broken homes." They are mosaic families, formed not from ease, but from courage. And while their beauty lies in their diversity, their challenges lie in their complexity.

To understand this sacred work, we must pause to explore the emotional architecture of these families and the pressures they face. We must understand why even the most well-intentioned love can unravel without preparation.

When viewed from a distance, mosaic families may appear as vibrant portraits of healing and hope. Inside the frame, they are often built on fragile seams of grief, unresolved identity, and hidden tension. Without intention, without healing, and a clear framework, these pieces cannot hold.

I did not enter this next chapter of life as a blank slate; I carried the scars of my past, the weight of my children's hearts, and the haunting fear of failing again. Furthermore, while I believed in the redemptive power of love, I soon discovered that belief alone was insufficient to fully realize its potential. I once believed that once the ink was dry on the divorce papers, the most challenging part was behind me. Healing after a fractured family takes more than time; it takes intention. The real work began not in dating someone new, but in meeting me again.

Here Is What I learned — Sometimes the Hard Way.

One of the most important lessons I learned was the importance of allowing myself the space and time to fully process my emotions before entering new romantic relationships. The initial loneliness and emotional turmoil following my divorce demanded deep introspection and consistent self-regulation. Jumping into dating too quickly could have led to choices shaped more by emotional vacancy than authentic connection. I came to understand that healing must take precedence over companionship. In time, I discovered that self-reflection during my single years did more than comfort me; it matured me. It enriched my ability to enter future relationships with clarity, steadiness, and integrity.

As I gradually regained emotional footing, I realized that regulation was not just for my benefit; it was essential for protecting the hearts of those most affected by my choices: my children. I knew I could not afford to repeat the emotional whiplash that divorce had already inflicted. The weight of forming a new relationship was not light; it carried with it the potential to shape not only my future but theirs.

"I thought I was ready, but looking back, I was just trying to not be alone. I hadn't really dealt with the pain from the divorce, and it showed up in how quickly I let someone new into our lives. My kids were confused, and honestly, so was I." — Jana.

Her words mirror what I had to learn, sometimes the hard way. Our children do not need a replacement parent; they need a steady one. They need us to be whole before we invite someone else into the fragile ecosystem of their recovery.

As I looked into the eyes of my children, still processing their loss, still recalibrating their place in a new family structure, I knew that any future decision had to honor their pace, not just mine. Emotional readiness was not only a matter of my heart, but a matter of theirs.

Taking Care with Introductions to My Children

Another critical insight was the significance of not hastily introducing my children to new partners or their children. Doing so can create emotional attachments that may lead to unnecessary confusion or heartbreak if the relationship does not last. My children had already weathered the storm of divorce; they did not need another disruption packaged as hope. Adding new individuals into their lives required thoughtful, compassionate consideration. I had to learn that protecting their emotional state and allowing them to adjust to new family dynamics on their own terms must take priority over my desire for companionship.

It was not easy. Loneliness often whispers temptations to rush. I realized that introducing someone new is not a milestone; it is a responsibility. Children cannot process adult decisions with adult reasoning; they feel every shift. They read emotional signals with sensitive hearts, and they build bonds quickly, sometimes far faster than adults do. When those bonds are broken, even unintentionally, the damage compounds. I had to ask myself: Is this person worthy of entering the sacred space of my children's lives?

"I brought my daughter around someone I thought I loved. We dated a few months, and it just did not work. But she had already called him 'Dad' once. That crushed me. After that, I told myself — never again until I know it is real." — Mark.

His words echo the quiet guilt many parents feel. That moment taught me to shift from impulsive connection to intentional discernment. The hearts of my children deserved more than introductions; they deserved stability.

Once I internalized that, I began to see dating not as a path toward blending, but as a test of trust, timing, and compatibility. The next step would be to ensure that the relationship itself could withstand the test before we ever merged our lives.

Focusing on One-on-One Relationships Before Combining

Once I began protecting my children's emotional space, I was also forced to examine the core of my own relationships. I came to understand that if I wanted a strong family unit, I first needed to build a strong foundation with my partner, one that was tested in private before being introduced in public. Time spent alone with a partner, away from the demands of parenting, allows the relationship to develop on honest terms. I was no longer interested in rushing toward blended bliss. I wanted something real, something resilient.

I realized that it benefits both partners to cultivate a relationship independent of children, at least initially. Those early moments of connection reveal values, vulnerabilities, and compatibility that are harder to detect in the chaos of blended life. Honest conversations about expectations, parenting styles, past wounds, and hopes for the future help lay the groundwork for shared understanding and mutual trust. This dating phase is not separate from building the family; it is what makes building the family possible.

"Before we ever introduced the kids, we went away for a weekend. Just us. That's when I realized we had very different ideas of parenting, of money, even of faith. I loved him, but I was grateful I learned that before our kids were in the mix." — Shara

Shara's reflection confirmed what I had learned: clarity in private leads to wisdom in public. Our families will reflect what we bring into them. If we want stability, we must start by creating it in the partnership itself, before any blending begins.

And yet, even the strongest new connection carries the past with it. Every new chapter brings with it unresolved pages from the ones before. That led to my next lesson, one that required courage, honesty, and deep emotional humility.

Recognizing the Weight of Past Baggage

Even in the warmth of a new relationship, the past does not disappear. It lingers in silent expectations, in financial stressors, in co-parenting negotiations, and in the invisible comparisons we make between what was and what could be. I came to understand that every person entering a new relationship after divorce carries unseen baggage, some of it manageable, some of it still bleeding.

I learned to name mine. Unresolved feelings toward my former spouse. Lingering shame over the failed marriage. I feel guilty about how the divorce affected my children. And sometimes, fear ... the fear that I would mess it all up again. I also came to understand that the person I was dating might carry their own burdens: court battles, child support tensions, grief, or a distrust rooted in past betrayal.

Instead of ignoring this weight, I chose to bring it to the surface. I wanted our connection to be honest, not idealized. That meant creating space for real conversations, not just about where we were headed, but about what we were dragging behind us, doing so allowed for compassion instead of judgment. It helped us meet each other not in perfection, but in our humanity.

"I was still dealing with my ex, and so was he. We both had kids, and money was tight. But the hardest part was learning how not to punish each other for what other people had done to us."— Carly.

That insight struck me deeply. The past does not vanish just because we find someone new. It travels with us until we face it with open eyes and gentle courage. If we want to build something lasting, we must acknowledge the weight we both carry and commit to lifting it together.

Still, even with emotional honesty and compassionate pacing, a relationship needs time. Not time to escape the past time to create something stronger and more resilient than what came before.

As I reflected on the lessons I had lived, not just studied, I began to recognize patterns. Through trial, patience, failure, and grace, certain principles emerged. These were not quick fixes or rigid formulas. They were anchors, habits, boundaries, and intentional practices that allowed me and others like me to build families not on fantasy, but on faith and thoughtful action. What follows are some of the most essential strategies I have learned and witnessed in creating a healthy mosaic family, one deliberate decision at a time.

Best Practice Tips for Navigating Your Instant

Building a mosaic family is not about following a rigid formula; it is about approaching each decision with care, wisdom, and heart. These best practices are drawn from lived experience, not theory alone. They serve as guideposts for those navigating the often chaotic yet deeply redemptive journey of forming a new kind of family. While every situation is unique, the following principles provide a compass for navigating the path ahead.

Take Time to Build a Strong Foundation -- Prioritize the relationship by spending quality time together and engaging in open conversations about expectations, responsibilities, and family dynamics before making long-term commitments.

Embrace Open Communication – Establish a culture of honesty and openness within the family. Encourage all family members, including children, to express their feelings and concerns in a safe environment.

Be Patient During Adjustment Periods -- Understand that blending families is a transition that takes time. Be patient with each other, especially children, as everyone adjusts to new roles, dynamics, and relationships.

Involve All Family Members in Decision-Making – When the day comes to introduce and combine the families, then encourage participation from all family members in discussions about family rules, boundaries, and activities. This inclusivity can help foster acceptance and reduce feelings of displacement before engagement and marriage.

Seek Professional Guidance—To navigate the complexities of a mosaic family, consider couples therapy or family counseling. Professional support can facilitate effective communication, resolve conflicts, and strengthen relationships.

Manage External Pressures Together - Address external stressors as a team. Discuss financial responsibilities, relationships with ex-partners, and other challenges openly to avoid misunderstandings and resentment.

Be Mindful of Children's Emotional Needs — When you are introduced to the other individual's children, acknowledge and respect their feelings. Build relationships with them gradually, ensuring they feel secure and valued in their new family structure. Do not try to win them over or "gaslight" them, as they will likely be aware.

Foster Individual Relationships - Prioritize establishing strong individual relationships between stepparents and stepchildren. Activities that encourage bonding can help integrate family members and build trust.

Create Family Traditions - Establish new family traditions that celebrate the unique nature of your mosaic family. Shared experiences can strengthen bonds and create a sense of belonging for everyone involved.

Stay Committed and Supportive - Remind each other of the commitment made to the family and support one another through challenges. Maintaining a united front can foster resilience and stability within the family unit.

By implementing these strategies, families can better navigate the complexities of being a mosaic family and work toward creating a harmonious and lasting family environment.

It is essential to note that these tips are not a one-size-fits-all solution but rather serve as guidelines for balancing your new family dynamics while pursuing a relationship. Always seek professional help if you feel anxious, uncertain, or need assistance processing your emotions. This can provide clarity and support as you navigate these changes.

Additionally, be mindful about expressing your frustrations to family members and friends; venting about minor issues can inadvertently escalate tensions and create misunderstandings. Aim to approach challenges with perspective to avoid "poisoning the water" in your relationships with loved ones.

"I wish someone had told me that going slow is not the same thing as being afraid. It is actually love — when you slow down for your kids, for each other. That's how trust starts."— Jana.

"You can't build a new family if you're still living in the rubble of the old one. Clean it up. Name it. Then build again — but do it with grace." — Mark.

In the depths of vulnerability, we unearth the strength to reshape not just our identities but the very fabric of family, weaving new connections in the mosaic of life after loss. In the delicate weaving of our lives, we reclaim our identities and create a sanctuary of love, resilience, and mutual understanding amidst the swirling chaos of new beginnings.

The truth is, mosaic families are not built in the grand moments; they are shaped in the pauses, in the patient decisions, and in the quiet courage to love again after loss. This chapter may be messy, yet it is not meaningless. And with time, truth, and tenderness, the pieces come together; not perfectly, but beautifully.

"A mosaic family is not proof that nothing broke, it is proof that what shattered can still be shaped into something new and sacred."

Understanding the Mosaic: A New Kind of Family Story

After the dust of divorce settles, what comes next is often more complicated than anyone warns you. I found myself trying to rebuild a life that no longer looked like the one I had. What emerged wasn't just a second chance at love. It was the beginning of something more intricate, more layered: a mosaic family.

Mosaic families form when individuals, often with children from previous relationships, come together to create a new family unit. Unlike the nuclear ideal, mosaics are shaped by grief, resilience, loyalty binds, custody schedules, and emotional scars that do not simply disappear with a new wedding ring. These families blend diverse parenting styles, inherited wounds, spiritual frameworks, and relational histories into a cohesive, living system. And yet, when treated with care, they become a canvas for grace, creativity, and healing.

Mosaic families are not broken families. They are re-formed families. They ask more of us: more patience, more clarity, more compassion, and a deeper understanding of emotional systems. I realized that if I approached this season as if I were repeating the past with a new partner, I would fail. If, however, I entered it with intention, acknowledging its complexity and honoring the individual pieces, it could become something sacred.

That realization marked a turning point in my life. Before I could love again, I had to prepare differently. Not perfectly, but honestly. I had to do the work that love required on the inside, before I could show up rightly on the outside.

And yet, insight alone does not bind a family together. Like a mosaic without grout, even beautiful pieces can fall apart without the glue that holds them in place. In the next chapter, I explore what it means to 'grout the pieces,' to hold the bonds with intention, and to make the fragile connections of a new family strong enough to last.

Mosaic Truth

The speed at which families form does not determine their strength. In mosaic families, depth is forged not by haste, but by intentional steps that honor every step of the journey.

A time-lapse image of a mosaic being assembled, tile by tile, on a weathered table, showing hands pausing between pieces. The early tiles are jagged and scattered, but over time, the pattern begins to emerge.

Families that form fast must learn to build slowly.

True belonging is not microwaved; it is marinated in patience, presence, and grace.

Reflective Questions

? What emotional patterns from your previous relationship might still be influencing how you show up in your current family?

? In what ways have you rushed into rebuilding without honoring the grief still present in your children or yourself?

? How do you differentiate between companionship that comforts and love that heals?

? What conversations are you avoiding, either with your partner, your children, or yourself, that might be holding back the formation of something lasting?

? Are there relationships in your mosaic family that need more time, more patience, or a redefined approach?

Key Takeaways

- Forming a family quickly can feel exciting, but emotional readiness cannot be rushed. Healing requires time, not just shared intentions.
- Children may comply outwardly while still grieving inwardly. Just because a family looks blended does not mean it feels bonded.
- Fast-forming relationships often skip essential stages of emotional safety. Grief, honesty, and boundaries cannot be bypassed if trust is to take root.
- Slowing down is not weakness; it is wisdom. Taking time allows space for clarity, alignment, and deeper connection to form naturally.
- Emotional timing matters as much as logistical timing. When two adults are ready for love, their children may still be navigating loss.
- Being in love is not the same as being equipped to lead a family. Leadership in a mosaic home requires emotional maturity, spiritual grounding, and a great deal of patience.
- The early season of forming a mosaic family is not about perfection; it is about laying a foundation that is honest, steady, and ready to hold the weight of love.

Chapter Ten

Lessons Learned: When grace becomes grout

Love does not always feel like enough, especially when you're standing in a courtroom trying to prove it. In the trenches of mosaic family life, I discovered that love is not only what we feel, but also what we build. It is what we protect. It is what we fight for when systems distort our motives, when others mislabel our efforts, and when the very people we love most begin to pull away.

After my divorce, fatherhood became a battlefield. I was handed fragments, court orders, weekend exchanges, and moments that used to be mine, now filtered through supervision or suspicion. What began as a custody battle quickly evolved into something more profound: a reckoning with identity, justice, and the kind of love that holds on, even when it has not chosen back.

In a mosaic family, love is not about ownership; it is about connection and unity. It is about building a home where every child feels valued and safe, regardless of their past.

I still remember sitting outside the courthouse, clutching photos of my children, wondering if my presence would be enough to keep me in their lives. Mark, a participant in my study, captured that ache perfectly: *"I thought if I just loved hard enough, the system would see that. But I felt invisible. No one saw what I carried — except maybe my kids. And even they weren't sure they were allowed to love me back."*

Parental bonds, especially those of fathers, are too often treated as optional, as something to be permitted, rather than preserved. In those years, I learned that showing up doesn't always mean you're invited, and staying present sometimes means standing alone. Sue told me, *"I watched my husband cry in silence after every drop-off. No one talks about the quiet grief of a dad who's treated like a visitor in his own child's life." Still, he showed up. Still, he loved. That is what love looks like when it has nothing left to prove it, only everything left to give.*

This is not a chapter about how things went right. It is a chapter about reality. About the kind of love that shows up bruised, doubted, and delayed — and shows up anyway. It is about what I learned in the aftermath: that love, to last, must be held together not with control or perfection, but with boundaries, grit, and grace.

Before I could rebuild anything that resembled a home, I had to look back not just at what broke, but also what shaped me. The past does not just explain where the cracks began; it holds the blueprint of how we carry love, grief, and identity into every relationship that follows. To understand what I needed to grout, I had to revisit what had first fallen apart.

The Past

I have always been profoundly grateful for my two children. Through the darkest moments of my life, they have remained my brightest light, my grounding purpose, my deepest joy. Loving them was never the hard part. Fighting for the right to remain in their lives was.

"I did not fight out of anger. I fought because my children deserved a father who would not disappear quietly."

The years following my divorce were marked by a battle I never expected to face. My former spouse began to engage in what I would later understand as parental alienation — subtle at first yet increasingly damaging. It was not just about missed phone calls or miscommunications — it was about the fragments of connection that kept breaking away.

It was about the slow unraveling of trust, the distortion of my role in their eyes, and the painful recognition that love alone would not be enough to protect my place as their father.

"Parental alienation does not just erase time, it erodes identity, one visit, one whisper, one false narrative at a time."

That pain lit a fire in me, not just for my children, but for every parent who finds themselves erased not by absence, but by manipulation and misrepresentation. In 2001, that fire led me to a courtroom not only for custody, but also for change. Under the leadership of Governor Frank Keating, I helped spearhead the Equal Access Law in Oklahoma, a legislative step toward correcting the imbalance that too often left fathers fighting uphill battles just to be present.

"Some people write legislation to make a name for themselves. I wrote to make sure my children remembered mine."

That advocacy gave me purpose; however, my personal journey was far from over. I returned to court; this time not to seek full custody, but to fight for joint custody because **I**

believed then, and still do now, that children need both parents.

My pursuit was never about revenge. I did not want my ex-spouse to feel the loss I had endured. This was not about evening the score. It was about restoring balance. My focus was not on what had been done to me, but on what was being taken from my children: the right to love and be loved by both parents, without fear, guilt, or manipulation.

To withhold a parent from a willing and capable child is not protective parenting; it is emotional abuse, no matter how justified it may feel in the moment.

I came to understand that what fueled the alienation wasn't just bitterness; it was a distorted lens shaped by unhealed wounds, perhaps even undiagnosed disorders, which misrepresented reality and redefined truth in damaging ways. Rather than respond with resentment, I chose a different path: compassion for my children.

Through empathy, I began to see the emotional trap they were caught in. That's why I pursued joint custody, not because I wanted control, but because I wanted connection. Not because I needed to win, but because I refused to let them lose.

The process was grueling, made more complex by my ex-spouse's remarriage. We underwent a comprehensive custody evaluation, one of the most invasive and emotional experiences of my life. What it revealed about their household deeply disturbed me; details I will not share here out of respect for my children's privacy, but they changed everything.

"No child should have to choose who to love. No parent should have to prove they are worthy of the love they already give."

What I learned through that process redirected the trajectory of my life. I realized I was not just meant to endure this; I was called to help others through it. Becoming a therapist was not a career move. It was a response to pain — a decision to stand in the gap for others who felt voiceless.

I hold a conviction that runs deeper than law or psychology: **no parent should have to fight tooth and nail to stay in their child's life.** PAS (Parental Alienation Syndrome) is not a gendered issue; it affects mothers and fathers, and it leaves children confused, fractured, and disconnected from the very love that's meant to stabilize them.

"The greatest tragedy is not the absence of love. It is when love is present and still pushed away."

Eventually, after exhaustive legal and emotional efforts, the court deemed me a capable and nurturing parent. I was awarded primary custody and the majority of visitation rights. And yet, the scars of the process remained; scars I have since turned into sacred spaces for helping others heal.

"Custody is more than a ruling — it is a statement to your child: 'I never gave up on you'."

Even after custody, life did not become simple. I chose to date with care, intentionally keeping my personal life separate from my role as a parent. I only introduced my children to a partner when I believed the relationship was stable and serious. I never asked my children what they thought about the women I dated; not because I did not care, because I did not want to burden them with choices they shouldn't have to make. My priority was always this: **to protect their peace.**

"Love your children in a way that asks nothing from them in return; not approval, not permission, not explanation."

These experiences forged something unshakable in me: resilience, yes — but more than that, clarity. A sacred responsibility to stand in the places I once felt most alone and offer direction to others stumbling through the same darkness. This is not just about my past; it is about the patterns, the systems, and the unseen wounds that continue to shape countless families today. I became a voice not only for fairness, but also for restoration. Not only for fathers, but for mothers. And most importantly, for the children silently caught between the stories that adults cannot resolve.

"I did not come through the fire unburned. I came through it lit with purpose."

Some of the most profound lessons came not in the courtrooms, but in the quiet, fragile spaces of second chances. Loving again and trying again and hoping that what broke before could somehow be built differently this time. In this next section, I want to step away from theory and advocacy to explain something more personal and human: what I learned the hard way when love formed quickly, and the questions I never asked when I should have.

Explanation

No one walks into love thinking it will collapse under the weight of unspoken histories. We fall in love with a person, not always realizing we're also stepping into their children's lives, their past wounds, their unhealed loyalties. In mosaic families, love is never just between two people; it is a layered dance of connections, some visible, some buried.

I thought I understood that. I had been a father. I had been through a divorce. I had lived the pain of being shut out and the joy of being chosen again. However, nothing prepared me for the way a child's unspoken grief, quiet resentment, or fierce loyalty could shape the atmosphere of a home. Love was present, but it was not enough on its own.

"I did not know I was walking into unfinished stories," said Tiffany, one of my participants. *"His kids loved their mom, and I was a reminder that things had changed. I thought we'd blend. What we actually did was clash, softly, silently, until we shattered."*

Looking back, I now see that the most significant misunderstandings came not from malice, but from the things I did not ask about. I assumed love would build bridges, that kindness would earn trust. I did not realize I was walking into a narrative I hadn't read from the beginning.

"They did not hate me," said James, "they just did not know where to place me. I wasn't Dad. I wasn't 'nobody.' I was ... in the way."

This is what I want to explain, not to blame, not to rewrite what happened, but to help others avoid the blind spots I missed. The truth is, if you're dating someone with children or becoming a stepparent, you are not just entering a relationship. You are entering a family system that is already in motion.

What follows are the lessons I learned, not from theory, but from experience. From missteps. From moments when love was present yet understanding was not. From the deep realization that in mosaic families, asking the right questions early on is not a suggestion — it is survival.

The Lessons I Learned

Some lessons do not come with clarity. They come wrapped in confusion, delayed by heartbreak, and only become visible in hindsight. I did not read them in a textbook or learn them in graduate school. I learned them in the tension at a dinner table where silence spoke louder than words. In the ache of being present and still not chosen. In the long nights of wondering how love could exist in a room yet never find a way to land.

These are the lessons I learned through trial, through missteps, and the sobering reality that no matter how much love you bring into a mosaic family, you are still walking into rooms built before you ever arrived.

No two families are the same, and these patterns repeat more than we care to admit. I hope that by sharing what I missed, misunderstood, or mishandled, someone else might feel less alone and better prepared to meet the complexity with grace.

The following is what I learned:

Children Share Selective Truths

What a child says and what a child feels are often two very different things. In mosaic families, this gap becomes even more pronounced. Children quickly learn which truths are safe to tell, which ones keep the peace, and which ones carry consequences they are not emotionally equipped to handle. So, they adapt. They filter. They protect themselves — and sometimes, the adults around them.

"I told my mom I was fine because I knew if I wasn't, she'd blame my stepdad," said Fawn, a young adult reflecting on her childhood. *"I did not want her to be mad at him, so I kept my mouth shut."*

Children are not being deceptive; they are being cautious. In homes marked by divorce, remarriage, and divided loyalties, they do not have the tools to process complex emotions. So instead, they share what they believe will keep their world stable, even if that means leaving parts of their truth untold.

"My stepson would hug me at bedtime but tell his dad later that I yelled at him," said Tori, one of the stepparents I interviewed. *"It wasn't that he was lying — he was trying to keep his dad's loyalty. I became the emotional buffer."*

What I have learned, personally and professionally, is that we must learn to listen with more than our ears. Children will tell their story, yet not always in words. Their behaviors, their body language, their silence, and shifts in mood often speak louder than anything they say out loud.

"Kids know how to read the emotional weather," said Judy, a mother of three navigating blended family life. *"They say what clears the skies, not what clouds the room."*

As a parent or stepparent, this means being slow to react and quick to observe. It means asking better questions, open-ended ones that invite honesty without fear. It also means creating emotional space where kids are safe enough to be messy, uncertain, and contradictory.

Children do not owe us polished answers. What they need is a safe relationship where their whole truth, even the uncomfortable parts, can eventually rise to the surface.

Insight: In mosaic families, the truth often arrives in fragments. Our job is not to demand clarity on our timeline; it is to remain present long enough for the whole story to be told.

Dual Loyalties and Manipulation

In mosaic families, love does not always travel in a straight line. It twists, intersects, and sometimes tears at the seams of loyalty. Children often feel caught between worlds, wanting to please a biological parent while also navigating a relationship with a stepparent they did not choose. In this tension, manipulation can emerge, not always out of malice, but out of survival, guilt, or unspoken pressure.

"My daughter would come home after a weekend with her dad and suddenly hate everything about our house," said Joyce, a mother of two. *"It was like someone had flipped a switch. I could feel her love for me getting quieter when he was louder."*

Dual loyalties are powerful. A child may feel disloyal for showing affection to a stepparent if they believe it will hurt their biological parent. That guilt often leads to passive resistance, subtle undermining, or emotional triangulation, where a child uses one adult's emotions to influence another's behavior.

"My stepson would say, 'My real dad doesn't make me do that,' right in front of my wife," *said James, a stepfather trying to build trust.* "It put her in a no-win situation — and it chipped away at our connection."

These behaviors, while difficult, are often a reflection of emotional confusion rather than manipulation in the malicious sense. Children are not trying to destroy relationships; they are trying to protect the ones that feel most fragile or are at the most significant risk. Nevertheless, in doing so, they may pit adults against each other or create emotional hierarchies that fracture the family's unity.

"I did not realize I was being used as leverage," said Tiffany, who later reflected on how her son would praise her and criticize his stepfather when he was angry. *"It made me feel closer to him, but at the cost of their relationship."*

The key is not to blame the child, but to understand the pattern. Adults must lead with emotional maturity. When triangulation arises, it must be addressed, not with punishment, but with honest conversation. Children must be reassured that loving one person does not require rejecting another.

"We told our daughter over and over: 'You don't have to choose between us. Your heart has room for all of us.' It took years, but eventually, she believed us." —Sue.

When parents and stepparents present a united, emotionally consistent front, the need for manipulation fades. Children will test boundaries, and they also long for the security of knowing the adults are not in competition. That stability permits them to love freely.

Insight: Dual loyalty does not mean divided love; however, when adults become emotionally reactive, children learn to navigate with control rather than trust. The antidote is unity, empathy, and the courage to confront subtle manipulation with compassionate truth.

Feeling Torn Between Parents

Some of the deepest wounds children carry are the ones we never see. In mosaic families, love can become a conflict zone, where every hug feels like a betrayal, every smile comes with a silent cost, and belonging is divided between two homes, two histories, and two very different versions of the truth.

"I used to hold my breath before switching houses," said Fawn, reflecting on her experience as a child of divorce. *"I had to mentally switch teams. What made one parent smile might make the other mad."*

This emotional tug-of-war is not always visible. It shows up in hesitation before hugs, in silence after a weekend away, in the child who withdraws rather than disappoint either parent. While adults may believe they are offering freedom, children often feel caught between their parents' pain, carrying the weight of emotional allegiance without having the words to explain it.

"My stepdaughter once asked me if hugging me meant she did not love her mom anymore," said Sue. *"It broke me. She was six."*

Even when conflict is not overt, children pick up on emotional tension. They recognize when one parent is being criticized, when one relationship feels conditional, or when another might use affection as a weapon toward one adult. As a result, they often default to the parent they fear losing and withdraw from the one who feels more secure.

The confusion further deepens when one parent tries to be a friend rather than a parent. In my own home, I saw this play out. The children's mother was emotionally close to my children, almost peer-like. She comforted and joked, giving without many boundaries. I tried to bring structure, guidance, and firm love. But instead of balance, it created confusion. To my children, her flexibility felt safe, and my structure felt harsh. In their eyes, I became the rule, and she became the refuge.

"My son always acted colder toward me after he visited his mom," said Mark. *"I used to take it personally — until I realized he was afraid to love both of us at the same time."*

Helping children name this experience is one of the most healing gifts an adult can offer. When we validate that it is okay to love both parents and that no child should have to choose between them, we create space for emotional freedom. We relieve them of a burden they were never meant to carry.

The result? Children lose the emotional freedom to love fully. They become peacekeepers. They carry the weight of adult insecurity and heartbreak as if it is their job to make everyone happy. No child should ever have to wonder whether their love will offend someone.

"My grandmother told me, 'You're not a traitor for loving them both.' That was the first time I cried in years," Becky said, in a therapy session, reflecting on her childhood wounds as we discovered the source of her people pleasing.

Children are not wired to navigate divided loyalty on their own. They need adults who are secure enough to absorb their confusion, steady enough to welcome their affection without control, and wise enough to separate the child's love from the adult's ego.

Our role in mosaic families is not to compete for love; it is to clear the path for it. And that means being strong enough to accept a child's confusion without blaming them for it and being wise enough to hold the line when a parent-as-friend dynamic sets unclear expectations. And being secure enough to offer consistent love that doesn't shift with approval.

Insight: Children should never be expected to bear the burden of adult heartbreak. They are not emotional referees. They are not peacekeepers. They are just children, longing for permission to love without guilt. And they do not need a parent who is their friend. They need a parent who gives structure, safety, and the freedom to love both worlds without having to choose.

Inquire About the Other Ex-Partner

Love can make us curious about the person in front of us, and it should also make us curious about the people who came before. When you're entering a mosaic family, you're not just joining a new relationship — you're stepping into an unfinished story. The presence of an ex-partner, especially one still co-parenting, shapes the tone, tension, and boundaries of the entire system.

What you don't know about your partner's ex can hurt you, and your relationship.

"I thought her ex was just absent," said James, *"but turns out, he was deeply involved — and deeply manipulative. I was blindsided by how much control he still had over our home."*

Understanding the history between your partner and their former spouse is not about digging for drama — it is about gathering emotional context. How do they communicate? Are boundaries respected? Is there unresolved trauma, resentment, or manipulation that still seeps into the parenting dynamic?

"If I had known her ex was still calling during dinner, still making her feel guilty, still threatening to fight for custody anytime we disagreed ..." said Mark, *"I would have asked better questions — and made more space for clarity."*

In mosaic families, silence about the past often creates space for misunderstanding in the present. You may believe you're starting fresh, but if the ghosts of former relationships still linger — through text messages, court battles, or passive-aggressive parenting moves, they will show up, whether you're prepared or not.

"My wife never told me how much her ex still influenced her decisions," said Sue. *"It was like he was still in the marriage—and I was the outsider."*

Asking about the ex-partner may feel invasive at first, but it is actually an act of wisdom and respect. You're not seeking gossip; you're seeking grounding. By understanding the patterns, behaviors, and emotional entanglements of that previous relationship, you gain a clearer map for navigating your role with empathy and emotional intelligence.

There is a word of caution that must be spoken here. What you're told about the ex-partner is often one side of the story, and sometimes, that side is shaped by unhealed wounds, resentment, or self-protection. It is easy to adopt your partner's narrative as truth, especially when your love for them makes you want to defend or believe in their pain. But love should never blind you to complexity.

One of the most revealing sources of truth in mosaic families is not just your partner's account; it is the children. How they speak about their other biological parent, how they behave before and after transitions, and how emotionally safe they seem with both adults, these are windows into the family system. Their words may not be complete, but they carry clues about loyalty, fear, and unspoken tension.

"Had I paid closer attention to what her kids said about their dad — and how guarded they were around me — I might have made a very different choice," I later realized. *"I wasn't just marrying their mother. I was walking into a battlefield I did not see."*

This is not about blame, it is about awareness. When we ignore the behaviors of children in favor of the version we're told, we risk becoming entangled in a family system we were never prepared for. The truth is rarely clean. Sometimes, what's left unsaid speaks louder than the stories told.

The best approach is twofold: **observe and listen.** Pay attention to what is being modeled, what is repeated, what creates tension, and what the children emotionally withhold. Watch the tone in conversations, the silence after exchanges, and the way your partner reacts when the other parent's name comes up.

"Looking back, I should have slowed down and observed more," said Tiffany. *"There were signs, but I wanted love to be louder than the red flags."*

Be careful not to rush to judgment or step into someone else's pain with assumptions. Empathy must be paired with discernment. Because once you say yes to a mosaic family, you say yes to all of it: the beauty, the brokenness, the bonds, and the battles.

Insight: Not every story is fully told at the beginning. In mosaic families, discernment means asking the hard questions, watching for emotional patterns, and listening closely to what children reveal when no one is prompting them. You are not just inheriting your partner's version of the past, you are stepping into a living system of old loyalties, layered emotions, and unfinished dynamics. Asking about the ex is not an act of suspicion; it is an act of strategy and care. Because you're not just building a relationship with your partner, you're building trust within a complex web of past attachments, present responsibilities, and future hope. Choose wisely. Listen slowly.

Discuss Disciplinary Approaches

Discipline is not just about consequences, it is about clarity, trust, and consistency. In mosaic families, where loyalties are divided and emotional undercurrents run deep, discipline can either bring unity or create fault lines. The way correction is handled can affirm safety, or trigger fear, resentment, or rebellion.

When two adults parent together, especially when only one is the biological parent, discipline must be intentional, collaborative, and deeply respectful of the family's emotional landscape.

"I felt like the villain no matter what I did," said Frank, a stepfather trying to maintain structure. *"If I corrected them, I was too harsh. If I stayed quiet, I was weak. There was no win."*

The truth is that children in mosaic families often navigate invisible lines of loyalty. When a non-biological parent enforces rules, it may be perceived as a threat to their bond with their biological parent. Even if the correction is fair, the emotional charge can distort how it is received or retold.

"I lost custody of my children because of a lie," a close friend once told me. *"The child was angry at the stepdad, but I paid the price. It started with discipline and ended in court."*

Stories like that stay with you. They remind us that discipline in blended homes must be more than fair; it must be **agreed upon**. Discussing disciplinary roles before conflict arises is not just good parenting, it is **protective**. It guards the child's emotional clarity and shields adults from being cast into roles they did not choose.

In my experience, I have learned that biological parents should take the discipline lead, especially in the early years of blending. This is not about diminishing the role of the non-biological parent. Quite the opposite. It is about preserving their ability to **build trust** without prematurely assuming a role that the child may resist. When the biological parent leads and the stepparent supports, it eliminates confusion and reduces the chance of relational sabotage or false accusations.

"When my wife disciplined my son, he accepted it," said Mark, *"but when I tried — even gently — he acted like I'd betrayed him. I did not understand the weight of that until it nearly broke us."*

The goal is not perfection; it is partnership. Before addressing misbehavior, parents should align privately. What will be the consequence? Who will speak? How can both adults reinforce the same message with the same tone?

When children see their parents, whether biological or non-biological, presenting a united front, it reinforces their emotional security. It says: we are in agreement, and we care about you enough to hold you accountable with love. Remember to ask yourself:

What conversations about discipline have I been avoiding?

What do I need to ask, or agree on, with my partner to bring clarity, consistency, and unity to our family's leadership?

Insight: In mosaic families, discipline without alignment can become a battlefield of blurred roles and broken trust. When parents, primarily biological and non-biological, communicate and correct together, it shifts discipline from a focus on power to one on protection. Clarity brings safety. Unity builds trust. And children thrive when correction comes not from control, but from care.

Create New Traditions through Compromise

Traditions are more than routines; they are emotional anchors. They tell us who we are, where we belong, and what matters to the people we call family. In mosaic families, however, traditions are not inherited; they are negotiated. They are built from fragments of the past, fused with hope for something new.

The challenge is this: everyone brings their version of "normal." Moreover, what feels sacred to one person may feel unfamiliar, or even threatening, to another. Blending traditions requires more than logistics. It requires listening, flexibility, and sometimes letting go of what once defined you to make room for something that now includes others.

"Christmas was always just me and my daughter," said Sharon. *"When I remarried, suddenly there were stockings for five. It felt chaotic and also beautiful. But I had to grieve the simplicity before I could love the new."*

In mosaic families, compromise is not failure. It is formation. Creating new rhythms doesn't mean erasing old ones. It means honoring the stories that shaped each person while choosing, together, what story you want to write going forward.

"My stepson hated Thanksgiving with us at first," said Jason. *"We did things differently than his dad's side. But when we let him*

bring one of their food traditions into our meal, his whole posture changed. He felt seen."

This process of co-creating traditions is not just about holidays; it is about identity. Children watch closely to see if their memories, cultures, and customs are welcome in the new family. When those parts are dismissed, they may emotionally retreat. When they are invited in, even in small ways, it sends a powerful message: *You matter here.*

"My daughter asked if we could light a candle for her grandma, like she used to with her dad," said Sharon. *"That one candle changed everything. She felt like this wasn't just my family, it was ours."*

Compromise requires humility. It may mean doing things differently than you're used to. It may mean sitting with discomfort while a new rhythm takes shape. When everyone has a voice, a vote, and a seat at the table, something beautiful begins to form, not perfect, but real.

Insight: In mosaic families, new traditions are not found; they are formed. They are built through compassion, flexibility, and a willingness to let old ways evolve into shared ones. When everyone brings a piece of their past and places it on the table with openness, belonging begins, not through sameness, but through shared meaning.

Equitable Treatment for All

In mosaic families, fairness is not just a parenting principle; it is a survival need. Children in blended homes are hyper-aware of how love, attention, and discipline are distributed. They notice who gets the extra hug, who's corrected more harshly, who's allowed to bend the rules, and who's expected to adapt. And they remember.

What may feel like simple parenting decisions to the adults involved can feel like favoritism toward a child trying to find their place in a new system. One shift in tone. One uneven consequence. One unspoken comparison. These can send a message that echoes louder than the words you speak: *you belong a little less than they do.*

Biological children often assume a sense of emotional security; they've been there longer. Yet that familiarity can quickly turn into entitlement or resentment when new children enter the picture. Meanwhile, non-biological children may test boundaries not out of rebellion, but out of fear: *Will I still matter if I push too far?*

"My stepson acted out constantly," said Frank, *"but I realized it wasn't because he hated me, it was because he did not trust that I'd stay. He was testing how breakable our connection was."*

And while discipline must be consistent, connection must be personal. Fairness does not mean sameness; it means meeting each child where they are while maintaining shared standards of respect, accountability, and love.

Still, **even with the best intentions**, equitable treatment can become complicated. Sometimes, a child feels left out and labels another as the favorite, when in reality, they are seeing a version of love or connection they wish they had. I remember a moment when one of my children was accused of being favored. The truth was, I had worked hard to stay balanced. As I watched the other child repeat the same pattern, unnoticed by anyone, it became clear how quickly one parent can get caught in the middle. Suddenly, fairness wasn't about actions; it was about perception.

"I did not want to discipline my son more softly," said Sharon, *"I found myself doing it. I felt more at ease with him until my stepdaughter noticed. That was a wake-up call."*

Children in mosaic families are looking for evidence:

Do I matter as much?

Will you protect me the same?

Do I have a place, or am I just visiting yours?

Every interaction answers those questions. Every double standard feeds division. Every moment of fairness builds trust.

Creating an environment of equity requires emotional honesty, patience, and a willingness to confront your own biases, whether intentional or unintentional. It means checking in with your discomfort, acknowledging when you feel more protective of one child over another, and doing the work to parent from love, not guilt or habit.

Consistency doesn't mean perfection. It means that every child knows where the lines are, and more importantly, that those lines exist to protect them, not punish them. When fairness becomes the foundation, children begin to feel at ease. Rivalries soften. Relationships deepen. And trust, absolute trust, takes root.

Insight: In mosaic families, fairness is the language of belonging. It tells each child: "You are safe here. You are seen. You matter." Equity builds the bridge between difference and unity, because love without fairness breeds resentment; however, love with fairness becomes a family. This is a topic I would bring up in a dating relationship with someone who has children. Along with the following:

Understand Parenting Styles

Parenting styles are not just about how we discipline, they are about how we see, respond to, and emotionally engage with our children. They reflect what we believe about love, protection, accountability, and identity. And often, they are shaped by our own childhood wounds, what we received, what we lacked, and what we're still trying to heal.

In mosaic families, this complexity is multiplied. This can be turned into a storm quickly if one is not proactive in de-escalating the situation. Two adults may love the same children but express that love in entirely different ways. One may be emotionally expressive, the other more structured. One may avoid conflict, the other addresses it head-on. And, in that tension, the child often becomes the quiet casualty, uncertain of the rules, unclear on where they stand.

"I did not grow up with structure," said Sharon, *"so I let a lot slide. My husband had a military background, and everything was rigid. Our kids did not know what to expect, and honestly, neither did we."*

The most important goal in any parenting system, especially in a mosaic family, is to create a home where children feel **seen**, **safe**, and **heard**. Such an emotional environment cannot be created if the adults are pulling in different directions. Children don't need perfection, but they do need clarity. They need to know the adults are on the same page and that love is not something they have to earn through behavior or manipulation.

Some of the most challenging moments I have faced as a stepparent and biological parent came when I realized our parenting styles were not aligned. One of us would correct; the other would comfort. One would draw a boundary; the other would override it. And the message to the children, even unintentionally, was confusion. Discipline started to feel like a guessing game. Respect became optional. Emotional safety unraveled.

This is especially dangerous when **a child's trauma history or emotional triggers are unknown**. What feels like a fair consequence to one adult may reactivate anxiety, fear, or shame in a child who's been through inconsistent or harsh parenting in another home. Without those conversations ahead of time, one adult may unknowingly recreate emotional harm while trying to help.

"My stepson shut down every time I raised my voice, even slightly," said Frank. *"It took months to realize his dad used yelling as intimidation. I wasn't angry. I was trying to be firm. But it did not matter. His body remembered what his mind couldn't say."*

At a basic level, parenting styles often fall into four categories: **authoritative** (firm and warm), **authoritarian** (strict and controlling), **permissive** (lenient and indulgent), and **neglectful** (disengaged). In blended homes, these styles don't appear in neat boxes. They crash into each other. They get blurred by guilt, fatigue, or unresolved pain. And without communication, those blurred lines become breeding grounds for power struggles, favoritism, and mistrust.

"My daughter knew she could play us," said Sam. *"If I said no, she went to her stepmom. If her stepmom said no, she came back*

to me with a softer tone. We thought we were co-parenting, but really, we were being played like instruments."

These behaviors aren't signs of a manipulative child. They are signs of a confused one. Children test systems when they are trying to figure out if the adults are safe, steady, and emotionally united.

"I realized I was overcorrecting because of how I was raised," said Sharon. *"When I finally shared that with my husband, he softened. He disagreed with my style, but he finally understood it."*

When adults take the time to share not just their preferences, but also the stories behind them, empathy grows. Judgment softens. Parenting becomes a partnership. And the children? They start to feel **Seen,** not managed. **Safe,** not monitored, and **Heard,** not dismissed.

That is what they need most, not control, but connection. Not sameness, but unity.

Insight: In mosaic families, parenting styles are not just methods; they are mirrors of our own unfinished stories. When adults communicate, align, and lead from a place of self-awareness and empathy, children gain the gift of emotional safety. When a child feels seen, safe, and heard, discipline becomes less about correction and more about connection.

Designate a Weekly Family Night

In mosaic families, transitions are more than physical moves between houses; they are emotional handoffs. Children don't just carry backpacks back and forth; they carry expectations, memories, tension, and questions. Establishing a consistent rhythm that helps them land emotionally after visitation is not just helpful; it is essential.

One of the most powerful tools I have found in creating connection and stability is designating a weekly family night, especially right after children return from time with their other biological parent. This intentional time acts as a soft landing, a place to reconnect, recalibrate, and remind each other what home feels like.

I remember the nights when all our kids, mine and hers, returned from their other homes. The air felt different. There was a quiet tension, a recalibration that had to happen each time. So, we made it a point to gather around the dinner table. No screens. No cell phones. No distractions. Just food, presence, and conversation.

We went around the table, asking each other how our week had been and what we were thankful for. It was simple, and grounding. Everyone had a voice. Everyone got to speak. We talked openly about what was coming that week, including homework, chores, and expectations. We were honest: there would be warnings if rules were ignored, and consequences would be applied if needed. They also got to share their desires. Each child had a "buy-in," something they wanted to do and looked forward to. It gave them a sense of choice in a world that often felt decided for them.

We made it a point to plan thoughtfully. We checked the weather before promising an outing. We wanted to avoid disappointment whenever possible. And while their mom and I always knew the weekly plan, this was a moment to help them remember their schedule, not just practically, but emotionally. It helped bring them back into rhythm.

Of course, there was pushback.

"I don't have to do that at my other house. Why do I have to do it here?"

It stung, yet it wasn't personal. It was the echo of divided norms. A child's attempt to understand why love and structure sometimes looked so different depending on which roof they were under.

That dinner table did not fix everything, but it anchored us. It gave us a place to reconnect, to reset expectations, and to remind each child: you matter here, and so does what we build together.

Before I became a therapist, I made my fair share of parenting mistakes. Mosaic families are pressure cookers, emotions run high, expectations clash, and not every day goes as planned. There were times I lost my cool. Times I reacted too harshly. Times I let frustration win over wisdom.

I wish I could say I always responded with patience. I did not. There were moments I raised my voice, handed out punishments that did not fit the behavior, or overcorrected because I felt out of control. In those moments, I did not feel like a leader; I felt like a failure. I felt like a heel.

However, here's what I learned: *staying in the wrong is far more damaging than admitting it.*

I made a conscious decision to own my mistakes in front of my children. When I overreacted, I apologized. When a punishment was too harsh, I corrected it. Not because I was trying to appear perfect, but because I knew what unacknowledged hurt could do to a child's heart.

"I'm sorry. I shouldn't have spoken to you that way. Let's talk about a fair consequence together."

Those words don't erase the moment, but they begin to heal it. They teach children that power is not about domination, it is about responsibility. And they remind them that even adults are still learning.

In a world where so many children are told to respect authority without ever seeing humility, I wanted my children to experience something different. I wanted them to know that love doesn't mean always getting it right; it means always being willing to make it right.

Apologizing did not diminish my authority. It deepened it. It taught my children that our home was a place where truth mattered, even when it was uncomfortable. And it reinforced the kind of emotional safety I wish every child in a mosaic family could feel: *you can be honest here, even when it is messy. Even when I mess up, I'm still for you.*

This is precisely why family night became so important to us.

It wasn't just a time to reset the calendar or plan the week. It was sacred space, a chance to hear each other, understand where we were coming from, and listen to perspectives we did not always see. Even when we came from different lanes, different homes, histories, and parenting styles, **family night helped us move forward together.**

This doesn't have to be elaborate. A movie night, a board game, cooking dinner together, or just sitting around the table with no distractions, what matters most is **presence**. It signals to the children: ***You matter. We're here. This is your place, too.***

Setting aside 30 minutes to check in with the kids when they return is equally vital. Ask open questions: *What did you enjoy? Was anything hard?* These conversations allow children to feel seen and heard, and they give parents insight into their emotional world without interrogating or competing with the other household.

"My daughter always acted differently after she came back," said Sharon. *"At first, I just gave her space. But when I started asking, gently, she opened up. She needed a bridge back to me."*

Routine plays a massive role in emotional security. When visitation weekends are predictable, with the same weekends each month and drop-off times, it reduces anxiety and helps children mentally prepare for the transition. Chaos around scheduling often shows up later in behavior, emotional withdrawal, or acting out. Structure is not control; it is a gift of peace.

While family night fosters connection with the children, parents also need intentional connection outside of their parenting roles. It is just as vital to designate a **night for yourselves** as a couple, a time to reconnect romantically and relationally without discussing parenting strategies, calendars, or problems.

"We started going out once a week — no kid talk," said Frank. *"At first, it was hard. Then we started laughing again. That saved us."*

In mosaic families, where stress and emotional complexity run high, couples can begin to feel more like co-managers than lovers. Over time, which wears down trust and intimacy. Protect your connection. Go on dates. Be lighthearted. Let joy back in.

The strength of your bond is not just good for you; it is grounding for your children.

Insight: In mosaic families, emotional security grows when rhythm replaces chaos. Family nights foster connection, check-ins build trust, and consistency calms the storm of transition. However, do not forget that your relationship as partners also needs time, laughter, and a sense of lightness. The family only thrives when the foundation between the parents is strong.

Acknowledge Potential Interference

Mosaic families are not built in a vacuum. They are formed in the presence of history, some of it healing, some of it still hurting. One of the more difficult truths I have come to accept is this: ex-spouses and extended family members from previous relationships can, and often do, significantly impact the emotional climate of your current marriage.

Sometimes the influence is subtle-a passive-aggressive text, a last-minute schedule change, a whispered comment to a child. Other times, it is more overt, undermining your authority, sowing mistrust, or even manipulating the child-parent bond to serve their own unmet needs.

"We would take two steps forward and then get a call from her ex, and suddenly we were back to square one," said Frank. *"It wasn't about the kids. It was about control."*

When outside voices start echoing inside your home, it becomes even more important to protect what you're building. That begins with awareness and continues with **unity between partners**. Being honest with one another about how outside interference affects you, how it shapes your reactions, and how it might be affecting the children is not just helpful, it is necessary.

You do not have to fight every battle. But you do have to stand together.

Insight: In mosaic families, interference is often a test of unity. When partners communicate, protect each other's emotional space, and respond as a team, external voices lose their power to divide.

The Kind of Love That Holds

Mosaic families are built piece by piece, and what holds them together is not luck, convenience, or even biology. It is the kind of love that is willing to do the invisible work. The kind of love that apologizes when pride would rather retreat. The kind that waits through silence, listens between the lines, and chooses presence over perfection.

This chapter has not been about easy wins or perfect formulas. It has been about grouting the pieces, with truth, empathy, and the willingness to stay at the table even when everything in you wants to walk away. It is about the hard lessons we learn not because we failed, but because we dared to show up in the fire.

I have come to realize that parenting in a mosaic family is not just a role; it is a calling. It is the art of holding space for grief while planting seeds of joy. It is knowing that some wounds will be carried forward, but love can still show up as a healing salve if we are brave enough to keep pouring it.

And that's the miracle of mosaic love: it doesn't erase the cracks. It holds them.

So, to every parent, stepparent, partner, and caregiver walking this road, please understand this:

You are not failing because it is hard. You are becoming something sacred because you continue to show up.

This chapter was about the lessons that carved wisdom into my bones. Wisdom alone is not what keeps families together. What holds them is the grout, boundaries, truth, forgiveness, shared vision, and quiet courage. That is where we are going next.

Because love needs something more substantial than feelings to hold it in place.

It needs structure.

It needs substance.

It needs grout.

Grout is not what you see first in a mosaic, but it is what holds every piece in place.

Mosaic Truth

Repair does not require perfection; it requires participation.

Just as grout binds broken shards into lasting beauty, so too do intentional acts of love, humility, and forgiveness seal the fractures within a mosaic family.

The healing of a home is not found in removing pain, but in honoring the effort to mend together.

Review Questions

- When have you shown up in love even when you felt uninvited or unseen?
- Have you ever misread a child's behavior because of what they did not say? What patterns have you noticed?
- How do you navigate the tension between discipline and connection in your family?
- What assumptions have you made about an ex-partner's influence, and how have those assumptions helped or hurt your current dynamic?
- Are there unspoken emotional "lanes" in your mosaic family, loyalties, grief, or habits that need to be named?
- What has been your greatest parenting regret, and what did you do to repair it?
- Have you and your partner intentionally aligned on parenting roles, correction, and boundaries, or are those conversations still waiting?

Key Takeaways

- Love alone is not enough; it must be supported by structure, alignment, and repair.
- Parental alienation distorts identity; truth and compassion must work to restore it.
- Children should never have to choose between the people they love.
- Discipline without unity creates confusion; alignment creates safety.
- Emotional manipulation often masks loyalty conflicts; adults must lead with steadiness.
- Fairness is not treating everyone the same; it helps every child feel they belong.
- The invisible work of mosaic families, boundaries, humility, and consistent love is the grout that holds it all together.

Chapter Eleven

Lessons Learned In Thresholds (Boundaries)

Boundaries are not walls that confine us; they are thresholds that define our values, guiding us toward what nourishes our spirit and protecting us from what diminishes it.

What happens when the very relationships meant to bring you life begin to drain the very soul out of you? What do you do when your desire to be loved turns into a pattern of pleasing, rescuing, or disappearing to keep the peace?

I learned the hard way: without boundaries or thresholds, even love becomes dangerous.

After the collapse of my second marriage, I wasn't just grieving the loss of a partner — I was unraveling. I had poured so much of myself into holding the family together that, when it ended, I wasn't sure who I was anymore. Health issues weakened my body, but codependency had weakened something deeper, my sense of self. I tried to fix everyone, manage everyone, and stay emotionally "needed" until I could no longer recognize where their pain ended and mine began.

Then a friend said something that shattered my illusions:

"You're not addicted to love. You're addicted to saving people who don't ask to be saved."

That sentence broke me open. I saw the trail of emotional over-functioning I had left behind ... patterns built not from strength, but from fear. I called it love. Yet, what I had actually built was an identity dependent on being needed.

This is not just my story. It is the silent pattern in so many mosaic families. We sacrifice boundaries in the name of unity. We abandon ourselves to avoid rejection. We confuse selflessness with self-erasure.

Boundaries (thresholds) are not selfish. They are sacred.

We often hear boundaries described as "lines in the sand." But sand shifts. It erodes. One wave and the line disappears. That's not what boundaries are meant to be, within oneself, a family, and not in a mosaic family, and not in a life where emotional safety matters.

Boundaries are not lines in the sand. **They are thresholds.**

Like the threshold of a door, they define the space between what is allowed and what is not. They signal where your values begin and where another person's expectations must pause. Just as a door may be open to some, closed to others, or locked when protection is needed, boundaries can — and should — shift based on context, trust, and emotional readiness. They are not rigid; they are firm. They are not cruel, they are clear.

Like any door, thresholds don't just keep harm out; they create space for safety within.

Here is what many overlook: **thresholds must be guarded.**

In Proverbs 4:23, Solomon offers a wisdom that is both ancient and eternally relevant:

"Above all else, guard your heart, for everything you do flows from it."

To guard your heart is not to wall it off; it is to keep it open. It is not to hide it behind fear. It is to station a watchman, a filter, a protector, a discerner of what gets in and what must stay out. Not everything deserves access. Not every voice deserves volume.

Imagine a prison guard, not just observing who enters and exits, but also watching the internal behaviors within the cell. Thresholds work the same way. They are not passive lines drawn once and forgotten. They require active observation, emotional awareness, and the courage to say no, when necessary, even to people you love.

A guard does not exist to punish. A guard exists to protect. In families, especially those with mosaic structures, where love, loyalty, and expectations often spill over emotional boundaries, **a well-trained inner guard is essential.**

Not to create distance ... to create definition.

Not to keep others small ... to keep yourself whole.

When boundaries or, as I say, thresholds are held with wisdom, some people may not like the closed door. That's okay. Not everyone will celebrate your clarity. Some may resist, manipulate, feel guilty, or withdraw. Thresholds are not about keeping others comfortable. They are about keeping your heart protected, your mind sound, and your relationships rooted in truth, not obligation.

So ask yourself:

Where is my threshold?

Who guards it?

And what am I still letting in that is draining the life I'm trying to build?

To effectively maintain these boundaries (thresholds), it is essential to develop "guarding actions" — internal and external strategies that protect your emotional and psychological space. These actions act as gatekeepers, ensuring that only those who respect your boundaries are granted access.

Imagine a guard standing at the doorway diligently performing specific tasks to protect your well-being. This guard embodies your internal mechanisms for boundary maintenance.

Ai generated.

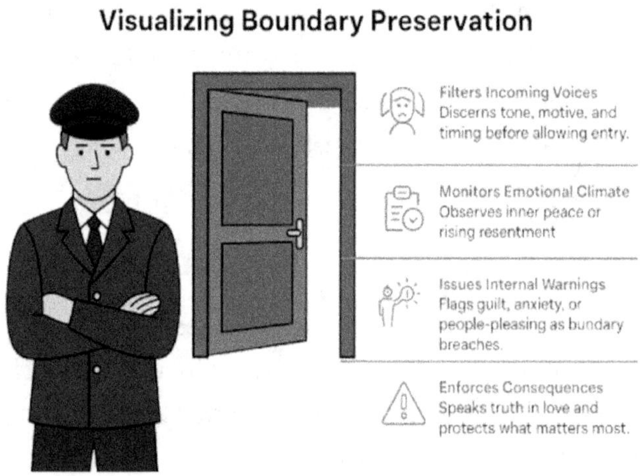

The guard of the mind will perform these duties:

- **Filters Incoming Voices:** The guard carefully discerns the tone, motive, and timing of interactions before allowing entry. This involves paying attention to the words used, the underlying intentions, and the context of the communication. Are they speaking with kindness and respect? Are they trying to manipulate or control you? Is this a good time for you to engage in this conversation? By filtering incoming voices, you can prevent harmful or draining interactions from breaching your boundaries.

- **Monitors Emotional Climate:** The guard constantly observes your inner peace or rising resentment. This involves being attuned to your emotional state and recognizing when your boundaries are being tested or violated. Are you feeling calm and centered, or are you experiencing anxiety, guilt, or resentment? These emotions can serve as early warning signs that your boundaries are being compromised.
- **Issues Internal Warnings:** The guard flags feelings of guilt, anxiety, or people-pleasing as potential boundary breaches. These feelings often arise when we are compromising our own needs and desires to accommodate others. Recognizing these internal warnings allows you to take proactive steps to reinforce your boundaries and protect your well-being. For example, if you feel guilty saying "no" to a request, it may be a sign that you need to strengthen your boundaries around your time and energy.
- **Upholds the Standard:** The guard speaks truth in love and protects what matters most. This involves communicating your boundaries clearly and assertively, while also maintaining compassion and respect for others. It also means prioritizing your own needs and values and refusing to compromise on what is important to you. Upholding the standard requires courage, self-

awareness, and a commitment to protecting your emotional and psychological well-being.

By understanding these threshold types and implementing these guarding actions, you can create a strong and healthy boundary system that protects your well-being and fosters fulfilling relationships. Remember that boundaries are not about building walls, but about creating safe and respectful spaces for connection and growth.

Threshold (Boundaries) Types and Their Meanings

We can visualize our personal boundaries as different types of doors, each representing a different level of access and protection. Understanding these "door types" can help us communicate our needs and maintain healthy relationships.

- **Open Door:** This symbolizes trust and welcome. An open door signifies that you are comfortable and secure in the presence of the person on the other side. It is reserved for emotionally safe people who honor your space and respect your boundaries. This doesn't mean you have no boundaries with these individuals, but rather that your boundaries are naturally respected and understood.
- **Closed Door:** This signals the need for privacy, emotional rest, or time to heal. A closed door is a necessary reset, not a rejection. It indicates that you need space to recharge, process emotions, or be alone. It is a temporary boundary that allows you to focus on your well-being without external influences or demands.
- **Locked Door:** This protects against repeated harm, manipulation, or boundary violations. A locked door is a

firm and unwavering boundary designed to safeguard you from individuals who consistently disregard your needs, disrespect your boundaries, or cause you emotional or psychological harm. It is a necessary measure to protect your well-being and prevent further damage.

- **Door with a Key:** This represents conditional access. Trust must be earned or rebuilt before re-entry is granted. A door with a key signifies that access is possible, yet not automatic. It requires demonstration of respect, understanding, and a commitment to honoring your boundaries. The key represents the conditions that must be met before the relationship can be restored to a more open and trusting state.

This chapter is not about rules. It is about reclaiming the space where your soul can breathe again. Whether you were never taught boundaries or yours have been trampled in the chaos of a blended life, it is time to draw new lines, not to keep others out but to find your way back in. Are you ready to stop bleeding for love and start building something sustainable?

Let's begin.

The Past

Before I found my way to a place of secure attachment, I wrestled deeply with anxious attachment. When my Mosaical-spouse left during a season when I was already facing serious health issues, I was met with a stark, sobering truth: living alone, I had only a 34% chance of living due to cancer, due to a military service-connected injury by 2021. (Thank God it has been eradicated and will not come back.) Yes, I had friends, family, and a supportive church community standing beside me, but the internal battle was deeply personal.

I will never forget a conversation I had with a friend about working in addiction counseling. I had been approached by an agency to work with individuals facing substance abuse issues. At first, I hesitated; I had never dealt with personal addictions to drugs, alcohol, or gambling. Growing up, no one in my immediate family ever really talked about or dealt with this issue — only the older generations, the "greats," and unfortunately, they were often the ones who caused pain on both sides of the family due to alcoholism.

My closest "vice" might have been a strong attachment to my morning coffee. My friend looked at me and said, *"You do have an addiction—you're addicted to relationships."* Her words stopped me cold. And she was right. My anxious attachment was, in its own way, a form of dependency.

In that moment, I realized how quickly anxious attachment can slip into codependency. I placed so much weight on relationships that I often lost sight of myself inside them. I constantly craved reassurance, validation, and signs I was still wanted. I lived in fear: Would they leave me like my spouse did? Would I still be loved if I were not perfect? That fear blurred my personal boundaries. I struggled to separate where I ended and others began.

In this codependent state, my emotional well-being became tied to others' feelings and actions. I felt responsible for their happiness and often sidelined my own needs to keep peace or feel secure. I was afraid to speak up, afraid that asserting myself would drive people away. I became the caretaker, the fixer, the one who always said yes. I thought I was being helpful — a "nice guy" in my marriages and relationships—but in truth, I was slowly losing myself.

Becoming a therapist helped me confront and rewrite this pattern. Through training, reflection, and real-world experiences, I began shifting from an anxious to a secure attachment style. I gained confidence — not just in my professional life, but also in how I present myself in relationships. I learned that love should never cost you your identity.

It is a painful realization that love can quietly become dependency when fused with anxiety. I have come to understand that healthy love honors both connection and individuality. Building secure attachments meant learning that my worth is not defined by who stays or leaves. I began to set boundaries, even when it felt foreign. I learned that protecting my peace was not selfish; it was essential.

In mosaic families, where multiple emotional histories converge, these attachment patterns become even more visible. Each person brings their past: old wounds, loyalties, and coping strategies. When I was still entrenched in anxious attachment, I found it difficult to establish healthy boundaries in such a complex dynamic. My longing for closeness clouded my awareness of my own needs. I took on the emotional burdens of others, often neglecting my own well-being in the name of maintaining connection.

This became especially confusing in mosaic families, where loyalties are complex and connections are constantly shifting. I tried to be the emotional glue, managing tensions, anticipating needs, softening the blow of discomfort. Trying to keep everyone happy left me emotionally depleted. My sense of value became tied to how well I could hold things together. I wasn't building a connection. I was exhausting myself in the illusion of control.

Without boundaries, misunderstandings multiply. In mosaic families, that instability is magnified. My people-pleasing tendencies led me to suppress my voice to maintain peace. When you silence your own truth, others cannot honestly know you, and that creates more disconnection, not less.

My anxious behavior did not just affect me. It sometimes created codependent patterns in the family system, where emotional reliance blurred individuality, and members became stuck in roles that stifled growth. Even though my intentions were rooted in care, the outcomes weren't always healthy.

I was seeking closeness, yet without clear boundaries, I created confusion. I acted from obligation rather than genuine affection. And that created friction, not intimacy.

What I now understand is that mosaic families thrive when each person is seen and respected as a whole individual. For someone healing from anxious attachment, this means committing to self-awareness, setting boundaries, and developing emotional maturity. It means allowing others their own space to grow, without trying to carry their journey.

Healing is not just about no longer feeling anxious; it is about embracing a new perspective. It is about choosing relationships that honor wholeness. It is about allowing love without losing yourself. Especially with the complexity of mosaic relationships, it means creating a home where connection and individuality can coexist.

If secure attachment is the foundation, boundaries are the framework. And for many of us, especially those raised in chaotic or codependent systems, boundaries were never modeled, let alone taught. Mosaic families, shaped by overlapping roles and shifting dynamics, often learn the hard way that emotional safety is not possible without structure. *"I kept feeling like I had to fight for my place,"* Carly shared. "I wasn't *just trying to co-parent — I was trying to protect my role as a parent from being erased."*

Jana echoed a similar struggle: *"There were days I did not know what my role was supposed to be. I was doing everything but still felt like I was in someone else's house."* Without clear expectations and defined roles, even love begins to feel like an obligation. Boundaries are what protect love from becoming burdensome. They are how we stay whole while staying connected.

That brings us to a critical truth ...**boundaries in mosaic families are not just helpful; they are essential.**

Explanation

Learning boundaries in a mosaic family is not automatic. Most of us were not raised with clear, compassionate models of how to hold space for ourselves while staying connected to others. We were taught to obey, to keep the peace, to serve, often at the expense of our own voice. For those who grew up in environments where love was conditional or chaotic, boundaries were either rigid and punitive or nonexistent. This silence created confusion in adulthood. We do not know what we are allowed to say, need, or protect. And in a mosaic family, this uncertainty is multiplied by layers of role ambiguity, loyalty binds, and emotional landmines.

"I did not know how to say what I needed without sounding like I was complaining," Mark admitted. *"So, I stopped saying anything at all."*

Carly added, *"I kept feeling like I had to fight for my place. I wasn't just trying to co-parent; I was trying to protect my role as a parent from being erased."*

Mosaic families carry the emotional weight of their parts, the pieces from previous relationships, inherited fears, and unmet expectations. Boundaries are the way we begin to differentiate *who we are* from *what we inherited.* They give shape to our identity in a system where everything feels fluid. But these boundaries are not learned overnight. They are taught slowly through therapy, modeling, honest communication, and intentional unlearning of old survival patterns.

We begin to learn boundaries when we notice what depletes us. We begin to teach them when we say, *"This is what I need to feel safe in this family."* In mosaic systems, this can look like a stepparent clarifying their role, a child learning to express their limits without guilt, or a biological parent setting expectations with an ex-spouse without emotional triangulation. Boundaries are not just about stopping harm — they are about creating space for *healthy, intentional love.*

In my clinical work and lived experience, I have seen it again and again: boundaries bring relief. They reduce burnout, anxiety, and emotional confusion. They foster self-respect, protect mental health, and empower individuals to live from a place of clarity rather than a state of constant reactivity. Most importantly, they teach children that safety is not just a feeling; it is a structure you help create.

Boundaries are how mosaic families move from emotional survival to emotional sustainability. They are not barriers. They are blueprints for belonging that do not require erasure. They are the only way to love without losing yourself.

Importance of Clear Boundaries

It is hard to understand why boundaries matter if no one ever showed you how to set them. If your life has been shaped by survival, people-pleasing, or confusion about your role in relationships, the concept of boundaries might feel foreign, maybe even selfish.

Nevertheless, here's the truth: boundaries are essential precisely because they help you discover *who you are* apart from what others need from you.

If you're constantly feeling drained, resentful, anxious, or uncertain in your relationships, that's a sign that something sacred is being compromised. That *something* is your boundary.

Clear boundaries are important because they protect your emotional and relational integrity. They help define:

- What you will allow.
- What you will not accept.
- What you need to feel safe, respected, and valued.

You may not know all your boundaries right now and that's okay. The starting point is noticing how you feel. Boundaries often manifest first in your body: a tight chest, resentment after saying yes, or anxiety before specific conversations. Those are clues that a line has been crossed or never drawn.

Boundaries matter because they prevent you from disappearing in your own life. They allow you to stay present without being overrun, to love others without losing yourself. They are how you teach people to honor who you are, not just what you do for them.

You know boundaries are important when their absence starts costing you your peace. When you feel invisible in a home you helped build. When you say yes and silently wish you had the strength to say no. Boundaries are not just tools for survival — they are the foundation of healthy love.

And if we want to raise children who know their worth, we must first learn how to protect our own.

When you begin to protect your own boundaries, everything around you shifts. Children learn what safety feels like. Biological parents find clarity instead of conflict. Stepparents are relieved of pressure and confusion. Boundaries do more than define roles; they dignify each relationship within the family mosaic. They remove the guesswork and give each person permission to breathe, belong, and grow in the space that is truly theirs. The following sections examine how boundaries operate in each of these relationships, not as barriers, but as bridges to trust, structure, and healing.

With Children

Children do not learn boundaries by being told or lectured; they learn them by experiencing them. And what they feel becomes their blueprint for self-worth, trust, and future relationships. In mosaic families, where love is real and roles may be unclear, boundaries provide the stability children cannot put into words but always recognize in their hearts. Clear boundaries create predictable rhythms in a world they are still learning to understand.

1. **Emotional Safety:** Children need to know that their needs and feelings will be respected. Clear boundaries provide a sense of safety, allowing them to express emotions without fear of punishment, silence, or shame. Emotional safety means a child knows where they stand with you. In therapy, I have seen children flourish simply because a parent consistently held to a specific bedtime or followed through on a promised consequence, not to punish; to protect the rhythm of the home.
2. **Understanding Relationships:** When a child doesn't know who's "in charge," they internalize that confusion as instability. In mosaic families, where a stepfather may discipline, a biological father reappears sporadically, and a grandmother often assumes the role of a mother, boundaries become clearer regarding who is responsible for what. This fosters respect and reduces anxiety. Teaching children how each adult fits into the family's design empowers them to feel secure, not conflicted.
3. **Encouraging Independence:** Boundaries are not limits to freedom; they are invitations to maturity. When parents set clear expectations, they enable children to

make age-appropriate decisions and experience the natural consequences that follow. This helps them develop problem-solving skills and emotional regulation. A child who knows their room is their responsibility learns autonomy and pride in managing it.

With Biological Parents:

Co-parenting without boundaries does not just strain the adults; it silently fractures the emotional landscape in which children are trying to grow. When biological parents lack clarity, unity, or respect, children absorb the tension in ways that distort their sense of safety and loyalty. Boundaries between biological parents are not just relational tools; they are emotional safeguards for the next generation. In mosaic families, those boundaries draw the line between cooperation and confusion, between healing and hostility. The success of any mosaic family rests on how well the biological parents manage their roles without waging war on each other through the child. When boundaries between biological parents are blurred, the child becomes the battleground. When boundaries are honored, the child becomes the bridge.

1. **Co-Parenting Clarity:** In mosaic families, biological parents must intentionally define their roles, especially when parenting from separate homes. Who makes educational decisions? Who disciplines? Who communicates with teachers or doctors? Boundaries around these roles reduce triangulation and resentment. When parents agree ahead of time on who leads what, children are spared the emotional fallout of parental ambiguity.

2. **Respect for New Relationships**: One of the most significant sources of conflict in mosaic families is the lack of respect for new partners. Boundaries help biological parents honor the influence of a stepparent while still maintaining their parental role. Healthy boundaries sound like: *"I'm the decision-maker for medical care, but I value your input."* They create emotional safety for everyone involved, including the child, who should never feel caught between loyalty and love.

With Non-Biological Parents:

Non-biological parents often step into families already in motion, loving deeply, yet unsure of their place. Their role is vital, and undefined without boundaries. With guidance, trust, and clarity, their presence becomes a gift rather than a threat in the mosaic design. Without clear boundaries, this love can turn into silent suffering. Too involved, and they may feel resentful. Too distant, and they feel irrelevant. Boundaries are the compass for non-biological parents. They define roles without diminishing heart. In mosaic families, boundaries offer non-biological parents the guidance and security to contribute meaningfully, without overstepping, disappearing, or losing themselves in someone else's story. Boundaries create space where non-biological parents can be present without pressure, involved without overreaching.

1. **Defining Roles**: Non-biological parents need clarity, not assumption. Are they a caregiver, a supporter, a disciplinarian, or a mentor? Boundaries help determine this with input from the biological parent and the children. Without this clarity, well-meaning stepparents

may do too much, or not enough, leading to confusion and conflict. A healthy role begins with a defined lane and grows through trust.

2. **Building Trust:** Trust is not automatic in mosaic families; it is earned through consistency, respect, and presence. Boundaries help build that trust by clarifying who does what and when. Children learn they can rely on a stepparent not just because of authority, but because of emotional safety. Adults learn to honor each other's roles, reducing jealousy and resentment.

Maintaining Healthy Boundaries

Boundaries are not a one-time fix; they are a rhythm. Like tuning an instrument, they require ongoing attention and adjustment as families grow, change, and face new seasons together. Ongoing attention to boundaries keeps the family emotionally flexible without falling into chaos.

1. **Regular Family Meetings:** These create structured spaces for each voice to be heard. In therapy, I have encouraged families to hold weekly 10-minute check-ins, not to fix problems, but to affirm presence and connection. Even simple rituals, such as "highs and lows of the week," reinforce emotional awareness.
2. **Open Communication:** Boundaries thrive in environments where emotions are not punished or ignored. That means parents naming their discomfort and inviting children to share theirs. This teaches children how to identify needs instead of acting them out.
3. **Reinforcement of Boundaries**: Consistency builds trust. If a boundary is only enforced when a parent is

tired or angry, children learn that limits are about mood, not love. Reinforcement is not rigidity; it is relational integrity.

4. **Modeling Healthy Behavior:** The most powerful teaching happens through example. Adults who respect each other's time, say no without guilt, and apologize when boundaries are crossed demonstrate emotional safety better than any rule ever could.

With Yourself:

The most important boundary you will ever set is the one that protects your relationship with yourself. Before you can teach others how to love, respect, or care for you, you must first believe you are worth protecting. Personal boundaries are not about isolation; they are about integrity. They remind you that your well-being matters and allow you to stop over-giving, over-explaining, and over-extending to feel valuable.

Protecting Emotional Health

Emotional health is not protected by chance; it is preserved with intention. Without boundaries, even the most compassionate hearts wear thin. When you give beyond your capacity, you begin to disappear beneath the weight of unmet expectations and unspoken exhaustion. Boundaries aren't selfish; they are how we stay whole in a world that often demands too much.

1. **Prevention of Burnout:** Boundaries help prevent emotional exhaustion by allowing individuals to set clear limits and say no when needed. This is particularly important for those who tend to overcommit or feel

pressured to accommodate others' needs at the expense of their well-being.

2. **Managing Stress:** Clear boundaries enable you to manage emotional stress by clearly delineating what is acceptable behavior from others. When you know your limits, you can avoid situations that overwhelm you.

Promoting Self-Respect

Self-respect begins where self-abandonment ends. You cannot value yourself when you constantly dismiss your own needs to make others more comfortable. Boundaries are the internal affirmation that your feelings matter, your voice deserves space, and your needs are not a burden.

1. **Acknowledging Personal Needs:** Setting boundaries helps you recognize and prioritize your own needs and values. This fosters self-respect and affirms that you deserve attention and care, just like anyone else.
2. **Encouraging Assertiveness:** By establishing boundaries, you learn how to advocate for yourself. This assertiveness builds confidence and reinforces your sense of self-worth.

Improving Relationships

Healthy relationships do not thrive solely on love; they require clarity. They are not built on guessing games, silent expectations, or emotional over-functioning. Without boundaries, love can become enabling, conversations turn codependent, and resentment slowly replaces respect. When, however, you stop forcing people to read your mind, you begin inviting them to know your heart honestly. Boundaries create the structure in which intimacy and individuality can coexist, allowing both partners to breathe.

1. **Fostering Healthy Interactions:** Boundaries contribute to healthier relationships by clarifying what is acceptable and unacceptable in interactions with others. This clarity can prevent misunderstandings and disputes.
2. **Encouraging Mutual Respect**: When you establish and communicate your boundaries, others are more likely to respect them. This fosters a culture of respect in your relationships, encouraging others to set their boundaries as well.

Enhancing Focus and Productivity

Your time, energy, and purpose deserve protection. Boundaries are how you give your best to what matters most without being consumed by everything else. When you know what to say yes to, your no becomes a doorway to freedom.

1. **Defining Priorities:** Boundaries allow you to prioritize your time and energy for the things that matter most. You can focus more effectively on what is essential by saying no to distractions or commitments that do not align with your goals.
2. **Creating a Balanced Life**: By setting boundaries between work, personal time, and social commitments, you can cultivate a more balanced and fulfilling life, increasing productivity and satisfaction.

Facilitating Emotional Regulation

Boundaries help you manage emotional storms before they turn into relational disasters. They allow you to prepare for triggers, guard your peace, and create safe spaces to reset emotionally, mentally, and spiritually.

1. **Managing Triggers**: Having boundaries helps you identify situations or behaviors that trigger negative emotions or stress. By recognizing these triggers, you can take proactive measures to either avoid them or prepare yourself emotionally.
2. **Establishing Safe Spaces**: Boundaries enable you to create emotionally safe spaces where you can reflect, recharge, and process your thoughts and feelings without interruptions or external pressures.

Encouraging Independence

Boundaries are not barriers to connection; they are bridges to personal growth. They teach you to stand tall in your own story, to meet your own needs, and to build a life that does not rely on the approval or control of others.

1. **Building Autonomy:** Setting boundaries teaches you to rely on yourself to meet your own needs, fostering a sense of autonomy and independence. This is especially important in relationships, where it is easy to become codependent if boundaries aren't established.
2. **Facilitating Personal Growth:** By setting boundaries, you allow yourself to explore your interests and passions freely, leading to personal growth and self-discovery.

Supporting Mental Health

Your mental health is not a luxury; it is a necessity. Boundaries protect your peace from the weight of overcommitment and emotional confusion. When you prioritize your well-being, you not only survive, but you also heal, grow, and thrive.

1. **Reducing Anxiety and Depression:** Clarity around your limits can help mitigate feelings of anxiety or depression that may arise from overcommitment or confusion in relationships.
2. **Promoting Self-Care:** Boundaries encourage self-care practices, reminding you to nurture your well-being, whether that means taking time for rest, engaging in hobbies, or seeking support when needed.

Establishing personal boundaries is not just about saying "no" to others; it is ultimately about saying "yes" to yourself. It is about honoring your limits without apology, claiming space for your emotional well-being, and living from a place of clarity rather than chaos. Healthy boundaries empower you to regulate your emotions, protect your mental health, enhance your relationships, and build a more balanced and purposeful life. By prioritizing your needs and creating structure in both your personal and professional spaces, you position yourself not just to survive but to thrive in a world filled with competing demands and expectations.

Understanding the impact of attachment disorders and choosing to prioritize clear boundaries within mosaic families has the power to transform emotional survival into lasting stability. This intentional work does more than improve communication, it creates a nurturing, resilient family environment where children and adults alike can grow, heal, and belong.

A Faith-Based Perspective on Boundaries

In a recent premarital session, I sat with a couple as they courageously prepared to form a new mosaic family. The man, divorced after betrayal, still carried the scars of broken trust. The bride-to-be, a widow, held the tenderness of grief. Their love was deep, and their faith sincere. They sought more than just structure for marriage, they longed to understand how to lead spiritually and emotionally in a mosaic family. Both serve in helping professions, teaching and healing, roles that often come with the temptation to fix what feels broken. However, in family systems, love cannot be forced into solutions. There must be yielding. Otherwise, love turns into collision.

As we explored spiritual leadership in the home, the conversation turned to a familiar but often misunderstood phrase: "head of the household." In many faith-based contexts, this phrase has been used to justify control, sometimes masking toxic masculinity in spiritual language. Nevertheless, leadership in the home was never meant to resemble dominance. And I invited them to consider a better model. I shared my thoughts on Jesus with them. He spent three years teaching His followers how to live and how to serve. Something was still incomplete. In His final hours, Jesus did not command from a place of superiority — He knelt. He washed their feet. It was not weakness. It was the highest form of love. This was servant leadership, rooted in humility. It was love poured into action. He teaches not only His disciples, but He teaches us that we need love in our service. Without love, service becomes an obligation.

Relationships are not obligations — they are a place of service in love.

For love does many things: it serves, it forgives, it gives grace and mercy, not out of duty, but as an offering of the heart. It is easy to serve without love. It is far harder, and far more powerful, to love in the way you serve. And that, I believe, is one of the greatest needs in mosaic families: the ability to serve one another with genuine love, not out of expectation or performance, but from a heart grounded in grace.

I offered the couple a reframe. In Greek and Middle Eastern cultures, the biblical word "head" does not mean "commander;" it means "source," like the headwaters of a river. He is not the ruler, but the source. Like the headwaters of a river, his emotional presence sets the flow. If he leads with fear or detachment, the family downstream dries up. If he leads with integrity, tenderness, and emotional maturity, he becomes a source of peace, nourishment, and life.

Likewise, the woman, formed from his side, not his shadow, carries her profound influence. She shapes the current. She enriches the flow. Her emotional awareness, like a mirror, reflects the tone of the relationship. If she becomes overwhelmed or emotionally blocked, it sends waves back to the source. In this mutual model, submission is not about subservience; it is about wisdom. It is the act of softening a strong response when two strong wills meet. It is yielding, not out of inferiority, but out of discernment, for the sake of peace.

And that peace? That is the piece that belongs to the mosaic. Boundaries hold that peace together. Boundaries in faith-based families are not about power or control. They are about stewardship. They define how we protect the sacred within our homes, shaping what flows through our families: truth, safety, grace, and love. In a mosaic family, boundaries do not limit love; they dignify it. How else can faith-based spiritual boundaries apply to any family or mosaic family?

Faith-Based Boundaries as Discipleship, Not Discipline

In the context of faith, boundaries are not barriers; they are invitations to discipleship. Jesus Himself modeled boundaries, not by building walls, but by walking away when necessary, retreating to pray, and refusing to let others' expectations shape His identity or mission. In the same way, families rooted in faith must learn to discern when to draw close and when to create sacred distance.

Boundaries are not a rejection of others. They are a reflection of self-awareness and Spirit-led stewardship. Parents who model boundaries teach their children how to guard their hearts, not to shut people out, and to keep wisdom in. They model how to say "yes" with intention and "no" without shame. They remind the family that we do not have to be everything to everyone, yet we are called to be whole before God.

Spiritual Boundaries Preserve Dignity

In any family, especially mosaic families where stories, past wounds, and loyalties overlap, boundaries help preserve the dignity of each person's story. They are not about correcting one another through control; they are about cultivating space for healing, individuality, and grace.

Boundaries say: *You are still your own person, even as we become an "us."*

They say: *We are not here to fix one another, but to faithfully love each other while God does the transforming.*

This applies to parents, children, stepsiblings, in-laws, and beyond. It honors the complexity of belonging while giving each person room to grow.

Spiritual Boundaries Help Avoid Idolatry of the Family

Without clear boundaries, even good things can become idols. Families can begin to prioritize harmony over truth or sacrifice their convictions for the sake of peace. The Gospel teaches us that real peace does not come from pretending. It comes from presence, from truth in love, and from honoring what is holy.

Spiritual boundaries remind us that we are not saviors to our spouses, our children, or our families. There is only one Savior. Our job is not to rescue; it is to remain rooted. Not to force outcomes, to be faithful in posture. In doing so, we release the family from performance and invite God's presence to do what only He can.

Boundaries are not just relational — they are spiritual.

For years, I wrestled with the idea of loving myself. Not in the self-help, motivational kind of way, but in a deeper, sacred way. I had heard people say, *"See yourself the way God sees you."* But what if the God you were taught to see was more condemning than compassionate? What if the voice of God in your mind sounded more like criticism than comfort?

For years, I wrestled with the idea of loving myself. Not in the surface-level, self-help, motivational way, but in a deeper, sacred way — the kind that rewrites the way you see your own reflection. People would say, *"See yourself the way God sees you."* It sounded simple enough, yet what if the God you were taught to see was more condemning than compassionate? What if, somewhere along the way, the image of God you carried was shaped more by human criticism than divine comfort? I came to realize that the voice I often thought was God's was not His at all; it was fear in a holy disguise, shame echoing from old wounds, and the residue of words spoken by imperfect people. God's true voice does not accuse; it calls. It does not tear down; it builds. His voice comes as a quiet, steady whisper that brings peace, even when it convicts. Faith and fear cannot share the same breath, and learning to tell them apart became one of the most important steps in learning to love myself as He intended.

That was my struggle. Boundaries seemed selfish because I had equated love with sacrifice, and sacrifice with silence. I thought setting limits made me less holy, less giving, less like Jesus. I missed the part where Jesus himself walked away from the crowds. Where He chose solitude. Where He refused to let others dictate His calling. He lived with fierce clarity, but never with condemnation.

Boundaries begin when we believe we are worth protecting — not from pride, but from grace.

When I finally began to *love myself through God's true eyes*, eyes not of shame, but of mercy, I discovered that boundaries were not walls of punishment, but thresholds of peace. And that peace does not come from pleasing everyone. It comes from being aligned with the truth that I am loved, I am not responsible for everyone's emotions, and I do not need to earn my worth by breaking myself for others. What if the most spiritual thing you can do is say "no" without guilt? What if God is not asking you to be a martyr, but to be a steward of your own soul?

Faith-Based Boundaries Anchor Mosaic Families in Purpose

Mosaic families often feel like they are starting in fragments; however, Scripture reminds us that God specializes in reconstruction. Faith-based boundaries allow each piece to take its rightful place, not by force, but by formation. They are the guardrails that help a family mature in love, especially when pain or past trauma tries to pull them apart.

Just as the body of Christ is made up of many members, each with unique functions, so too is a family. Boundaries honor that diversity. They allow each member to function freely and fully, without threat of collapse. In this way, boundaries are not only emotional, but they are also deeply spiritual. They make room for the Spirit to dwell richly among us, not just within individuals, but within the family as a whole.

The Boundary Between Judgment and Love

As described earlier in this chapter, I defined boundaries not as rigid lines in the sand, but as thresholds, dynamic entry points that determine what we allow in and what we keep out. Boundaries are not walls to keep people away; they are sacred spaces we guard with discernment. Like a threshold to a home, they require a sentry, a mental and spiritual "guard" who filters what enters, what exits, and what lingers too long within. This guard does more than protect; it observes, evaluates, and preserves the integrity of what lies within the heart. With that in mind, there is one threshold that often goes unexamined, the one between judgment and love.

Boundaries are not just thresholds between people; they are thresholds within the soul. They define the space where we end and where God begins. They separate the urge to control from the call to care. They distinguish judgment from discernment, condemnation from compassion.

In every family, especially those with mixed heritage, there will be moments when someone is not fulfilling their role. A child rebels. A co-parent detaches. A spouse withdraws, and in those moments, it is tempting to slam the door of correction. To cross the threshold of grace and enter the room of judgment. Spiritual boundaries, however, invite us to pause at the doorway.

They remind us:
We are not the judge.
We are not the jury.
We are stewards at the threshold of mercy.

Just because someone steps out of alignment does not mean we step out of love.

Just because the picture is incomplete does not mean we abandon the frame.

The test of spiritual maturity is not how we respond when everything fits ...

It is how we hold the threshold when the pieces still shift.

The boundary of the believer is this:

To guard the door of your heart without closing it.

To speak the truth without throwing stones.

To make room for change without demanding control.

Because sometimes the most sacred threshold is the one where grace stands waiting — not to fix, but to welcome.

Not to punish, but to restore.

And that ... is the threshold where mosaics are made whole.

Whether you grew up in a broken family, are single, married into a mosaic family, or serve in any form of leadership, spiritual boundaries matter. We must define them clearly and hold one another accountable, always in love and respect.

In this light, boundaries are not about who holds power. They are about how we steward the sacred. They define the emotional current of the home. They shape what flows through our families: truth, safety, grace, and love. In a faith-based mosaic family, boundaries do not limit love; they dignify it.

Love does not ignore the cracks; it honors them. In mosaic families, love overlooks the messiness, not to dismiss it, but to seal it with grace. Boundaries become the mortar, holding each piece in place, not perfectly, but purposefully, so the whole can be stronger than what was once broken.

You don't have to be a believer or a person of faith to understand the concept behind the imagery of a man and woman equating to the flow of a river in the household. It is not about hierarchy; it is about emotional and spiritual responsibility. In my version of Scripture ... *Steve's version*, that is. I often reframe the phrase *"head of the household."* Too many times, we've heard this used to justify toxic masculinity or outdated control dynamics in relationships. What if being the head is not about control, but about source?

In 1 Peter, the writer addresses husbands specifically, advising them to be careful in their response to their *wife's emotions.* That's not a light warning. That's spiritual accountability. Then, later, Scripture reminds the man: Be mindful not to emotionally agitate your children, as *it builds walls, not trust.* And finally, he is told to love his wife — not only when she's easy to love, but especially when she is emotional, beautifully complex, and unpredictable, or what I like to say is the *roller-coaster version of her.* (*That's the tongue-in-cheek part, of course.*)

God placed boundaries upon man not to restrict him, but to require restraint, to call him to lead with emotional wisdom, not ego. Logic without compassion becomes a weapon. Authority without purpose becomes control. When a man knows his place and his purpose, provision follows. His presence becomes peaceful rather than reactive. And when a woman feels seen, safe, and supported, she multiplies everything she's been given. That's how blessing flows throughout a mosaic family. But even rivers need banks. Even blessings need boundaries.

Before I could teach these truths to others, I had to wrestle with them myself. Because spiritual leadership is not just about what we pour into others. It is about what we are willing to face within.

And the most sacred boundaries I ever set were the ones I had to carve from the rubble of my own experience.

The Lessons I Learned

Not all battles leave visible scars. Some are fought in silence — at kitchen tables, behind closed doors, in the spaces where voices rise and hearts retreat.

I was trained to hold a line in combat, yet no one trained me for the war within: The war of staying kind while feeling unheard.

The war of choosing growth over reaction. The war of learning how to love without losing myself. I have come to see that personal growth is not linear. It is sacred. It is messy. And it is often born in the very places where our peace was once violated.

What I have learned about boundaries, for myself and others, did not come from textbooks. It came from soul-tugging nights, relational fractures, and moments of grace that held me when I could not hold myself.

If these lessons speak to anything, it is this:

Boundaries are not barriers. They are bridges.

They help define where we end and someone else begins; not to isolate, but to love without disappearing. They are not about power. They are about presence.

I remember standing guard one night in the military. We were at the National Training Center in the California desert, preparing to deploy to the sands of Iraq. The air was bitterly cold, and the silence was deafening. It was the middle of our war games — full-scale exercises meant to simulate the realities of combat. I had been assigned to watch the entry point to our camp, positioned on a high hill that overlooked everything. The stars were sharp, yet the ground below was black. No moon. Just dust, stillness, and responsibility. I flipped down my NVGs (night vision goggles) and scanned the terrain. Suddenly, I saw movement. A coyote, maybe five hundred feet out, crept silently across the sand. It startled me, not because it was a threat, more because it reminded me that something could cross the line when you least expect it.

That line I was guarding wasn't just physical. It was symbolic. It marked the boundary between what was allowed in and what needed to stay out. And it was mine to hold. I did not know it then, but that moment would later become a metaphor for life. Because some of the most brutal battles I would face would not be in warzones, but in living rooms.

Years later, I found myself standing guard again, not in the desert, but in my own home. Not holding a weapon but holding emotional weight. It was a Sunday after church, and we were standing in the living room. The tension had been brewing, and something small turned sharp. The kids' mom and I began to argue. I asked for space. Repeatedly. Pleading for her to back off. The more I tried to set a boundary, the more she pressed in. Until I snapped. I yelled. Loud. And I hate yelling. Because yelling takes me right back to childhood, when everyone shouted and no one really listened.

That day, I crossed my own threshold. I reacted instead of responding. And I became the very thing I swore I never would. What's ironic is how easily we marry what's familiar, even when it hurts. I had chosen a partner whose emotional patterns mirrored the chaos I grew up with, someone who charged when overwhelmed, someone who did not recognize the threshold. And in doing so, she overwhelmed the line I was trying to hold.

That day became an awakening. I did what I could, and I apologized for my reaction. I went through therapy and became a therapist. Processing these wounds and pulling out the splinters helps. In the presence of my therapist two decades ago, I went inward. I asked myself, why did I explode? What was touched underneath? As I processed that moment, I found what I now call my splinter. In my therapy practice with couples and individuals, we often talk about triggers, but for me, "trigger" can shift the focus onto what was done to me, rather than what still lives inside me.

A trigger says *it made me angry.* A splinter says, *this is where I still hurt.* My splinter was the deep ache of not feeling heard. Not feeling safe. Not feeling emotionally protected as a child. And because I had never been taught boundaries, I had no internal compass to manage them now. So, I have learned, sometimes painfully, that boundaries are not just external; they are internal. They are not just about saying no to others. They are about saying yes to self-awareness. They are not about power. They are about presence. Control is a knee-jerk reaction. Management is a thoughtful practice. Control tries to force change.

Management invites transformation. And in both war and relationships, knowing your post can mean the difference between survival and collapse. In the military, we were trained to hold the line, never to retreat without cause and never to advance without clarity. Boundaries were not seen as weakness; they were understood as protection. Positioning mattered. Discipline mattered. And I would come to learn that in relationships, the stakes are just as high. Boundaries are not barriers. They are bridges. They define where we end and someone else begins ... not to isolate, but to love without losing ourselves. They don't exist to keep people out; they exist to keep us from disappearing. They protect what is sacred, what is still healing, what needs space to grow.

So, as I share these lessons, not just as a therapist, but as a man still learning, I offer them not from a place of superiority, but from a place of grace. Because growth is not linear. It is sacred. Messy. Hard. It is forged in late-night soul-searching, in broken conversations, and in the kind of grace that holds you when you cannot hold yourself. If anything I have shared resonates with your own journey, I hope you remember this: You have the right to guard your peace. You have the right to name your splinters. And you have the responsibility to hold your line, because it is sacred.

To My Reader:

Thank you for understanding that life is a process. Growth is not a straight line, and change is real, and lasting change takes time, reflection, and courage. I recognize that not everyone is ready to change, and not everyone can receive healing in the same season.

To those whom my actions may have impacted, I want to say this sincerely:

If you are reading these words and are carrying pain because of something I have done, please accept this as a formal apology. I may not know every person I have hurt, but I know hurt leaves an imprint. I offer this olive branch not as an excuse, but as a sign of peace, of maturity, and of a heart that is still learning to love better.

In this journey of becoming, whether through failure, faith, or forgiveness, I hope these pages reflect a more profound truth: that we are all works in progress, mosaics in the making. Growth does not come from perfection—it comes from reflection. And reflection begins with self-awareness.

Before we can change how we relate to others, we must first understand what lives within us: our patterns, our wounds, our blind spots, and our deepest longings. This next part of my journey required me to stop managing impressions and start examining my intentions.

The Importance of Self-Awareness

In the military, we were trained to stay alert, to study terrain, sense threats, and always remain aware of our surroundings. Situational awareness could save lives; however, no one taught us how to scan inward.

No one taught us to read the emotional terrain of our own hearts.

I knew how to detect an ambush. I did not yet know how to recognize when my soul was under fire. I could protect a perimeter, but I hadn't learned how to protect my peace. And until I turned that same discipline inward, I kept crossing my own emotional boundaries, mistaking exhaustion for weakness, compliance for kindness, and burnout for bravery.

Understanding my own needs, feelings, and limits has become essential. Self-awareness is the flashlight in the dark places. It helps me recognize when I'm overwhelmed, when I need space, and when my "yes" is actually a "no" in disguise. Without this inner compass, boundaries blur and burnout becomes inevitable.

Self-awareness teaches us where the line is. However, it is saying no to that which teaches us how to hold it. For years, I thought saying no was selfish. That meant disappointing people, causing conflict, or closing a door that should stay open. In the military, we were trained to follow orders — personal preference did not matter. And in my personal life, that mindset carried over. I said yes even when I was breaking inside. I overextended, overcommitted, and over functioned. Eventually, I learned: a yes that violates your peace is not kindness; it is self-abandonment.

Saying No is Empowering

Every "no" you speak in truth is a deeper "yes" to your worth. It is not rejection. It is a revelation. It reveals what you value, what you need, and what you refuse to sacrifice to keep the peace. Saying no is not about being difficult; it is about being deliberate. It is about reclaiming your voice after years of silence. It is how you protect your peace without apology. It is how you draw a line — not to shut people out, but to stay true to the person you are becoming.

Many of my clients, like me, grew up with childhood wounds that taught them to equate love with compliance. When you're raised to keep the peace at all costs, saying no doesn't feel like a boundary; it feels like betrayal.

I remember one moment clearly. A friend asked me to help with a project for which I had neither time nor capacity. I was exhausted, emotionally spent, but I said yes anyway, smiling on the outside while resenting it on the inside. That night, I stayed up late helping, even though I had a full day of sessions the next morning. I wasn't being kind. I was being compliant. I wasn't being generous. I was afraid of disappointing someone.

When I looked back, I realized what was underneath it all: I was still that little boy who learned that love could be withdrawn. That rejection could come quickly. That "no" might mean abandonment.

I remember growing up and being told to say "sorry" right away for things I did wrong, whether I was ready or not. It did not matter if I understood what I had done or had time to process my feelings. If I hadn't apologized immediately, I would have been punished. That taught me early on that saying no wasn't safe. That having boundaries was disrespectful. That my emotions had an expiration date.

And so, as an adult, I carried that forward. I became a people-pleaser, not because I did not care about others, but because somewhere inside me was still that little boy trying to avoid rejection, trying to keep the peace, trying to avoid punishment for not being "ready."

I had to retrain my mind. I had to learn that a delayed response is not a sign of disrespect. The need for space doesn't make you selfish.

That a sacred "no" can be just as loving as a "yes."

And one of the most powerful confirmations I found was in the story of Jesus with Mary and Martha.

Their brother Lazarus was sick, and they begged Jesus to come quickly to heal him before it was too late. They expected urgency; however, Jesus did not move right away. He loved them deeply, and yet — He stayed right where He was. He waited.

Not because He did not care. Because He was not led by pressure; He was led by purpose. He said no to their timeline because He was aligned with the Father's. He delayed, not out of coldness, but with intention. And in that delay, something deeper was revealed — not just a healing, but a resurrection.

Sometimes I wonder — was the delay also a boundary?

A holy pause that asked: *Will you trust My timing, even when I do not move on yours?* Was the waiting a test, not of their faith in what He could do, but of their willingness to surrender what they thought He should do?

Sometimes, the most complex boundary we ever learn to hold is the one between our timeline and God's. Between urgency and trust.

Between taking control and letting go.

Jesus could have rushed to fix what was breaking. Instead, He stayed in alignment and in doing so, He showed us that love does not always look like immediacy. Sometimes, love looks like waiting. Sometimes, love says no, not to punish, but to reveal a purpose we could not yet see.

Saying no may disappoint people but saying yes when you're not ready will destroy your peace. And peace is not a luxury. It is a calling. Every "no" you speak in truth is a deeper "yes" to your worth. It is not rejection. It is a revelation. It reveals what you value, what you need, and what you refuse to sacrifice to keep the peace.

Saying no is not about being difficult; it is about being deliberate. It is about reclaiming your voice after years of silence. It is how you protect your peace without apology. It is how you draw a line, not to shut people out, but to stay true to the person you are becoming.

Learning to say no with purpose and peace reshaped how I relate, not just to myself, but also to others. Because once we stop managing people's expectations, we can start building relationships on something deeper than performance: truth, trust, and emotional safety. Healthy relationships are not built on compliance or control; they are built on clarity. And clarity begins with the courage to be honest about who we are, what we need, and where we stand.

Boundaries Foster Healthy Relationships

When you communicate your limits clearly, you are not being difficult; you are creating a space where respect, clarity, and trust can grow. Without boundaries, love turns into obligation. With them, love has structure and direction. Please consult with each other as parents before agreeing to children's requests, whether they are yours, theirs, or ours. In mosaic families, unity between adults is not just a parenting tactic ... it is a survival strategy.

One of the quickest ways kids test that unity? Simple requests.

Can I go to the party? Can I stay up late? Can I skip chores this once? These questions may seem harmless in the moment, yet they carry a hidden weight. Because behind every child's question is another, unspoken one:

"Are the adults in agreement — or can I split the system?"

James, one of the participants in my research, shared a moment that hit this point hard:

"When I told my stepson he could go to his friend's overnight without checking with his mom, I did not think it was a big deal. Turns out she had already said no. That one moment of 'yes' unraveled three weeks of trust between us."

That's how fast unity can crack. A well-meaning yes, spoken without alignment, can cause more division than any discipline issue. Kids are smart. They know who will say yes. They know when one parent is frustrated with the other. They know when there's tension, and they know how to use it.

When, however, a parent pauses and says, "*Let me check with your mom/dad first,*" something powerful happens. It sends a message that often matters more than the answer itself: We are not divided. We are a team even when we disagree.

This is especially crucial in mosaic families, where two or more households may have totally different rhythms, rules, or expectations.

When adults fail to communicate, even good intentions can backfire into confusion, resentment, or power struggles. When adults choose consultation over convenience, they model something much deeper than decision-making; they model integrity.

When children watch adults check in with one another, seek clarity, and honor each other's voice — even after divorce, even through strain — they are not just learning about rules. They are learning about respect. Restraint. And relational maturity.

That's something they will carry long after they leave your home.

Insight

In mosaic families, saying yes without alignment can do more damage than any consequence. When adults choose to consult first, before making a decision, they protect trust, reinforce unity, and model the kind of emotional integrity every child deserves to witness.

Communication is Key

Boundaries without communication are like doors without hinges; rigid, hard to open, and even harder to trust. Open and honest dialogue helps others understand where you stand and reduces the assumptions that so often lead to unnecessary conflict. It is not about controlling the narrative; it is about protecting the relationship by making your needs known.

Self-Care is Not Selfish

There was a time I believed that rest had to be earned. That saying no meant letting someone down. I have learned the opposite is true: self-care is the most honest way to show up fully in a relationship. When I honor my limits, I can be more present for others. That is not selfish; it is sacred. You cannot pour from an empty cup. You cannot give what you no longer have.

Respecting Others' Boundaries is Vital

Just as we long to be heard and honored, others do too. Boundaries are not one-sided. Respecting the lines others draw, whether spoken or silent, is how trust is built. In mosaic families, this includes children, ex-partners, stepparents, and even extended relatives. It takes maturity to realize that someone else's boundary is not a rejection of you; it is, rather, a reflection of what they need to feel safe.

Boundaries Evolve Over Time

Life is not static, and neither are our needs. What worked last year may no longer serve your emotional well-being. Healthy boundaries are not carved in stone; they grow with you. Re-evaluation is not weakness; it is wisdom. As your seasons change, so will your capacity, your priorities, and your relational bandwidth. Permit yourself to adapt.

Not Everyone Will Understand

Letting go of people-pleasing often means disappointing someone, and that can be terrifying, especially for those of us who were conditioned early on to keep the peace, to say yes, to stay silent. Some people will push back when your "no" disrupts their expectations. That is okay. Their discomfort is not your failure. Stand firm — not in defiance, but in integrity.

When I set boundaries, I do not do it to punish. I do it to preserve my peace, my values, and the sacred spaces I have fought to heal. Communication helps soften the edges. Using "I" statements, remaining calm, and allowing others time to adjust may not guarantee acceptance. It does, however, open the door for mutual understanding.

Reflection Leads to Growth

Every moment you pause and reflect becomes a moment you reclaim. Reflection is how we transform boundaries from rigid lines into meaningful practices. Ask yourself: Where did I say yes when I meant no? Where did I speak out of fear instead of truth? Who helped me honor my worth, and who ignored it?

Surround yourself with people who honor your growth, not just your compliance. The more you reflect, the more you align. And the more aligned you become, the more at peace you will feel; even when others do not get it.

Best Practice Tips for Navigating Boundaries

Clarify What You Need - Journal about situations that leave you feeling resentful, drained, or anxious. These emotions are often indicators that a boundary has been crossed.

Speak It, Don't Just Feel It - Use *"I feel ..."* or *"I need ..."* instead of *"You always ..." or "You never ..."* It diffuses blame and invites dialogue.

Practice Assertiveness - Start small. Say no to the unnecessary; decline with respect. Hold the line gently but firmly.

Stay Consistent - Inconsistency confuses others and erodes trust.

When you waver, you send mixed signals about what is acceptable.

Seek Support - Whether through therapy, peer support, or trusted mentors, let others help you strengthen your voice and clarify your values.

Conclusion

Thresholds are the invisible framework that shapes healthy relationships. They define where we end and others begin, not to divide, but to dignify. Especially in mosaic families, where layers of history and complexity run deep, boundaries are what hold the design together.

They are not about perfection.
They are about peace.
They are not about isolation.
They are about clarity.
They are not about saying "no" to love.
They are about saying "yes" to loving well.

"True connection begins when we embrace our individuality and set boundaries, not as walls to keep others out, but as bridges that allow us to engage authentically without losing ourselves."

Let your thresholds speak of your values. Let them reflect your healing. And most of all, let them create the space where love, trust, and truth can thrive.

You are not selfish for setting boundaries.
You are not unloving for needing space.
You are becoming.
And that ... is sacred work.

Before I could learn to trust others again, I had to learn to trust myself. Boundaries were the beginning, and trust was the bridge that connected them. The bridge between fear and freedom. Between control and surrender. Between self-protection and sacred connection.

Because even the strongest boundaries mean nothing ...

If you don't trust who you are when they are tested.

Thus, the following lessons I learned weren't just about relationships. They were about trust, how it breaks, how it rebuilds, and what it means to trust again when the past has taught you to brace for disappointment.

"I kept making the same mistakes because I never healed properly," James admitted. His words echo a truth many of us live but rarely say out loud. Healing is not just about letting go; it is about looking inward, honoring the wounds that shaped us, and choosing to do the work before inviting anyone else into the space we're still trying to make sense of.

That is the truth I carry into this next chapter.

Boundaries taught me where I end.

But trust? Trust is how I begin again.

Mosaic Truth

Boundaries are not walls to keep others out; they are the lines that honor where healing begins.

In mosaic families, boundaries do not break connection; they create it.

When each piece is held with clarity and care, the entire design holds stronger.

Love without boundaries leaks; love with boundaries leads.

Reflective Questions

- ? Where in your life have you said yes out of fear instead of authenticity?
- ? When was the last time you honored your emotional limits, even when it made others uncomfortable?
- ? What boundaries have you struggled to communicate, and why?
- ? Are there relationships in your life where your "no" has been ignored or dismissed? How did that affect your trust?
- ? What part of your story still believes that setting boundaries will cost you love?
- ? How have you responded to the boundaries of others? Did you respect them or resist them?
- ? What would it look like to protect your peace without guilt or explanation?
- ? Where might God be inviting you to realign your boundaries, not as rejection, but as restoration?

Key Takeaways

- Boundaries are not barriers to love; they are bridges to honest, respectful connection.
- Self-awareness is the foundation of healthy relationships and allows you to honor both your needs and your limits.
- Saying no can be one of the most powerful ways to say yes to your emotional and spiritual well-being.
- Boundaries evolve over time; what protected you in one season may need to be redefined in the next.
- Not everyone will understand your boundaries, and that's okay. Their discomfort is not your assignment to carry.
- Learning to respect the boundaries of others is just as important as holding your own. The courage to set boundaries is the first step in learning how to trust yourself again.

Chapter Twelve

Lessons Learned In Trusting

Boundaries taught me where I ended. Trust taught me how to begin again. Trust was never easy for me. I could love deeply and serve faithfully yet still brace for disappointment.

Growing up, I learned to scan for danger, anticipate the shift, and perform to connect. Over time, that became my version of safety. Trust required me to stop overanalyzing and start listening to what was true. It meant honoring my instincts without assuming the worst. Rebuilding trust became a process of surrender, a decision to believe that not everyone is here to harm or abandon.

These lessons were not theoretical. They were shaped through lived moments, through brokenness, therapy, and grace. Trust became the next step in healing the mosaic. Trust is the quiet confidence that bridges the distance between hearts; it is both a gift and a choice, built over time and strengthened through vulnerability.

Imagine growing up in a world where stability is a fleeting illusion, where each new school, neighborhood, and friendship is brushed aside by looming military deployments and constant change. This was my reality, a battleground where deep-seated fears of abandonment clashed with a longing for authentic connection. As a child raised in a Christian home, I was taught to embrace kindness and love, yet that very goodness often opened the door to heart-wrenching disappointment.

Now, as I face the intricacies of blended families and navigate the emotional turbulence of co-parenting, I find myself caught between loyalty to my children and the complexities of trust with my partner. The echoes of my anxious attachment shadow me, making every relationship feel like a delicate dance on a tightrope, balancing between vulnerability and the fear of betrayal.

In this chapter, I will explore the profound lessons from my fractured past, how the very fabric of love can become entangled with codependency, and how building trust in a mosaic family requires courage, effective communication, and a commitment to understanding.

Step into my journey as I navigate the emotional minefield of parenthood, relationships, and the battle for a stable family environment, and discover how the scars of the past can ultimately lead to a stronger foundation for the future. As we delve into the intricate dance of loyalty, trust, and love, are you ready to confront the complexities of your relationships and embark on a new beginning?

The Past

Growing up in a military environment, I experienced constant change, frequent moves, new schools, and the instability that came with my father's deployments. These experiences made it hard for me to form lasting connections and left me with an underlying fear of abandonment before my healing. On the one hand, I learned the importance of camaraderie and loyalty. Still, on the other hand, I often found myself overly trusting or overly cautious, never quite sure how people might respond to my openness.

Being raised in a Christian home, I was taught to treat others with kindness and love, anticipating that this goodness would be reciprocated. That expectation, however, sometimes led to disappointment when others did not meet those hopes. It created a conflict within me: I wanted to connect genuinely, but my past experiences and the unpredictability of military life left me hesitant.

When I was dealing with my anxious attachment style, I often grappled with the fear that others would reject me or leave, which ignited an intense desire to connect and also a deep fear of being let down. It is a struggle to forge authentic relationships while wrestling with the nagging anxiety that accompanies my history.

Being remarried, I had significant trust issues, especially when it came to trusting my children or spouse during conflicts. There were times when my daughter would say one thing, and my spouse would insist she was lying, claiming that was not what had happened. This constant back-and-forth put me in a difficult position and made it increasingly hard to figure out whom to trust. Often, my choice of whom to believe would make the other person angry at me, leaving me in the middle of a conflict between two important relationships in my life.

As a result, I started to lean more toward believing in my children, driven by my fear of losing them. This instinct, unfortunately, complicated matters even further because it intensified the parental alienation I was already facing from their mother. There were times when visitations would be sabotaged; I worked in telecommunications and would need to change scheduled dates, yet she would not accommodate those changes. Then I would receive an email saying how sad my children were: *"I had their bags packed, and they were waiting on you, but you did not show up. That was a big disappointment for them."* I asked how a mother could be so cruel and was the reason I fought and won custody was to ensure equality in what was in the best interest of my children.

Those moments hurt deeply, making it even harder to know whom to trust. I felt caught in a web of conflicting loyalties, and I was constantly worried about losing my children, especially since I was navigating all this before gaining custody. This entire experience has been overwhelming, and it has been a challenge to establish trust in any of my relationships during such tumultuous times.

Questions often arise when we consider the dynamics of focusing on the children and establishing trust with the other parent. I trusted her when she assured me, *"My (her) children come first, and that is my (her) priority."* However, I soon realized that while marriage is traditionally viewed as a lifelong commitment to a partner, this is not always our reality.

In many cases, parents can become overly protective, which I believe stems from a deep-seated desire to shield their children from potential hurt or disappointment. This overprotection can manifest in various ways, whether it is making decisions without consulting the other parent or creating an environment where the children may feel they have to choose sides. While the intention is often to safeguard the children's well-being, it can sometimes lead to complications in co-parenting relationships and diminish the role of the non-parent spouse.

We must remember that while parenting is a vital aspect of our lives, nurturing the relationship with our spouse, who is not the biological parent, should also be a priority. Building a strong foundation as partners is essential for creating a stable family environment. Marriages thrive on trust, communication, and shared goals. When we focus on each other, we foster a partnership that supports effective co-parenting.

By working together as a unified front, we can collaboratively address the challenges that arise in parenting, ensuring that the emotional needs of both the children and the relationship are met. My experience has taught me that a partnership based on mutual respect and trust strengthens the bond between spouses and creates a secure, loving environment for the children. Ultimately, when trust and communication are prioritized in the relationship, it becomes easier to navigate parental responsibilities together with confidence and clarity.

Explanation

Blending two nuclear families into a new marriage can be an enriching yet intricate process. It is often complicated by the influences of ex-spouses, extended family members, and other external parties who may hold biased viewpoints. These external influences can disrupt the harmony of the new family unit, making it essential for all members to establish a solid foundation of trust and understanding.

Ex-spouses, for instance, may hold lingering feelings about the divorce or separation, leading to behavior that undermines the new family dynamics. They might project their biases onto the children, instilling feelings of loyalty conflicts or negative perceptions about the new spouse or family members. Such dynamics can create significant emotional stress for children, who may feel torn between their biological parents and their new family. Parents in a mosaic family must maintain open lines of communication with their children, ensuring they feel safe expressing their feelings while working to minimize loyalty conflicts.

Extended family members, often called "law family members," can also impact the newly formed family structure. Grandparents, aunts, uncles, and cousins might harbor preconceived notions about what is best for the children or express skepticism about the new family dynamics. Their biased viewpoints can lead to unwarranted judgments or interference, making it challenging for the new couple to establish their parenting style and traditions. In many cases, these relatives may inadvertently reinforce division instead of promoting unity, creating a rift between the mosaic family members.

Navigating the pressures from ex-spouses and extended family members requires intentional dialogue and boundary-setting. The new couple must present a unified front, clearly communicating their goals and parenting strategies to both children and external family members. Establishing boundaries helps protect the family's emotional health while fostering an environment where children can thrive.

Additionally, open discussions about family dynamics can help mitigate external bias. Engaging family members in conversations that address their concerns and encouraging them to understand the new family structure can be beneficial. While it is important to acknowledge their feelings, the new couple must gently guide these relatives toward recognizing the value of the changes taking place rather than viewing them through a lens of bias or resentment.

External influences such as ex-spouses and extended family members can significantly disrupt the blending process through biased viewpoints and preconceived notions. Fostering a strong foundation of trust, maintaining open communication, and setting clear boundaries can help navigate these challenges. By prioritizing emotional well-being and creating an inclusive, supportive environment, families can enhance their chances of successfully integrating their unique histories while building a cohesive and loving new household.

Attachment disorders can significantly impact the trust-building process between spouses and children in a mosaic family. Understanding these disorders, which arise from inconsistent or insufficient caregiving during critical periods of emotional development, is essential for navigating the complexities of family dynamics.

These invisible wounds do not disappear on their own. They show up in the spaces between us, in our tone, our timing, our expectations, and our silence. Attachment disorders are not just psychological terms; they are lived patterns that can shape how we love, how we protect ourselves, and how we respond when conflict arises.

Impact on Trust Between Spouses

When trust is strained between spouses, the ripple effect often extends to the children, especially in mosaic families where emotional loyalty is already divided. Children do not just observe the disconnect between adults; they absorb it. And when attachment wounds exist within the child, the dynamic becomes even more delicate. What follows is not just a behavioral challenge but a relational one. To build trust with a child who has experienced inconsistent care or emotional instability, parents must move beyond correction and toward connection.

Hindered Trust

If one or both spouses have experienced attachment disorders, feelings of insecurity and fear of rejection may surface in their relationship. This can lead to difficulties in fully trusting one another, which in turn impacts communication and collaboration in parenting. For example, a spouse with an anxious attachment style may constantly seek reassurance and exhibit jealousy or possessiveness, creating tension and conflict within the family dynamic. Their partner might become frustrated or overwhelmed, leading to a breakdown in mutual trust.

Awareness and Growth

On the positive side, spouses who recognize their attachment issues can use this self-awareness as a catalyst for growth. They can develop healthier coping mechanisms and enhance their emotional connection by openly discussing their challenges and seeking therapy or support. This shared vulnerability can strengthen their bond, fostering trust as they navigate challenges together.

Impact on Trust Between Parents and Children

Learning how to earn a child's trust, especially one shaped by inconsistency, is not a sprint. It is a slow walk of presence, patience, and perseverance. In mosaic families, the process of building trust is rarely a linear one. One day may feel like progress, the next like regression. Yet, every moment of attuned care, every consistent response, every safe boundary becomes a brick in the foundation of trust. Healing in children does not begin with words; it begins with presence that does not flinch, and love that does not leave.

Hindered Trust:

Children with attachment disorders, such as anxious, avoidant, or disorganized attachment, may struggle with establishing trust in their new family environment. They may also struggle to express their feelings or fears, which can lead to emotional withdrawal or resistance to forming relationships with stepparents or new siblings. Their behaviors can be interpreted as defiance, unpredictability, or lack of respect, further straining relationships within the mosaic family.

Healing Through Support

Conversely, when parents (both biological and stepparents) are attuned to the needs of children with attachment disorders, they can help facilitate healing and build trust. Consistent, responsive caregiving that is patient and empathetic allows children to gradually feel secure in their new environment. When parents demonstrate reliability and understanding, children can begin to form healthier attachments, fostering trust and emotional connections over time.

When trust begins to grow, even in the smallest ways, it opens the door to deeper reflection. These experiences, raw, often painful, but deeply formative, taught me more than any textbook ever could. Through trial, failure, repair, and grace, I began to recognize the deeper truths shaping my relationships.

The Lessons I Learned

Trust is not something I mastered overnight. It was tested, torn, and slowly rebuilt in the quiet spaces of reflection, conflict, and grace. In mosaic families, where loyalty pulls in multiple directions and old wounds resurface at unexpected times, trust is both fragile and essential. I did not learn these lessons in a classroom. I learned them through loss, misunderstanding, reconciliation, and the decision to keep showing up.

Jana said it plainly: *"I carried so much baggage from my first marriage into my second."*

Her words reflect what many of us experience: the unspoken grief we carry into new beginnings, often without realizing how much it shapes the way we relate, protect, and withdraw.

Joy, on the other hand, shared what helped her begin again:

"I learned by attending individual therapy that healing must happen before stepping into something new."

Trust is not a leap. It is a layered process. And for me, it began with the most challenging lesson of all — learning to trust myself.

Trusting Myself

One of the most invaluable lessons I have learned through my experiences is the importance of trusting myself. Navigating the complex emotional landscape of mosaic families has taught me that, despite external pressures and conflicting loyalties, I must rely on my instincts and values to make the best decisions for myself and my children. This self-trust lays the foundation for healthier relationships. Having professional help can also foster trust within myself.

Clarifying Communication

I have found that clarity in communication is crucial for building trust among family members. Clear, honest dialogue can minimize misunderstandings and misinterpretations. By expressing my thoughts and feelings openly, I create an environment where others feel safe to do the same, reinforcing a culture of trust and transparency. I should not be afraid to express myself and to stand up for myself.

Understanding Children's Perspectives

I have learned to recognize that children often express what they think we want to hear or what they think will benefit them in the moment. This insight prompts me to approach their statements with sensitivity, recognizing that their emotions and circumstances may influence their words rather than reflecting the complete truth.

Collaboration Between Parents

Both biological and non-biological parents play a crucial role in fostering trust within the family. We must work as a team, creating a united front and communicating consistent expectations and values. This cooperation establishes trust between us and reassures children that they are in a stable and loving environment.

Recognizing Manipulation and Anger

I realized that children sometimes lie about a parent, either to manipulate the situation or out of anger, in an attempt to shift blame or garner sympathy. Understanding this behavior helps me navigate family conflicts with empathy rather than frustration. It reminds me to approach such situations delicately, avoiding punitive reactions and fostering open conversations about emotions and honesty.

Navigating the challenges of creating mosaic families is a journey that offers opportunities for growth and deeper understanding. By embracing self-trust, fostering clear communication, collaborating as parents, recognizing the complexities of children's behaviors, and setting healthy boundaries, we can build a foundation of trust that nurtures a loving and resilient family environment. Each lesson learned is a step toward creating a cohesive unit where everyone feels valued, understood, and secure.

Trust is not restored by theory alone; it is rebuilt through consistent action, humble correction, and intentional connection. Each step I took became part of a framework that others can follow. What follows are not just suggestions. They are the practical anchors that helped turn broken pieces into something whole.

Best Practice Tips for Navigating Trust

Trust may begin as a feeling, but it is sustained through intentional practice. In mosaic families, where every member carries a different history, trust must be built with care, clarity, and consistency. Emotional safety is not created by chance; daily choices cultivate it. The following are some suggested strategies.

Strategies to Build Trust

To promote trust among all family members, several strategies can be helpful:

Open Communication

Encourage honest discussions about feelings, fears, and experiences. Creating a safe space for all family members to express themselves candidly can foster mutual understanding and trust. This will be discussed more in the next chapter.

Consistent parenting

A consistent parenting style is crucial in building trust as it establishes clear expectations and boundaries for children. When parents maintain a uniform approach to rules, discipline, and emotional support, children experience a sense of stability and security that is vital for their development. This predictability is especially important for children with attachment issues, as it allows them to feel safe in their relationships and reduces anxiety about the unknown. Trust is reinforced by fostering an environment where children can rely on their parents to respond in the same way regardless of the circumstances, enabling healthier emotional connections and a stronger family bond.

Seek Professional Guidance

Therapy can benefit individuals and families. Professional support can help address attachment issues, teach healthy communication skills and coping strategies, and build trust within the family.

Establish Rituals and Routines

Building family rituals and routines can reinforce a sense of belonging and stability, helping ease anxiety rooted in attachment disorders. When family members engage in regular activities together, whether it is a weekly game night, shared meals, or bedtime routines, these predictable moments can alleviate anxiety, which is often associated with attachment disorders. Consistency in interactions helps individuals feel secure and valued, reinforcing their emotional connections and trust in one another. As family members know what to expect from each other, trust naturally deepens, enhancing overall family cohesion.

Model Healthy Relationships

Modeling healthy relationships is fundamental in building trust because it provides children with a tangible example of engaging with others constructively. When parents consistently demonstrate trust, empathy, and respect in their interactions, children learn to recognize these qualities as essential components of any relationship. This modeling helps children internalize the behaviors needed to cultivate healthy connections, fostering a sense of security in understanding how relationships work. Children feel more confident in forming relationships when they observe their parents effectively communicating, resolving conflicts, and showing vulnerability. This creates a reliable foundation of trust, encouraging open communication and emotional intimacy within the family, which also extends to external relationships.

Conclusion

In conclusion, building trust within a family requires a multifaceted approach that emphasizes open communication, consistent parenting, professional guidance, established rituals and routines, and modeling healthy relationships. Trust is not merely a leap into the unknown; it is the delicate bridge we build with our vulnerability, where open communication paves the way for genuine connection and mutual understanding. To trust others is to embrace the beauty of our shared imperfections, recognizing that the strength of our relationships lies in the courage to be real with one another.

As you ponder this statement, consider what trust means in your own life. How willing are you to be vulnerable with others? Are you ready to communicate openly, even when it feels uncomfortable? Can you embrace the imperfections within yourself and others as a pathway toward more profound, meaningful connections? In reflecting on these questions, you can build stronger bridges of trust that enrich your relationships and transform your experience of love and connection.

And if trust is the bridge, then communication is the path we walk when crossing it. Because trust cannot grow in silence, it needs words. It needs presence. It needs the courage to speak, not just to be heard also to be understood.

The following lessons I learned were forged in moments when my voice shook, conversations felt risky, and silence was no longer an option. These were the moments that taught me what accurate communication truly requires: not just clarity, but also connection. Not just speaking but listening. Not just honesty, but humility.

Let us now step into the sacred work of learning how to speak the truth in love, and how effective communication can heal what silence once divided.

Mosaic Truth

Trust in a mosaic family is not built all at once; it is layered, cracked, and repaired with time.

Every moment of honesty, every act of follow-through, and every graceful repair adds gold to the lines between us.

In these families, trust is not the absence of mistakes; it is the courage to keep rebuilding.

Reflective Questions

? What past experiences have shaped your ability to trust others today?

? In what ways has mistrust affected your relationships with your spouse, children, or family members?

? When was the last time you truly trusted yourself to make the right decision, even if it cost you approval?

? How do attachment wounds show up in your communication, your silence, or your need for control?

? Have you ever misinterpreted a child's behavior without understanding the deeper story behind it?

? Are you building your relationships on reaction or restoration? What does trust look like when it is rebuilt intentionally, not instantly?

Key Takeaways

- Trust is not restored in a single conversation. It is rebuilt through consistent presence, clarity, and emotional safety.
- Self-trust forms the foundation for all other trust; if we cannot trust ourselves, we will struggle to trust anyone else.
- Children often act out of emotional confusion rather than deliberate defiance. Connection must come before correction.
- Attachment wounds can significantly impact how we communicate and respond in adult relationships; awareness is the first step toward healing.
- Mosaic families require both parents to act as a united front, balancing empathy for the child with integrity in the marriage.
- External influences like ex-spouses or extended family can erode trust unless boundaries and unity are clearly maintained.
- Trust is strengthened through rituals, consistency, and modeling vulnerability in everyday life.

Chapter Thirteen

Lessons Learned In Communication

Actual vulnerability in communication arises not just from what we say. It arises from the courage to observe, the subtle shifts in silence, the unspoken fears behind the words, revealing the more profound truths we often overlook. What if the very fabric of your relationships unraveled under the weight of unspoken fears and unresolved pains? For many, communication serves as the lifeline that connects us; it has the power to heal, nurture, and build bridges across even the most turbulent waters.

In this chapter, I delve deep into my journey from the precision of military telecommunications to the emotionally charged world of family dynamics and counseling. As I navigated the complexities of mosaic family life, I encountered a stark truth: the silent battles of childhood wounds often dictate our adult connections, leading us to misinterpret intentions and struggle with trust. Through personal anecdotes of turbulent custody disputes and the profound lessons learned in the counseling room, I reveal how the language of love can quickly shift to misunderstanding. Join me as I unravel the secrets that can turn chaotic communication into a conduit for healing and connection, showcasing the vital methods for fostering trust and understanding within our families. Are you ready to transform the way you connect, speak, and ultimately, love?

The Past

I joined the United States Army to pay off my student loan debt, and I am proud to say that I financed my education (BA, MA, Ed.D.). The Army placed me in telecommunications, where I worked on engineering communication systems for land, air, and sea operations during combat. Fortunately, I did not witness active combat but instead focused on providing support.

When I moved to Tulsa in 1996 to work for a large telecommunications company, I learned a saying that rings true both in military and civilian life: *"A failure to communicate."* In my current role, I support couples in various types of relationships, whether they are engaged, married, or part of a blended family. A common question I ask is, *"What led you to seek professional help?"* The typical response is, "*We don't communicate.*" My perspective is that they do communicate, as that is what initiated their relationship. However, somewhere along the way, communication became complicated, often overshadowed by childhood wounds. These experiences can evoke reactive responses such as shutting down, fear of abandonment, or feeling unheard.

When couples argue, it is often a manifestation of unresolved childhood pain; they don't feel heard, leading to heightened emotions. I believe that fear fundamentally drives communication breakdown. I work with couples, both individually and together, helping them thrive by addressing their fears while also unraveling their childhood hurts. This process allows them to rebuild trust and navigate the pain from their past experiences.

I also help men understand that a woman's communication often stems from her emotions; the logical mind must remain calm and avoid reactive interpretations by the male. Addressing these fears and wounds can lead to improved communication. Misunderstandings often arise when one person projects their assumptions onto another.

I teach couples that effective communication becomes nearly impossible during moments of anger because blood flow shifts from the brain to the muscles, preparing the body for a fight-or-flight response. It can take approximately 30 minutes for the brain to regain its function after such a reaction. To address this, I recommend the "timeout" approach, where the person requesting the timeout must responsibly check in to see if the other party is ready to resume the conversation.

A pivotal experience that highlighted ineffective communication for me involved my custody of my children and the challenges with my co-parent. As I mentioned earlier, the misunderstanding over the martial arts became a courtroom battle. Even more than that, it exposed a breakdown in communication that had begun long before the judge's gavel fell. The other parent was exhibiting signs of parental alienation, and she falsely claimed that I would harm our daughter if she pursued martial arts. My daughter asked to try it, and while I was supportive, I explained my need for trust regarding her ability to adhere to safety protocols, given our past experiences. This led to a heated argument, with my daughter hanging up on me.

A few days later, I was in court due to the false allegations. Thankfully, the judge saw through the claims, and I had the support of a licensed professional counselor who testified in my favor, vouching for my character. This experience underscored the importance of prioritizing children's best interests, regardless of personal conflicts between parents.

Through my training as a professional counselor, I learned that parents can significantly influence children's memories based on what they say in front of them. I frequently advise couples and parents to avoid discussing adult issues with children, as parents cannot effectively be friends and authority figures simultaneously. I had established structure and routines for my children, which they needed; unfortunately, the other parent offered them a more relaxed environment, contributing to their preference for staying there when they came of age by the court's language.

Despite silences from my children, I consistently sent emails, cards, and gifts during holidays and birthdays to communicate my love for them. My hesitation to fight harder in custody matters stemmed from my insecurities about voicing adult concerns around them. My children were unaware of the extent of my struggles, such as hiring a detective or advocating for equal access to them. I aimed to be a mentor and guide rather than trying to be their friend, and this approach ultimately paid off. I am proud to see my daughter thriving as a teacher with a master's degree and my son successfully running his own arborist business. Communication is crucial in all situations, and my experiences have profoundly shaped my understanding of facilitating better connections among individuals.

What is particularly interesting is that I hold a degree in communication, yet my personal experiences often made me feel inadequate. Clear communication is essential in a mosaic family. The non-biological parent should be a mentor and support figure for the other parent's children. On several occasions, my stepchildren approached me with questions or concerns, often fearful of how their mother might react. I learned the importance of maintaining their trust; I would discuss matters with their mother in a way that did not betray their confidence, reassuring them that both parents were committed to supporting them.

There were moments of joy and effectiveness in both biological and mosaic family dynamics, and I also faced challenges. As a man, I had to learn to manage my reactions to a woman's emotions, as responding reactively only escalated tensions. It was more effective to give her space and avoid questions like *"What's wrong?"* during arguments, as this often made things worse.

I am grateful for my career change, which has led me toward healthier, secure attachments and enables me to help others thrive in their relationships. Often, couples come into my office to discuss where communication breaks down. I typically ask, *"If you were running home and encountered two men wearing masks, what would you do?"* Most respond, saying they would run away, confront them, or call the police. I then ask, *"What if you were at a baseball game? What would you think?"*

On occasion, one partner would argue about words, saying, "You said 'house,' but I said 'home.'" This illustrates how easily communication can falter in any context. In a mosaic family, practicing patience and listening without jumping to conclusions is especially crucial, as there are many moving parts to navigate.

Explanation

Effective communication is particularly critical in mosaic families, often referred to as such, where multiple dynamics and relationships intertwine. My experiences, both personal and professional, underscore the importance of careful communication in these settings.

First, mosaic families often include non-biological parents who are essential to mentoring their partner's children. This requires an environment built on trust and open dialogue. Children in mosaic families may feel torn between loyalty or fear how their biological parents may react to issues they raise. Communication can easily become complicated in mosaic family dynamics. Unresolved issues from childhood or previous relationships can surface during disagreements, leading to heightened emotions and misunderstandings. In my work with couples, I emphasize that fears often underlie these communication breakdowns.

When one partner reacts emotionally, it can escalate the situation instead of resolving it. Providing space was more effective, allowing for more transparent communication once emotions had settled. Additionally, I have found that misunderstandings can arise from simple misinterpretations. In a mosaic family, where multiple perspectives and sensitivities exist, phrases like "house" versus "home" can take on profound significance and lead to conflict. This highlights the need for patience and careful listening, ensuring that assumptions are not projected onto others.

Understanding Communication Differences

The differences in communication styles between women and men have been extensively studied, and while individual variations exist, specific general patterns often emerge. Here are key distinctions:

Content vs. Process Focus

Women: Women often prioritize the process of communication and the relational aspects of conversations. They seek connection and empathy and may use conversation to explore feelings and build relationships. When women communicate, they often focus on sharing experiences and emotions.

Men: Men typically emphasize content more than process. Their communication might be more direct and solution-oriented. In discussions, men may focus on arriving at conclusions or fixes rather than exploring feelings, often viewing conversation as a means to an end.

Empathy vs. Problem-Solving

Women: Women are generally more inclined to express empathy and support during conversations. They may use phrases like "I understand" or "That sounds difficult" to validate the emotions of others. Emotional connection and understanding are often primary goals in their communication.

Men: When faced with a conflict or emotional discussion, men often engage in problem-solving. Instead of validating emotions, they might instinctively search for solutions. This can sometimes lead to women feeling unheard if the emotional nuance of a conversation is overlooked.

Indirect vs. Direct Communication

Women may adopt a more indirect approach, using subtle cues, hints, or nonverbal signals to convey their thoughts and feelings. This is sometimes rooted in a desire to avoid confrontation or to maintain harmony in relationships. Some seem to portray "mind reading" as something the men should already know, or as I was told by a spouse, "read the room."

Men often communicate more directly. They tend to appreciate straightforwardness and may interpret indirect communication as confusing or evasive. This difference can lead to misunderstandings, with each party misinterpreting the other's intent.

And in those moments, men often assign meaning to a woman's emotion rather than leaning in to understand it. They hear the tone yet miss the heart. Instead of asking *"What do you need right now?"* they hear criticism, control, or shutdown. Emotion becomes misread as manipulation or drama when it may simply be an unspoken cry for safety or connection.

Sharing vs. Disclosure

Women: Women typically share personal experiences and feelings without hesitation, often using storytelling to engage and connect with others. This sharing creates an avenue for intimacy and understanding. The conversation can start with A to D, C to W, and back to A, and it becomes too much for a man to listen.

Men: Men may be more reserved about sharing personal disclosures, particularly when it comes to emotions. When they do share, it may be more guarded, often tied to specific contexts or issues rather than open sharing. Their conversation begins with A to B straight to the point, and it does not provide enough details for a woman to follow.

Conflict Resolution Styles

Women: In conflicts, women may seek collaborative resolutions and prioritize maintaining the relationship. They might prefer discussing the problem in depth to gain a comprehensive understanding of all the perspectives involved.

Men: Men may lean toward resolution and closure, often wanting to address the issue quickly and move on. This can result in a quicker return to normalcy, but sometimes at the expense of emotional resolution for both parties.

Body Language and Non-verbal Communication

Women: Women often use more expressive body language, maintaining eye contact, nodding, and using facial expressions to indicate engagement and empathy. Non-verbal cues are crucial in conveying understanding and support.

Men: Men may employ more closed body language and are less expressive with facial cues. Their non-verbal communication might be more about asserting presence than conveying empathy or connection.

Understanding these differences in communication styles can significantly improve interactions between men and women. Recognizing that such differences stem from various social and cultural conditioning can foster empathy and reduce misunderstandings. Building practical communication skills that appreciate these distinctions can help create more harmonious and fulfilling relationships.

The Lessons I Learned

The insights I have gathered about communication dynamics, particularly between men and women, have profoundly shaped my understanding of relationships. I did not learn this from a textbook. I taught it in the tension of honest conversations, in the ache of being misunderstood, and in the quiet recalibration it takes to truly hear someone else without losing yourself.

Women Enjoy Sharing Stories

I learned that women often find joy and solace in the act of storytelling. It is not just about conveying information; it is about sharing experiences and feelings that foster connection and intimacy. I have come to appreciate the importance of listening attentively and allowing others the time to express themselves. Rushing or interrupting can cut off their flow and diminish the value of the experience they are sharing. By practicing active listening, I create a supportive environment that validates their feelings and enhances our bond.

Ask: "Do You Want Me to Fix It or Listen?

A pivotal discovery in my communication journey has been learning to clarify intentions in emotionally charged conversations. Before jumping in with solutions, I have learned to ask, *"Do you want me to fix this—or just listen?"* That one question can diffuse defensiveness and build trust. It gives her the power to define the kind of support she needs, and it helps me step into that role without having to guess. This one shift has saved many conversations from spiraling into confusion or unintended conflict.

Men Often Carry Emotion in Silence

I also learned that men, including myself, often carry emotion in silence. We've been taught to be strong, composed, solution-driven, sometimes to our emotional detriment. Many men don't lack emotion; we lack permission to express it. We process things more slowly, and we don't always have the words to express what we feel in the moment. That delay can be misinterpreted as detachment when we're still trying to understand what's happening inside.

Men Need Validation Too

I had to learn that being a man doesn't mean being a fixer or protector at all times. Sometimes we need to be seen in our vulnerability, not be judged for it. We need to hear that it is okay not to know what to say right away, that our quieter processing is not avoidance but a different emotional rhythm. For many men, being asked, *"What are you feeling?"* feels intrusive, but being told, *"Take your time, I'm here when you're ready,"* feels like a sign of safety.

Misread Emotion Creates Distance

And perhaps one of the most significant communication breakdowns I have witnessed, both in my relationships and my work, is this: men often assign *meaning* to a woman's emotion. In contrast, women often assign *intention* to a man's silence. She may say something emotionally charged, and he hears it as criticism. He shuts down, and she interprets it as rejection. Neither meant harm. Both felt hurt. And yet, without clarity and grace, emotions become weaponized, and silence becomes misinterpreted.

We Both Want the Same Thing — Connection

At the end of the day, I learned that despite all our differences, we both want the same thing: to feel seen, heard, valued, and safe. We speak different dialects. Love, then, is learning the language of the other, not to lose ourselves, but to build a shared vocabulary of trust.

Men Are Like Stick Shift Cars

Men, in many ways, are like stick shift cars. We don't always move smoothly from one emotional gear to the next without a small quantity of intentional coordination. If you want a shift in response, thought, or emotion, there's a pre-step that's often forgotten: you have to engage the clutch.

What's the clutch? It is the pause. The grace. The emotional space a man needs to disengage from one mental gear before shifting into another. Skip that pause, and what happens? You grind the gears, the engine jerks. Nothing moves forward the way it should.

For many men, especially those raised to value logic, protection, or physical performance, emotional processing can be a challenge. We don't constantly multitask emotionally, especially not in high-conflict situations. That doesn't mean we don't care. It means we need a moment. We need to engage the clutch.

The best conversations I have had in my relationships did not come because I was forced to change gears. They came when I was given the grace to pause, when someone gently pushed in the clutch and said, *"Take your time. I'll wait."*

Women Are Like Weather Systems

And if men are like stick shifts, then many women are like weather systems, deeply attuned to pressure, sensitive to atmosphere, and constantly communicating something, even when it is subtle.

A weather system doesn't just change out of nowhere. It builds. It shifts. It gives signs, changes in tone, temperature, and pressure. And, if no one's paying attention, the emotional "storm" can seem sudden, even though the cues were always there.

Women often feel things before they find the words for them. They sense a disconnect before it is spoken. And when ignored or invalidated, that emotional system grows, until it breaks open. However, when someone stops to observe, to attune, to say, *"I feel the temperature changing—what's going on?,"* the system doesn't have to erupt. It can soften. Stabilize.

Where men often need the clutch, women often need the radar. They don't need you to fix the weather. They need you to notice it, without running for shelter or pretending it is sunny.

The Power of Both

Neither metaphor is better. They are just different systems. Different needs. Both require attunement. Both require patience. And, when honored, both can lead to deeper connection, smoother communication, and emotional safety. The clutch and the radar aren't just tools; they are acts of love.

Communication as Water and the Bottle

Another powerful illustration I have come to understand is this: communication between men and women is like the dynamic between water and the bottle.

Women, in many cases, are like water. They move and respond based on emotional currents, such as stress, connection, fear, safety, or even hormonal shifts. Water doesn't wait to be analyzed; it reacts. It reflects what's happening in the atmosphere around it. It can flow gently or surge with intensity. It is alive. Responsive. And sometimes, unpredictable.

Men, on the other hand, often function like the bottle — not in a controlling way, but in a containing way. At our best, we provide structure, grounding, and stability. We try to support, to hold, to be present. However, when a woman is emotionally surging and we try to seal it off, to fix it, to cap it, to contain it without understanding, we miss the point. Water wasn't meant to be trapped. It was meant to be understood.

If we grip too tightly or try to hold too much without openness, the pressure builds. The emotional lid pops off. The water spills. And then we're left soaked in confusion, wondering why our presence wasn't enough.

Here is the truth: we were never meant to stop the water. We were meant to **feel it**, to **respond to it**, to be strong enough to say, *"I'm here. Let it pour."*

And for women, the challenge is just as sacred: to recognize that his silence is not always resistance — sometimes it is his way of holding space for you. However, even the most substantial containers will crack if they are left unappreciated or misunderstood.

Offering Comfort Without Words

When emotions run high, I have come to recognize the power of nonverbal communication. Instead of feeling pressured to say the right thing, I have learned that a simple hug can convey immense support. In those moments, saying, "It will be okay," reinforces my presence without the risk of dismissing her feelings or offering unwanted solutions. Emotions are often complex, and sometimes, just being there is enough to provide comfort.

Encouraging Open Expression

Letting her speak her mind without being reactive has been a profound lesson in emotional intelligence. It is essential to allow her the space to express her feelings fully, thereby empowering her and fostering a deeper understanding between us. I have made a conscious effort to separate her emotions from my childhood hurts, ensuring my past doesn't dictate my reactions. This practice creates a healthier dialogue where both of us feel heard.

Understanding Different Communication Styles

Recognizing that men and women often communicate differently has been one of the most enlightening and humbling lessons in my relational growth. These differences are not simply a matter of personality, life experiences, upbringing, emotional wiring, or social expectations that shape them. What I once interpreted as confusion or contradiction, I now see as emotional fluency expressed in a different dialect.

By learning to appreciate these differences, I have gained the ability to better empathize with her perspective, even when it doesn't match mine. I have discovered that women often process through emotion first, needing space to release and be witnessed before solutions ever enter the picture. It is not irrational; it is relational.

Men, on the other hand, tend to engage through containment and control, not to suppress, but to stabilize. We may go silent not because we don't care, but because we're trying to process before speaking. Like a stick-shift car, we need that moment to push the clutch in and mentally shift into the right gear. Without that grace, everything grinds.

In the same way, a woman's emotional world is often like water, always moving and responding to the unseen changes in her atmosphere. She may not need me to fix her emotions; she needs to know I can hold space without spilling. And I, in turn, need her to recognize that while I may not respond instantly, I am still present, just shifting gears internally.

This journey of seeing things through each other's lenses and honoring our respective rhythms has transformed the way we connect. It has given us the ability to interpret silence with compassion and emotion, and to approach it with curiosity. When we understand the motivations behind each other's communication styles, we stop reacting and start relating. We move from assumption to intention. From defensiveness to dialogue.

And that's where real connection begins.

Managing Reactive Behaviors

One of the most significant lessons I have had to learn is how to manage my reactive impulses, especially around emotionally charged topics like conflict, identity, and the threat of divorce. In the heat of an argument, it is easy to throw out ultimatums, shut down emotionally, or weaponize words like "divorce" to feel a sense of control. Nevertheless, I have discovered that the moment I speak from fear instead of purpose, I shift the energy of the entire conversation.

I have made a conscious decision to remove the "D word" from my emotional vocabulary, not as denial, but as protection. Because every time it surfaces in a moment of conflict, it plants a seed of fear. It signals instability, even when resolution is possible. By guarding that word, I protect the emotional safety of the space we share. Conversations can then focus on resolution rather than defense. Repair, not retreat.

Nature often becomes my model for how to respond. I think of reactive behavior like the tension between a grizzly bear and a rattlesnake. Both are fierce. Both are capable of incredible damage. But both also give a warning. If neither creature walks away, instinct takes over, and the outcome is destructive. One strikes, the other charges, and what could have been diffused becomes fatal. That is what reactive communication feels like. We posture. We swell. We bite. And then we wonder why love limps away from the battlefield.

In relationships, especially when leadership feels absent or misaligned, I have seen this dynamic play out time and again. When men emotionally withdraw, women often step into the masculine role, not out of ego, but out of necessity. Someone must steer the ship. However, if a woman carries that role too long without reprieve, it can breed resentment. And if a man finally reacts, rather than leads with calm presence, he risks showing up like the grizzly: loud, overwhelming, and emotionally unsafe.

I have learned that strength is not proven in how loud I get. It is shown in how still I can stay. Sometimes leadership is not about raising your voice; it is about lowering your tone and refusing to strike. It is knowing when to step up and when to step back, when to offer shelter and when to give space.

Honesty and Vulnerability in Communication

Learning to be honest with myself about my feelings has transformed my approach to communication. When I express my emotions honestly and directly, it opens the door for genuine conversations. I no longer shy away from vulnerability and recognize that sharing my feelings is not a sign of weakness but a strength. By modeling this behavior, I encourage her and others to do the same, creating a culture of openness and authenticity in our relationships.

The hardest part about communication is not the speaking — it is the 'staying soft' when everything in you wants to shut down, strike back, or walk away. That's what I had to learn, and relearn, again and again. Not just how to talk, but how to remain open when I feel misunderstood. How do I ask questions when I would rather assume the answer? How do I stay present when my instincts want to protect?

These lessons have taught me more than language; they've taught me humility. They've taught me that understanding another person's heart doesn't begin with answers. It begins with empathy, with patience, with choosing connection over control.

I'm still learning. I know this: when communication becomes a safe place, not a battleground, something sacred begins to grow. Intimacy. Resilience. Trust. These are not built into the noise. They are born in the pauses, in the courage to ask, *"What did you need to feel safe with me?"*

As I continue to grow in this area, I strive to create an environment where both partners feel seen, heard, and valued. Where differences are not threats, but invitations. And where love is not just felt—it is communicated, clearly, and without fear.

Best Practice Tips —Navigating Communication

Effective communication is essential for building strong relationships in any family structure, including mosaic families where diverse backgrounds and experiences come together. Here are seven practical tips for fostering positive communication between men and women, children, and within mosaic families:

Practice Active Listening

Tip: When someone is speaking, focus entirely on what they are saying. Avoid interrupting or formulating your response while they are talking. After they finish, paraphrase their points to show you have understood.

Application: In a family discussion, ensure everyone has space to share their thoughts and acknowledge each person's feelings.

Be Clear About Intentions

Tip: Before discussing an issue, clarify your intentions. Ask questions like, *"Are you looking for advice or someone to listen?"* This helps set the tone for the conversation and ensures everyone is on the same page.

Application: When addressing a problem or discussing feelings, have both partners express their needs upfront.

Create Safe Spaces for Sharing

Tip: Designate regular family meetings where everyone, including children, can express their thoughts and feelings without fear of judgment or retaliation.

Application: Use "talking objects" where only the person holding the item can speak, ensuring everyone gets a turn to voice their opinions.

Encourage and Model Vulnerability

Tip: Be honest about your feelings, even when they are challenging. Share your experiences and emotions to model vulnerability, which will invite others to feel comfortable doing the same.

Application: In mosaic family settings, share personal stories that highlight the challenges faced in adapting to the new family structure, helping everyone relate and open up.

Stay Calm and Avoid Reactivity

Tip: Cultivate self-awareness and recognize when you are feeling defensive or triggered. Take a moment to breathe and collect your thoughts before responding.

Application: In times of conflict, agree to take a "pause" if emotions escalate and revisit the conversation when everyone is calmer.

Use "I" Statements

Tip: Frame your thoughts using "I" statements to express feelings without sounding accusatory. This helps prevent defensiveness and encourages constructive dialogue.

Application: Instead of saying, *"You never listen to me,"* try saying, *"I feel unheard when I'm interrupted."* This can help others engage more openly.

Celebrate Differences and Common Ground

Tip: Acknowledge and celebrate each family member's unique perspectives and backgrounds. Highlight common interests and values to foster unity.

Application: Regularly engage in family activities that allow for shared experiences, such as game nights or outings, to enhance bonding through mutual enjoyment and understanding.

Conclusion

These practical tips can significantly enhance communication within diverse family systems, encouraging empathy, understanding, and connection. By fostering a culture of open dialogue and mutual respect, families can navigate challenges more effectively and create stronger, more resilient relationships. Communication is a bridge that, when built thoughtfully, connects hearts and minds across all family dynamics.

Genuine connection begins not with words spoken, yet with the courage to listen deeply, understand vulnerably, and communicate authentically; relationships transform and thrive in this sacred space.

The quote embodies the fundamental difference between passive and active engagement in communication. When we "listen to speak," we are often preoccupied with our thoughts and the words we plan to say next. This form of listening typically reflects a desire to respond, defend, or fulfill a conversational obligation. The listener may nod or offer simple acknowledgments while their mind races with their personal commentary, arguments, or solutions. In this mentality, the spoken word takes precedence over the profound understanding that authentic listening requires — an openness to truly absorb and process what the other person is expressing.

Conversely, to "speak to listen" means approaching communication with a genuine intent to understand. In this mode, the listener prioritizes the speaker's words over the impulse to reply. This involves clearing the mind of distractions, providing undivided attention, and tuning into the speaker's emotions, tones, and body language. It is a holistic engagement that values the other person's perspective, experiences, and feelings.

This more profound listening is rooted in empathy and vulnerability. It acknowledges that every exchange of words is not merely about sharing information; it is about sharing experiences, emotions, and the complexities of human existence. It involves recognizing that behind every statement lies many emotions and histories that shape how individuals express themselves.

When we "speak to listen," we create a safe space where individuals feel valued and understood. This leads to more meaningful conversations and fosters trust and connection. Relationships, whether personal, familial, or professional, are strengthened in this space of active engagement, where challenges morph into opportunities for understanding and growth.

Listening deeply transforms communication from a transactional exchange into a relational bond. Through this transformative process, we cultivate empathy, sharpen our understanding, and lay the groundwork for authentic relationships to flourish. A genuine connection is built not just on what we say, but on how fully and openly we listen.

At the intersection of love and pain, accurate communication demands that we dismantle the walls of fear, embrace vulnerability, and listen not just to respond, but to understand; for it is in this sacred dialogue that relationships are not only rebuilt but transformed into bonds of resilience and trust.

Mosaic Truth

Boundaries in mosaic families are not barriers to love; they are doorways to dignity.

They protect what is sacred, clarify where we begin and end, and invite connection without control.

In the mosaic, a boundary is not rejection; it is the frame that holds the beauty in place.

Reflective Questions

- When was the last time you paused before reacting, and what changed as a result?
- Do you listen to defend, or do you listen to understand?
- What recurring communication patterns in your relationships may actually be rooted in old wounds or unmet needs?
- How often do your words come from fear rather than from truth or love?
- Are you willing to repair a broken conversation even if you were not the one who broke it?
- What splinters in your emotional history still shape the way you respond during conflict?
- Have you created emotional space for others to be candid with you, without fear of correction or withdrawal?

Key Takeaways

- Effective communication is not just about clarity, it is about safety, trust, and timing. It requires presence, not perfection.
- Communication without emotional self-awareness often becomes projection. Knowing your own wounds is essential before speaking into someone else's.
- The words we choose shape the emotional climate of our families. Tone, timing, and truth must align to avoid unintentional harm.
- Silence can protect peace or punish presence. Learning when to speak and when to pause is a sacred skill in any mosaic relationship.
- Repair in communication is more potent than always being right. Owning your part and creating space for dialogue opens the door to healing.
- Misunderstandings multiply when assumptions go unchecked. Clarifying intentions can prevent days of emotional distance.
- Healthy communication requires humility. It is not about winning; it is about witnessing the other person's heart without losing your own.

Chapter Fourteen

Lessons In Faith

Sometimes faith is not something we inherit. Sometimes it is something we must rebuild after the storm, after the silence, after the shame. I remember my grandfather with a quiet kind of reverence. He only had a third-grade education and grew up picking cotton in the sun-scorched fields of West Texas. His father was emotionally and physically abusive, a man who left more bruises than blessings. And yet, my grandfather broke the curse.

He learned Spanish alongside the other farm workers. He worked with his hands. He worked with his heart. Later, while employed at Walker Air Force Base in Roswell, New Mexico, he met a man who treated him like a son. That man baptized him. And from that moment on, something in his life shifted.

It wasn't perfect. But it was holy. A cracked beginning was placed in different hands, and somehow, God made something whole from what was broken.

That is the heart of a mosaic. Pieces that shouldn't fit, due to pain, loss, or abandonment, which become part of something sacred when grace enters the story. My grandfather did not pass down a perfect legacy. He was able to pass down something more powerful: redemption. He taught me that faith is not about what we escape. It is about what we're willing to rebuild.

How much more can we learn when we begin to understand that we are not broken beyond repair? The fractures do not define us; we are shaped by what we choose to do with them. We are more than the pieces; we are the hands that hold them, the hearts that carry them, and the grace that binds them.

In mosaic families, faith is not only spiritual; it is relational. It is with faith that love can still be found after betrayal. That connection can be rebuilt after silence. That humanity still holds goodness even after we've seen its worst.

It is the kind of faith that believes in each other, even when trust has been tested. It is the kind of faith that says: I will show up for you, not because you're perfect, but because you're worth it.

When we build mosaic families, we are not just crafting households. We are becoming co-creators with a God who restores. A God who does not discard what has been dropped. A God who, so like my grandfather, sees potential where others saw failure. Who baptizes pain with purpose. Who whispers, *"You are more than the pieces — you are mine."*

This is not just family. This is redemption in motion. This is what faith looks like, one piece at a time.

Like *kintsugi*, gold is not just what holds us together; it is the story of how we refused to let the fractures define us. Our scars are not a source of shame; they are symbols of strength, sealed with grace.

Faith reminds us that healing is not instant, but it is possible. It tells us that the pieces can come together, even when we cannot yet see the design. Faith does not ignore the cracks; it declares that something beautiful can still be made through them.

And faith is more than belief in a distant deity. It is the decision to trust when logic says give up. It is the courage to hope when you have every reason not to. It is the daily choice to believe that love still matters, that forgiveness still heals, and that people can still change.

If we stay silent or live as victims, we forfeit the power of language to connect and to heal. When we speak, when we tell the truth of where it hurt and believe that love can still reach us, we begin to partner with the sacred.

Collaboration begins when we find the courage to name what once wounded us, and the faith to believe that what once broke us can now bind us together.

Faith is the quiet strength that binds us to ourselves, our families, and a greater purpose; it is the unwavering belief that in the depths of uncertainty, love, and divine guidance illuminate our path.

In a world where traditional values often clash with modern realities, many of us grapple with the complexities of love, relationships, and self-acceptance. Growing up in a Christian household, I was taught that men were meant to be the heads of their families, a notion that shaped my understanding of leadership as more about control than collaboration.

As my life journey led through a divorce and into the rich mosaic of blended family dynamics, I uncovered profound truths about grace, forgiveness, the transformative power of love, and how to rid toxic masculinity from a partnership of co-creating. Now, I invite you to embark on this journey with me as we strive to dismantle toxic beliefs, cultivate vulnerability, and foster lasting connections founded on mutual respect and understanding.

The Past

Growing up in a Christian household, I understood that my father was the primary breadwinner while my mother was a stay-at-home parent. Among the teachings I absorbed was the idea that "men are the head of the household," which often led to a misunderstanding of leadership as controlling rather than collaborative management. My perspective diverges from what is typically regarded as "traditional norms."

We must detach ourselves from toxic thinking that has led to household divisions. Currently, we observe a rise in the number of single individuals compared to married couples, which can largely be attributed to detrimental beliefs surrounding gender roles and relationships. These extreme views have impacted adult relationships and pose a significant threat to the foundations of future generations.

During my upbringing, I experienced a form of legalism that dictated behaviors and roles to adhere to strict interpretations of faith. However, I now find myself liberated from those constraints, living instead under the grace of Christ.

This grace offers a far more compassionate and understanding lens through which we can view relationships and interactions. Within the Christian community, we must refrain from allowing differing interpretations to create factions that divide the body of Christ. Instead, we should strive to remain subject to Him and embrace the biblical principles of love and respect in relationships.

Legalism can muddy the waters surrounding divorce, generating feelings of shame and guilt. I do not intend to air dirty laundry within the community; instead, I believe this topic needs to be addressed thoughtfully to cultivate a unified perspective. When I went through my divorce, there was a significant rift between my parents and me concerning the very word "divorce." Christianity should be about reconciliation and transformation, not about guilt and shame. It is about encouraging one another in our journeys.

In my counseling work, I often reference the scripture that advises us to "confess your sins to one another." However, I have seen this phrase as problematic, as it evokes a condemning viewpoint that reinforces separation from God. While it is true that sin can create division, it is equally important to recognize that it is an inherent part of our human experience.

I have witnessed divisions arise among people who argue over whose sins are worse, resulting in factions and a contentious atmosphere that fosters arrogance rather than love. This competitive mentality only exacerbates feelings of superiority or inferiority. Instead, I prefer to rephrase this idea as "confess your humanity to one another." This approach levels the playing field, allowing us to support one another in our struggles without judgment.

Unfortunately, I have encountered Christians who look down upon others facing difficulties and are quick to condemn rather than engage in conversation. When I remarried, my mother told me I was living in sin and warned me I would go to hell. This harsh judgment almost drove me away from Christianity entirely. Eventually, however, I realized that my mother is human, too, and her misunderstandings and biases shaped her conclusions.

I do not intend to get caught up in semantics, yet it is essential to recognize that redemption and reconciliation with the Creator are always within reach. God desires that none should perish. Of course, it invites difficult questions about divine justice and human suffering, questions I cannot answer as I am not God. I can share, as a parent, the profound love I have for my children; I truly wish to shield them from the pain that can come from unhealthy choices. This is the same with our Creator.

Divorce is indeed a sensitive topic, just as premarital relationships can be. Ultimately, I want to emphasize that if you have experienced divorce, it does not mean you are condemned. If you find yourself remarried, commit to honoring your vows and work through the challenges that may arise in a mosaic family. Your relationship with God is what truly matters, and it is built on love, grace, and a personal connection, not on rigid rules or guilt. Now is not the moment to delve into all the stories that have shaped my journey, but I hope to convey that faith and relationship go hand in hand, offering the promise of healing and hope.

Moving Away from the Toxicity of Male and Female Thoughts

In counseling, I often illustrate the principle of submission by referring to the scripture: *"Wives, submit to your husbands,"* and *"Husbands, love your wives."* These passages emphasize mutual respect rather than a hierarchy of control. When a man fails to step into his role as a provider, caretaker, and leader, it often forces the woman to take on those responsibilities. I have observed relationships where traditional dynamics are reversed; the woman makes most of the decisions and becomes frustrated that her husband does not take the lead.

In therapeutic conversations, I emphasize that men are meant to lead by offering emotional safety and support, allowing their partners to connect more fully. When this connection is absent, women may withdraw from physical intimacy, leading to a vicious cycle that can ultimately dismantle the relationship.

What does it mean to submit truly? As a man, I recognize that one aspect of submission is learning to temper my dominant masculine traits when my partner is upset, creating space for nurturing and empathy. Similarly, when women approach their male partners, they must set aside their more assertive, masculine characteristics in favor of nurturing and understanding. This exchange creates a balanced dynamic, fostering connection and intimacy.

From my observations, the essence of submission lies in mutual respect and understanding, where both partners collaborate to create an environment of support and love. In healthy relationships, both partners actively contribute to the well-being of the partnership, appreciating each other's strengths and vulnerabilities.

The Transformative Power of Love in Serving

When we think about the moment Jesus washed his disciples' feet, our minds often jump to the idea of service. Many sermons highlight how this act was an act of humility and a teaching moment for His followers, emphasizing the importance of serving others. I think something even deeper is at play here, something that invites us to rethink what it means to serve in our lives.

Imagine the scene: Christ takes on the role of a lowly servant. This act was radical in a culture where washing feet was reserved for the least among them. It was not just about getting dirty or performing a task, but about establishing an intimate connection with His disciples. Feet, as anyone who has ever had to wash them can attest, are a sensitive part of our bodies.

They represent a kind of vulnerability.

By kneeling to wash their feet, Jesus was not simply performing an act of service; He was sharing a profoundly intimate moment with them and submitting the dominant side of himself to the nurturing, caring side (submission within).

What strikes me is how this act speaks to the heart of what it means to serve. Yes, Jesus was demonstrating humility, but more importantly, He was inviting His disciples — and us — to infuse our acts of service with love. Serving others out of a sense of duty is one thing, but it is a whole different ballgame when your service is driven by genuine love.

This love transforms the act itself; it elevates even the simplest tasks from mere obligation to heartfelt expression. It is the motivation that should lie behind our actions, not just in our interactions within the church community, but also in our families and among our friends.

When we serve each other in love, something beautiful happens. We foster deeper connections, creating a nurturing environment that enables relationships to flourish. Think about your own family. The little things ... a kind word, helping out with chores, listening when someone needs to vent, are moments when love fuels our actions. They may seem minor or insignificant, but these acts of love hold immense power in strengthening our bonds.

One aspect of love-driven service that resonates with me is the understanding that we often cannot control the outcomes of our actions. In our fast-paced world, we may feel pressured to achieve tangible results, yet Jesus teaches us to focus less on the outcome and more on the intention behind our actions. Whether or not our efforts are recognized or returned, serving from a place of love enriches both the giver and the receiver. It helps alleviate the weight of expectations and reminds us of the intrinsic value of love in everything we do.

As you go about your day-to-day life, I encourage you to reflect on how you can embody the message of loving service. Think about how love can transform even the most mundane tasks at work, within your family, or in your community. Let us embrace the challenge of washing feet in our unique ways, allowing love to permeate our acts of service, and, in turn, make the world brighter for those around us. After all, as Jesus demonstrated, it is not just about serving; it is about serving with love.

Finding Worthiness in Love and Acceptance

Divorce can leave profound scars. It can make us question our worthiness of love, leading us to believe that if our first marriage failed, we would be undeserving of deep, meaningful connections in the future. This perspective, however, is untrue and can also sow seeds of doubt and dysfunction in our next relationship. Through my own journey, I have realized that stepping out of a legalistic mindset and re-examining my faith can pave the way for healing and growth.

Now, I understand that many of you reading this may not identify as believers or may even struggle with the concept of God. However, let us find common ground: we can all agree that love is essential in our families. Each of us yearns for connection, understanding, and acceptance. Through my experiences, I learned that expecting my loved ones to meet my emotional needs without first pouring love into the relationship can lead to disappointment. Instead, I focused on growing a secure attachment with my family members. I began accepting them as they were while also praying they would come to recognize the significance of love and connection in their lives.

Navigating the complexities of a mosaic family is no small feat. The challenges can feel overwhelming as we balance new relationships, differing parenting styles, and past hurts. In a society that often promotes a "throwaway" mentality, it can seem as if the notion of working through difficulties has been all but forgotten. Yet, in a mosaic family, the key is not to be right or wrong but rather to come together as a unit and find solutions that work for everyone involved.

One of my favorite conversations with parents, children, and couples revolves around the idea that making a point to be right can often lead to more hurt than resolution. I use a simple analogy: imagine two people who fervently argue about the moon's composition; one believes it is made of rock, while the other insists it is made of cheese. Neither has ever been to the moon, so their debate becomes a dance of stubbornness without evidence.

What if they stepped back and looked at the larger picture? They could agree that the moon rises in the east and sets in the west, that it appears differently depending on atmospheric conditions, and that its phases change according to its position relative to the Sun and Earth. In this scenario, there is more common ground than disagreement.

Finding such common ground is crucial in mosaic families. It is about recognizing that while our perspectives may differ, we can unite overshared values such as love, respect, and mutual support. As I have deepened my understanding of these principles through my faith, I have come to see how they enrich my relationships and nourish my personal growth.

Reading the New Testament has grounded me in the understanding that love transcends our flaws and encourages us to strive for deeper connections. I often hear from my clients how much they appreciate my approach. They tell me it means a lot that I'm not judgmental, allowing them to feel vulnerable and open during our conversations.

Despite the challenges of blending families, I have witnessed countless success stories from my practice. Families thrive because they choose to remain united in faith. These families often support each other through trials, fostering an environment where love and understanding can flourish.

It is important to remember that our past does not dictate our future. Each day presents a new opportunity to grow, love, and build relationships based on acceptance. By stepping into love, we can cultivate healthy connections and experience joy, rather than allowing shame or fear of unworthiness to cloud our vision. The journey through a mosaic family may be complex, yet it can lead to extraordinary beauty when we approach it with an open heart and a commitment to love.

Explanation

Faith can play a vital role in keeping mosaic families together by establishing a shared set of values, instilling a sense of purpose, and providing a supportive community. The shared beliefs held by family members create a strong binding force, guiding decisions and reinforcing the importance of commitment.

Many faith communities offer resources, counseling, and activities that help mosaic families navigate their unique challenges, offering emotional and spiritual support and reducing feelings of isolation during difficult times. Additionally, faith traditions often emphasize forgiveness and grace, which are crucial for overcoming conflicts and misunderstandings inherent to mosaic family dynamics. Engaging in faith-based rituals and traditions can help foster deeper connections and a sense of belonging among family members.

Serving one another is equally important within mosaic families, as it nurtures trust and strengthens relationships. Kindness and support demonstrate love and care, laying a foundation for healthy interactions. Serving one another also encourages cooperation and teamwork, reinforcing that each family member is vital to the family's overall well-being. This practice opens communication channels, allowing family members to express their needs and feelings constructively and creating lasting memories that solidify bonds.

As well, the impact of acceptance over expectation cannot be overstated. Accepting family members for who they are fosters a positive environment, reduces feelings of resentment, and encourages individual growth without undue pressure. This acceptance cultivates empathy, allowing family members to understand each other's perspectives and experiences more deeply.

When individuals are freed from the burden of meeting specific emotional needs, they can interact more authentically, paving the way for genuine and meaningful connections. Ultimately, the intertwining of faith, service, and acceptance creates a nurturing atmosphere essential for the resilience and harmony of mosaic families, enabling them to thrive despite their complexity.

The Lessons I Learned

1. **Not Letting Bible Bullets Affect My Relationship with Christ**: One of the most significant lessons I have learned is the importance of not allowing what I refer to as "Bible bullets" – the select verses or people's interpretations that can be weaponized to judge or condemn – to influence my relationship with Christ.

It is easy to become entangled in the rigid interpretations of scripture, which can create feelings of inadequacy and guilt. Instead, I understand that my relationship with Christ is personal and should be built on love, grace, and understanding rather than fear or shame. This realization has allowed me to approach my faith with a sense of freedom, embracing a connection with Christ that is grounded in compassion rather than dogma.

2. **Not Letting the Judgment of Others Affect My Thoughts on Divorce and Remarriage**: Society often places harsh judgments on divorce and remarriage, leading to feelings of shame and

isolation. I have learned that the opinions of others should not dictate my beliefs or feelings about my life choices. My journey through divorce and subsequent remarriage is a personal narrative guided by my experiences and lessons.

Rather than allowing the judgment of others to weigh heavily on my heart, I now focus on my journey of healing and growth. This shift in perspective empowers me to live authentically and celebrate my choices without fear of external condemnation. This book was developed out of wisdom and personal experience of divorce and remarriage of a blended family.

3. **Accepting that It Is Okay to Be Divorced**: In a world where divorce can carry a stigma, I have learned to affirm that it is okay to be divorced. This acceptance has been liberating. Each person's journey is unique; sometimes, even with the best intentions, relationships do not work out. Recognizing that divorce does not diminish my worth or my capacity to love has transformed my self-perception.

I have come to realize that endings can lead to new beginnings and that my past does not define my future. This understanding has been crucial in fostering a more compassionate view of myself and others who have walked similar paths. Someday, there is a chance that the right woman will walk into my life.

4. **Acknowledging That I am Doing the Best I Can in My Faith**: A vital lesson I have been learning to be okay with where I am in my faith journey. I have come to understand that faith is not a linear path but a dynamic and evolving process. I may not have all the answers, and that is perfectly all right.

What matters is my continual striving to grow and learn. I have learned to recognize the effort I put into nurturing my relationship with God, allowing myself grace when I fall short. This acceptance fosters a more profound sense of peace, knowing that I am doing my best, and it reminds me that growth takes time.

5. **Embracing Vulnerability in My Spiritual Journey**: I have learned the power of vulnerability in my faith journey. By being open about my struggles and imperfections, I have found a deeper connection with God and a greater sense of community with others who share similar experiences.

Vulnerability fosters authentic relationships, encouraging meaningful conversations about faith, love, and acceptance. It reminds us that we are all on this journey together, learning and growing. People often ask if I am concerned about how this book might affect my counseling practice. My answer is no ... because I have done the necessary inner work. As we say in the army, the sergeants in the trenches make the best officers understand how to adapt and overcome challenges. Embracing vulnerability allows me to foster deeper understanding and cultivate healthier relationships. Taking accountability empowers me to own my mistakes and prevents others from having power over me. I know my past is forgiven, and I continue approaching life with forgiveness and love.

6. **Choosing Not to Judge Others for Their Past or Current Circumstances**: One of the most pivotal lessons has been recognizing that we are all in different stages of our journeys. Instead of judging others for where they have been or where they are now, I strive to approach each person's story with empathy and understanding. Acknowledging that we all have

struggles helps create an environment of support and love, reminding me that everyone deserves grace on their path. The world can be better with marriages thriving if we take this stance to help instead of hindering.

7. **Leading with Gentleness as a Man**: I have learned that leadership in my home and community must be characterized by gentleness and kindness. In a world that often equates leadership with authority and power, I value the strength of leading through compassion and understanding. This approach encourages collaboration and fosters deeper connections, allowing others to feel safe and respected.

8. **Supporting Household Responsibilities**: In a mosaic family (or any family), I have realized the importance of actively participating in household responsibilities. Being present and supportive in daily tasks strengthens family bonds and models teamwork and shared responsibility. This commitment fosters a stable and nurturing environment for all family members, providing a foundation for love and cooperation.

9. **Infusing Service with Christ-like Love**: I have learned to integrate Christ's example of unconditional love into my service to others. By approaching my responsibilities and interactions with love rather than obligation, I find greater joy in what I do. This shift in perspective helps me serve without complaint and creates a more positive atmosphere around me.

In conclusion, each of these lessons has enriched my faith journey. They remind me that faith is not merely about adhering to rules or expectations; it is more about cultivating a deep, personal relationship with God grounded in love, acceptance, and authenticity. Each insight is a foundation for resilience, allowing me to navigate life's challenges gracefully and confidently. Ultimately, my faith in Christ has sustained me through much, affirming that it is okay for me to be divorced today, as it is just one aspect of my journey, not the entirety of who I am.

Best Practice Tips for Navigating Faith

Navigating faith within blended families can be both rewarding and challenging. Here are five tips to help blended families successfully integrate their faith:

Open Communication: Foster an environment where family members can openly discuss their beliefs and feelings about faith. Encourage regular family meetings or discussions where everyone can express their thoughts, ensuring all voices are heard and respected.

Find Common Ground: Identify shared values or beliefs that can be a foundation for your family's faith practices. This might involve selecting a denomination or faith tradition that resonates with most family members or finding universal spiritual principles, such as love, kindness, and forgiveness.

Incorporate Faith into Daily Life: Look for ways to integrate faith into everyday situations. Whether it is through prayer, reading scripture, or discussing moral lessons, find simple, meaningful practices that can involve everyone in the family and create a sense of unity.

Be Patient and Flexible: Understand that blending families with different faith backgrounds takes time and patience. Be open to different perspectives and willing to compromise. Recognize that it may involve adjusting expectations and remaining supportive of each family member's unique faith experience.

Forgive, Accept, and Love Yourself: Encourage each family member to embrace self-forgiveness and self-acceptance. Recognize that everyone has a unique past and may carry emotional baggage. Lead by example; share your experiences of forgiving yourself and accepting your imperfections. Foster an atmosphere where individuals can reflect on their journeys, acknowledge their mistakes, and celebrate their growth. This self-love enhances personal well-being and creates a more compassionate and supportive family dynamic.

By implementing these tips, blended families can create a supportive and nurturing environment that honors individual beliefs while fostering a communal sense of faith. Incorporating faith into daily life enriches the family's spiritual environment and reinforces their collective identity. Simple practices, such as mealtime prayers, family readings of spiritual texts, or discussing moral lessons and ethical dilemmas, can seamlessly integrate faith into everyday routines. This consistent practice of faith, no matter how informal, reminds family members of their shared beliefs and encourages them to live out those values collectively.

Moreover, recognizing the need for patience and flexibility is crucial as mosaic families navigate the complexities of integrating different faith backgrounds. Family members need to understand that blending beliefs may require time, effort and sometimes compromise. Each person's unique perspective on faith is an asset, and patience fosters an environment where individual voices can be acknowledged and celebrated. This acceptance can lead to deeper connections and understanding within the family, allowing everyone to feel comfortable exploring their spiritual journeys.

Lastly, encouraging family members to forgive, accept, and love themselves creates a culture of grace and understanding. Everyone has a past, and acknowledging this shared humanity can reduce feelings of isolation or inadequacy. By leading by example and modeling self-acceptance, family members empower one another to embrace their imperfections. This healthy self-love enhances individual well-being and, in turn, contributes to a more compassionate and supportive family dynamic.

I have had conversations with ministers about the importance of teaching love for God and our neighbors, but we lack teaching and ministering to the church on how to love and accept ourselves in our humanity.

While that message is vital, we also need to place more emphasis on accepting and loving ourselves. Nurturing self-love can enhance our ability to love others more fully. While the teachings of loving God and loving others are central to faith, the journey of self-acceptance and self-love is just as important. By prioritizing and advocating for these themes within their sermons and teachings, ministers can foster a healthier faith community where individuals are empowered to love themselves so they can extend that love authentically to others. This holistic approach will strengthen individual and communal bonds, ultimately reflecting the true essence of a faith grounded in love.

Through my experiences of trauma and feelings of unworthiness, I had to learn how to love and accept myself. I realized that I needed to let go of hatred and regret — whether for what has been done to me or for my actions toward others. I discovered that embracing forgiveness is a divine act, and learning to love myself has enabled me to give so much more to others through selfless service. This journey has equipped me to serve others more selflessly and compassionately. Ultimately, this led to the discovery that loving myself is not only valuable for your healing but also enhances your ability to connect with and support those around you.

These strategies honor individual beliefs and actively cultivate a vibrant, collective faith that uplifts and nurtures each family member. This supportive environment helps blended families navigate their unique challenges while reinforcing the importance of love, acceptance, and connection, ultimately creating a home where both faith and family can flourish harmoniously.

Remember, our past does not define us; every day is a new opportunity to grow, love, and build relationships rooted in acceptance. As you reflect on this journey, I encourage you to embrace the beautiful mosaic of your own life. Let go of the chains of guilt and judgment and step into the freedom that comes from love, acceptance, and a desire to connect authentically with yourself and others.

Mosaic Truth

Healing in mosaic families is not about erasing what happened; it is about restoring how we hold it.

The frame may crack, but it can be rebuilt with grace, humility, and shared intention.

Restoration begins not with perfection, but with the courage to stay present in the places where we once fell apart.

Reflective Questions

- ? What messages about faith and worthiness did I inherit, and how have they shaped my relationships?
- ? How do I define spiritual leadership within my family, and does that definition align with love, service, and grace?
- ? Where have I allowed shame, guilt, or judgment, either from others or myself, to distort my view of God, family, or self?
- ? How can I begin serving my family with love rather than obligation?
- ? Where do I need to offer myself more grace in order to offer it to others?

Key Takeaways

- Faith in mosaic families is not about perfection but about restoration. It is built one piece at a time, through vulnerability, shared struggle, and grace.
- Love and service are most powerful when infused with intention and humility, not obligation or performance.
- Healthy spiritual leadership is grounded in emotional safety, mutual submission, and shared responsibility.
- Releasing legalistic shame opens the door to authentic faith, more profound healing, and more compassionate family dynamics.
- Redemption is not reserved for the sinless but for those willing to rebuild with grace and truth.

PART FOUR

THE REVEALING OF THE MOSAIC

"Picture a mosaic, where each vibrant tile tells its own story, held together by the grout of boundaries that unite the fragments into a breathtaking masterpiece. Like life itself, it is the blend of unique experiences and respectful limits that creates extraordinary beauty."

Chapter Fifteen

The Reveal

Becoming Whole, Piece By Piece

Each person is a unique piece of a mosaic, and together we form a breathtaking image. Only by embracing our differences can we reveal the beauty of the whole. Understanding our sense of belonging within this dynamic is fundamental. When all parts of a family function harmoniously, each person understands their role and supports one another, and the entire unit benefits.

This cohesive approach can bridge gaps that toxic thinking has created, allowing us to shape a brighter future for our children, free from the burdens of harmful traditional views. By fostering an environment of grace, understanding, and mutual submission, we can build relationships that uplift and empower, ensuring that future generations are equipped with healthier partnership models.

Constructing a supportive framework where both partners can thrive and be heard, ensuring that love and respect are at the core of their interactions. Embracing this mindset strengthens relationships and cultivates a genuine sense of belonging that nurtures the family and reflects the heart of Christian teachings.

The Beauty of Differences

A mosaic beautifully mirrors the journey of life — a vibrant life, woven from countless, diverse pieces that each contribute to a larger story. Like a mosaic artist carefully selecting an array of tiles, some smooth, some textured, some bright, and others muted, life offers us a myriad of experiences, each with its shape, color, and significance.

Guarding the Mosaic from Outside Influence

In mosaic families, both men and women face unique challenges and opportunities as they navigate the complexities of their new relationships. In managing a mosaic family, the advice to "not poison the water" is a crucial reminder to avoid discussing minor disputes or misunderstandings with friends or family members who may inadvertently exacerbate the situation. When conflicts arise, especially those rooted in minor disagreements, venting to outside parties can lead to skewed perceptions and unnecessary drama, potentially damaging relationships, and fostering resentment.

It is more beneficial to handle these situations internally by having open and honest conversations directly with your partner or by engaging a neutral third party, such as a mental health professional, who can facilitate constructive dialogue and offer unbiased perspectives. This approach enables a deeper understanding and resolution without introducing outside opinions, thereby preserving the integrity of family bonds. If professional help is not immediately accessible, consider confiding in a trusted friend who respects your commitment to keeping family matters confidential. Protecting the sanctity of your relationship from external interference promotes healthier communication and fosters a more resilient family dynamic.

Gender-Specific Wisdom in Mosaic Families

Here are important lessons for each gender to learn to foster a thriving and harmonious mosaic family environment:

Lessons for Men in Mosaic Families

Emotional Intelligence

Emotional awareness can help men understand and empathize with their partners' and children's feelings. This includes recognizing heightened emotions and approaching situations with sensitivity and not reactivity. If there is reactivity, then the process from which these wounds stem occurs before engagement.

Developing emotional intelligence is paramount for men navigating relationships within a mosaic family. Emotional intelligence involves more than simply acknowledging one's feelings; it encompasses the ability to be aware of, understand, and empathize with the emotions of others, including partners and children. This skill set allows men to create a supportive environment where family members feel heard and valued.

By honing this awareness, men can recognize when emotions run high, in conflict, or during discussions about sensitive topics. Such recognition encourages a thoughtful approach rather than a reactionary response, helping to diffuse potentially volatile situations. If a person finds themselves reacting emotionally, it is crucial to pause and reflect on the underlying issues or wounds that may be influencing their behavior. Engaging in self-reflection, perhaps through journaling or meditation, can illuminate the roots of these reactions, empowering him to address them constructively.

By processing these feelings before engaging in family discussions, men can approach their partners and children with the sensitivity to foster meaningful conversations and resolutions. This will ultimately strengthen familial bonds and promote a more harmonious household dynamic. This conscious effort to connect emotionally enhances interpersonal relationships and sets a positive example for children, teaching them the value of emotional awareness and empathy in their own lives.

Active Listening

Learning to listen without interrupting fosters open communication. This skill is vital in addressing concerns and validating feelings within the family. Active listening is a powerful tool for men seeking to enhance communication within their families, particularly in mosaic family dynamics. It means fully concentrating on what is being said rather than waiting for your turn to speak. Women tell men, *"Do not try to fix it!"*

This involves maintaining eye contact, offering verbal affirmations such as "I understand" or "Tell me more," and avoiding interruptions. By practicing active listening, men create an environment where partners and children feel safe and comfortable expressing their thoughts and emotions. This validation is essential for addressing concerns, as it signals to the speaker that their feelings matter and are being taken seriously.

Active listening requires patience and mindfulness; it encourages men to set aside their judgments or responses until the speaker has finished sharing. This approach allows for better understanding and fosters trust within the family, as members feel respected and heard. When issues arise, whether related to family dynamics, personal feelings, or day-to-day challenges, active listening can help de-escalate tensions and clarify misunderstandings.

A man demonstrates his commitment to supportive dialogue and conflict resolution by signaling that he is fully present in the conversation. Over time, this practice can shift communication patterns within the family, promoting more open and honest discussions. These healthy communication habits can strengthen relationships and create a more cohesive family unit where all members feel valued and understood. Ultimately, active listening addresses immediate concerns and builds a foundation of respect and empathy that benefits the family as a whole.

Flexibility and Adaptability

Men should learn to be flexible in their roles and expectations, recognizing that blending families often requires adjustments in parenting style and daily dynamics. Men can handle conflicts more constructively by remaining open-minded, considering alternative solutions, and adjusting their roles as needed, such as sharing household responsibilities. Building relationships with stepchildren requires patience and flexibility, which helps earn their trust. Supportive men provide emotional and practical support to their partners, thereby enhancing family stability. Flexibility encourages personal growth and promotes a nurturing environment, enriching family life and strengthening connections among all members.

Sharing Parental Responsibilities

Men must understand that parenting in a mosaic family is a joint effort. Actively participating in household tasks, childcare, and discipline can ease the transition for everyone. Women are more likely to engage with a man when they feel supported and valued in a partnership, especially in the context of a mosaic family.

Understanding that parenting is a shared responsibility is essential; when men actively participate in household tasks, childcare, and discipline, it not only lightens the load for women but also fosters a sense of teamwork and mutual respect. This collaborative approach facilitates a smoother transition for everyone involved, enabling stronger emotional connections and a healthier family dynamic. Women are drawn to partners who demonstrate their commitment through active involvement, reinforcing that parenting is a joint effort that benefits the entire family.

Father Roles

Navigating the dynamics of a mosaic family can be challenging for fathers, particularly when it comes to fostering healthy relationships with non-biological children. One of the foundational strategies is open communication, which involves actively listening to children and encouraging them to express their thoughts and feelings without fear of judgment. Validating their emotions is crucial for establishing trust and understanding. Building relationships gradually is equally important; taking the time to nurture connections through quality one-on-one activities that the children enjoy can lead to deeper bonds and shared experiences.

Supportiveness and encouragement play a significant role in fostering a positive family environment. Celebrating small milestones and recognizing each child's strengths can promote a sense of accomplishment and self-worth. Establishing clear boundaries and consistency by involving the children in crafting family rules fosters cooperation. It gives them a sense of ownership in the family structure, while consistency in expectations provides a sense of security. Emphasizing teamwork through family projects or shared goals can teach valuable life skills, such as cooperation and communication, while also reinforcing unity within the mosaic family.

Encouraging individuality is another essential aspect of creating a nurturing environment. Supporting children in pursuing their interests and hobbies shows that their unique identities are valued, and it is equally important to respect their existing relationships with their biological parents. Fathers can model positive behavior by demonstrating patience, kindness, and accountability, which often serve as a guide for children. If mistakes occur, acknowledging them can foster a culture of humility and responsibility.

Creating a safe environment where honesty is encouraged will further bolster relationships. Ensuring that children feel both physically and emotionally secure lays a solid foundation for deeper, more meaningful connections. Involving children in decision-making processes can empower them, allowing their opinions to be heard and validated, which boosts their self-esteem and encourages a sense of belonging. If challenges arise that seem insurmountable, seeking professional help through family counseling or therapy can facilitate improved communication and understanding among all family members.

Building robust relationships with non-biological children in a mosaic family requires time, patience, and a genuine commitment to fostering a supportive and nurturing environment. By focusing on these strategies, fathers can foster a harmonious family dynamic that enables all members to thrive, embracing the complexities and joys that come with blending their lives and families.

Respecting Boundaries

Men need to learn the importance of respecting the existing relationships and boundaries that children have with their biological parents. This fosters trust and allows for smoother integration. Respecting boundaries is crucial in mosaic families as it acknowledges the existing relationships children have with their biological parents. When men understand and honor these boundaries, it fosters trust between themselves and the children, making it easier for everyone to adapt to new family dynamics. This respect prevents potential conflicts and feelings of divided loyalty, allowing for smoother integration into the family. Children feel more secure when they see their parents honoring these connections, which can lead to healthier relationships and a more harmonious home environment. Recognizing and respecting boundaries is essential for building strong, trusting relationships within the mosaic family structure.

Nurturing the Couple's Relationship

Prioritizing time with their partner and engaging in activities together can strengthen the couple's bond, providing a stable foundation for the entire family. Men play a pivotal role in setting the tone for the family dynamic, and one of the most important ways to nurture the couple's relationship is by prioritizing quality time together. By reducing reliance on electronics and limiting game playing, couples can create meaningful interactions that deepen their bond.

Engaging in activities together, such as cooking, taking walks, or simply enjoying a quiet conversation, allows partners to connect more personally, thereby enhancing communication and understanding. This intentional focus on nurturing the couple's relationship strengthens the bond between partners and establishes a stable foundation for the entire family. A strong, supportive partnership creates a positive atmosphere at home, which is essential for the emotional well-being of all family members. By fostering a loving and engaged relationship, men can significantly contribute to a harmonious family environment where each person feels valued and connected.

Embracing Vulnerability

Understanding that it is okay to show vulnerability can help men connect with their partners and children on a deeper level, cultivating a nurturing environment. When men embrace vulnerability, it creates a profound impact on women's emotional well-being and their ability to connect deeply with their partners. By opening up, men establish a safe space where women feel comfortable sharing their thoughts and feelings, fostering trust and intimacy. This emotional openness validates women's emotions, making them feel understood and appreciated, which strengthens their bond. As men model vulnerability, they reduce anxiety about emotional intimacy, allowing women to express themselves more freely.

Additionally, this dynamic teaches women that vulnerability is acceptable, encouraging them to overcome their fears and inhibitions. By showcasing empathy and understanding, men cultivate a sense of unity and connection in their relationships, creating a nurturing environment where both partners can thrive emotionally.

Lessons for Women in Mosaic Families

Communication Skills

Women should hone their ability to express their thoughts and feelings clearly and constructively, promoting open dialogue within the family. Women can significantly enhance family dynamics by focusing on their communication skills, yet they must be mindful of their word choices and use language that is respectful and inclusive. By expressing their thoughts and feelings clearly and constructively, they can foster open dialogue within the family. This intentional approach not only helps prevent misunderstandings but also creates an environment where every family member feels heard and valued.

Careful articulation of ideas and feelings encourages collaboration and understanding, allowing families to navigate the challenges that often arise in mosaic situations. Ultimately, effective communication can cultivate stronger relationships among family members, paving the way for a more harmonious and supportive family life.

Encouraging Inclusivity

Women need to facilitate the inclusion of all family members in decision-making and activities, ensuring that everyone feels valued and heard. She must be inclusive with her husband, as this significantly enhances his ability to connect with her on a vulnerable level. By fostering an environment of inclusivity, she invites him to share his thoughts and feelings openly, thereby deepening their emotional bond. When she actively involves him in conversations, decisions, and family dynamics, it encourages him to feel valued and understood. This sense of inclusion helps him drop his guard and promotes trust and intimacy within the relationship. Ultimately, by prioritizing inclusivity, she paves the way for more authentic and vulnerable connections, which are essential for a healthy and thriving partnership.

Managing Expectations

Learning to set realistic expectations for the mosaic family dynamic will help women cope with challenges and avoid disappointment. Managing expectations in a mosaic family is essential, as unrealistic expectations can lead to disappointment and negatively impact a woman's self-esteem. When she sets high expectations for her husband or the overall family dynamic, she may find herself frustrated if those expectations are not met. This can result in feelings of inadequacy or self-doubt, as she might internalize the notion that her family's struggles reflect her shortcomings.

She needs to recognize that while it is natural to hope for harmony and connection, expecting her husband to change behavior or adapt to her ideals can strain the relationship. Instead of attempting to correct or change him, it is more beneficial to practice acceptance. By embracing him as he is, she fosters a healthier atmosphere where both partners can feel secure and valued, allowing for a more genuine connection.

And it is vital to emphasize that acceptance does not mean tolerating any form of abuse or maltreatment. No one should endure behavior that is harmful or degrading. Mutual respect and safety are non-negotiable elements of a supportive relationship. In such cases, seeking help, setting boundaries, and prioritizing personal well-being is essential. Establishing a loving and respectful partnership involves understanding each other's limitations and working together to build a supportive environment, free from any form of harm.

Balancing Roles

Women should recognize the importance of balancing their roles as partners and parents. They must prioritize their relationships while also ensuring their children's needs are met. Fostering a balance between being a partner and a parent is crucial for women in mosaic families, as this balance supports their well-being and the overall health of the family dynamic. Understanding the importance of both roles can create a harmonious environment where relationships can thrive.

Quality of Partnership

At the heart of a mosaic family is the partnership between the adults involved. By prioritizing their relationship, women can ensure their bond with their partner remains strong and nurturing. A healthy collaboration serves as a foundation for the entire family structure, providing stability and consistency for the children. When couples invest time in their relationship, through date nights, open communication, and shared activities, they model a positive partnership to their children, teaching them the importance of relationships and emotional connection.

Fulfillment of Parent Roles

Meeting children's needs is a critical aspect of parenting, requiring attention and dedication. However, when women overly focus on parenting at the expense of their partnership, it can lead to feelings of neglect or resentment in the relationship. It is essential to strike a balance that acknowledges the vital importance of both roles, partner and parent. When couples work together as a team, they can support each other in fulfilling their parenting responsibilities while also prioritizing their emotional connection.

Modeling Healthy Relationships

By balancing their roles, women demonstrate to their children what a healthy relationship looks like. Children benefit from seeing their parents or guardians interact positively, make decisions together, and treat one another with respect and affection. These observations influence their understanding of personal relationships and their future connections.

Mental and Emotional Well-Being

Caring for oneself and nurturing the partnership can significantly enhance a woman's mental and emotional well-being. When individuals prioritize their romantic relationships, they often experience lower stress levels, increased happiness, and a greater sense of fulfillment. This emotional health spills over into their parenting, as a content partner is typically more present, patient, and engaging with their children.

Conflict Resolution

The dynamics of a mosaic family can be complex, and conflicts inevitably arise. A well-balanced partnership fosters better communication and practical conflict-resolution skills, allowing issues to be addressed constructively. When couples prioritize their relationship, they are more likely to work together to navigate challenges, providing a united front for their children and helping them feel secure.

Time Management and Self-Care

Finding a balance requires effective time management and prioritization. Women should recognize the importance of self-care, including making time for themselves and their partners. In doing so, they set an example for their children about the importance of caring for one's own needs while also being attentive to the needs of loved ones.

Ultimately, balancing the roles of partner and parent involves recognizing that both are integral to a fulfilling family life. By nurturing their relationship and being attentive to their children's needs, women can create a supportive and loving environment that benefits everyone involved. This balance is not only achievable but necessary for fostering a harmonious mosaic family dynamic that thrives on love, respect, and emotional connection.

Fostering Independence in Children

Encouraging independence in children, including those with stepparents, can help build their confidence and emotional resilience, ultimately aiding them in adjusting to new family structures.

Fostering independence in children, including stepchildren, is essential for their confidence, emotional resilience, and overall adjustment to new family structures. Encouraging children to take on responsibilities, learn to solve problems, and make choices for themselves can empower them and help them transition more smoothly into mosaic family dynamics.

Building Confidence

When children are encouraged to be independent, they develop a sense of competence and self-efficacy. Each time they complete a task, whether managing their homework, participating in household chores, or making decisions about their activities, they gain confidence in their abilities. This self-assurance is especially crucial in mosaic families, where children may feel uncertain about their place or role within the new structure. Fostering independence allows them to navigate their environment with confidence.

Emotional Resilience

Independence helps children build emotional resilience. By learning to face challenges without relying entirely on their parents or stepparents for solutions, they develop coping skills to handle disappointments and setbacks. For example, when children learn to manage their emotions after a disagreement with a peer or a failure in school, they cultivate resilience that will serve them throughout their lives. This resilience is particularly valuable in a mosaic family context, where children may experience a range of emotions related to new relationships and changes in family dynamics.

The Importance of Not Rescuing or Enabling

While it may be intuitive for parents and stepparents to protect their children from disappointment or challenges, rescuing or enabling them can hinder their development. It can create a reliance on adults, preventing children from learning to handle situations independently. For example, if a child struggles with schoolwork, a parent may feel compelled to intervene and help with their assignments. While this may yield immediate results, it ultimately deprives the child of the opportunity to learn perseverance, time management, and accountability.

Instead, adults should provide support and guidance without taking over tasks for their children. Encouragement to try complex tasks, engage in problem-solving, and seek solutions independently can foster a sense of agency. For instance, rather than immediately intervening during a sibling conflict, a stepparent might encourage the children to discuss their feelings and work toward a resolution, thereby teaching them valuable conflict resolution skills.

Encouraging Decision-Making

Fostering independence also means allowing children to make decisions. By involving them in family discussions, such as choosing weekend activities or planning meals, children learn to express their opinions and consider the needs and viewpoints of others. This involvement strengthens their decision-making skills and helps them feel valued as family members, which is especially important in mosaic families where they may feel a lack of control or agency.

Allowing Natural Consequences

One of the most effective ways to encourage independence is to allow children to experience the natural consequences of their actions. When children make choices, such as forgetting to do homework or choosing not to participate in chores, they learn about responsibility and the impact of their actions. While it may be difficult for parents or stepparents to watch their children face the repercussions of their choices, this experience is instrumental in teaching personal accountability and the importance of learning from mistakes.

Creating a Supportive Environment

Fostering independence does not mean abandoning children when they need support. Parents and stepparents should create an environment where children feel safe to express their feelings, seek guidance, and discuss their challenges. Open lines of communication foster trust, and children are more likely to feel comfortable approaching their parents for support rather than relying on them for everything.

Encouraging independence in children, including stepchildren, is vital for their development and adjustment to mosaic families. By avoiding the tendency to rescue or enabling them, parents can help instill confidence, emotional resilience, and problem-solving skills in their children, which will serve them throughout their lives. Fostering a sense of independence allows children to feel more secure in their identities and roles within the family, leading to healthier relationships and a more harmonious family dynamic.

Promoting Healthy Relationships

Women play a pivotal role in shaping the emotional climate of the home, especially in mosaic families where pre-existing bonds, loyalty conflicts, and unspoken grief often lie just beneath the surface. Rather than competing for affection or control, women, whether biological mothers or stepmothers, can become bridges of empathy and stability. When a woman actively nurtures healthy relationships between her partner and his children, she creates space for unity, not rivalry.

This doesn't mean forcing closeness or demanding loyalty. It means modeling respect, affirming each child's worth, and choosing humility in moments of tension. It is a quiet strength, one that speaks with consistency, not control. By promoting a culture of emotional safety, curiosity, and mutual care, women help shape an environment where stepchildren feel seen, not replaced, and where partners feel supported, not pulled apart.

In these sacred efforts, women help piece together what many believe is irreparably broken. Moreover, through these relationships, something new can emerge, not a replica of the past, but a reimagined future built on trust, patience, and grace.

Restoring Harmony Through Shared Purpose
Both Partners

Regardless of gender, both partners must take intentional responsibility for fostering connection, not competition, within the family. In mosaic families, love is not inherited; it is built. That construction requires both partners to lead with humility, emotional maturity, and a willingness to unlearn old patterns that no longer serve the new family design.

Both individuals must learn to listen, not just to words, but to silence, body language, and what the children are not yet ready to say. They must check their egos at the door, knowing that leadership in the home is not about authority; it is about stewardship. That means holding space for grief without demanding performance. It means embracing flexibility over control and modeling how to apologize, repair, and reconnect when things go wrong.

Unity is not achieved by one partner doing all the emotional labor; it takes both. Whether navigating discipline, household roles, or family rituals, partners must show up as teammates, not adversaries. Their bond becomes the emotional blueprint for the entire household. When both partners commit to consistent communication, mutual respect, and shared values, the foundation for trust is laid, not just between them but for everyone watching.

Core Strategies for All Couples

Regardless of gender, both partners should focus on

Teamwork

Effective collaboration in parenting, household responsibilities, and decision-making is essential for fostering a cohesive family environment. Teamwork in a mosaic family fosters a sense of unity and shared purpose between partners, allowing them to collaborate effectively on parenting, household responsibilities, and decision-making. By working together, both partners can leverage their strengths and perspectives, creating a supportive environment that benefits all family members.

This collaboration alleviates stress and confusion, setting a positive example for children that teaches them the importance of cooperation and communication. A strong team dynamic ultimately enhances emotional connections, builds trust, and contributes to a harmonious family atmosphere where everyone feels valued and included.

Conflict Resolution

It is essential to develop healthy ways to handle disagreements. This includes practicing patience, understanding, and compromise. Conflicts are inevitable in any relationship. It is, however, crucial to learn how to resolve them healthily and constructively. This not only strengthens the bond between partners but also sets a positive example for children.

A Mosaic Guide to Conflict Resolution

The art of resolving conflict in a mosaic is understanding that

conflict is not the enemy of love; unresolved, but unacknowledged conflict is. In mosaic families, where roles are often unclear and emotional histories run deep, disagreements can become amplified. What begins as a miscommunication can quickly spiral into cycles of blame, resentment, or silent withdrawal. That is why developing healthy conflict resolution skills is not just a recommendation — it is a requirement.

Unlike the neatly defined edges of a puzzle, mosaic pieces are jagged, uneven, and imperfect. That is also true of the people who form our families. Conflict allows us to chisel and shape our responses, not to cut one another, but to refine the connection between us. When conflict is navigated with care, it becomes a tool that polishes the relationship rather than fractures it.

Here are some essential tips to promote healthy conflict resolution in mosaic families:

Practice Patience

Conflicts can escalate quickly, but it is essential to take a deep breath and remain calm. Avoid reacting impulsively and give each other space to express their feelings.

Understand Each Other's Perspective

Try to see things from your partner's perspective. Put yourself in their shoes and try to understand their feelings and thoughts.

Compromise with Courage

No one wins every argument, so be willing to find common ground and meet in the middle. Compromise is key to resolving conflicts amicably.

Conflict in Front of Children

Additionally, there are some common mistakes to avoid when dealing with conflicts in front of children: ***Do not fight in front of the children.*** Children are sensitive to conflict, which can create anxiety and uncertainty. Try to resolve issues when they are not present or when they are old enough to understand the situation.

Avoid criticizing each other in front of the children. Put yourself in your child's shoes and think about how it would make you feel if your parents were critiquing you. Instead, address issues privately.

Do not use "wait till the parent comes home" as a threat: This can create a sense of powerlessness and fear in children. Instead, work together as parents to resolve conflicts fairly and respectfully.

Do not give away your power: Do not let your partner dictate the outcome of a conflict or make you feel wrong. Stand up for yourself and work together to find a mutually beneficial resolution.

By following these tips, you can foster a healthy and respectful environment for conflict resolution, ultimately benefiting your relationship and your children's well-being. Remember, conflicts are opportunities for growth and improvement, so approach them with an open mind and a willingness to listen.

Seeking Support

Both partners should openly discuss the need for external support from friends, family, or professionals and not hesitate to seek help when necessary.

By cultivating these vital skills and understandings, both men and women can contribute to the success of their mosaic family, fostering an environment of love, respect, and stability for all members involved.

In summary, the successful integration of mosaic families is analogous to crafting a mosaic; each unique piece, with its distinct colors and shapes, contributes to a beautiful, unified whole. By removing fear and incorporating these key strategies, mosaic families create a loving and supportive atmosphere, harnessing the strength found in diversity to ensure that each member feels honored and connected within this multifaceted family landscape.

The quest for belonging within mosaic families can be especially challenging, mirroring the chaos of a mosaic before it finds harmony. Identity can feel disjointed amid the numerous roles one assumes. Understanding our sense of belonging is essential as we piece together the puzzle of our lives, with each role contributing to our overall understanding of who we are.

The Power of Individual, Kid, and Family Time

Families must balance individual, kid, and family time to foster lasting connections. Each component is imperative for overall well-being. Finding time for oneself is vital for self-care and personal growth. It allows each member the space to recharge, reflect, and enhance family dynamics. Kid time is about prioritizing quality time with each child and strengthening trust and emotional security, which is crucial in mosaic families. Finally, family time is about sharing experiences to cultivate unity. Activities ranging from outings to dining together contribute significantly to the collective sense of belonging.

When In-Laws Cross the Line

Managing a mosaic family can be both rewarding and challenging, especially when external family members, such as in-laws, become involved. To navigate these complexities, open and honest communication between partners is essential. Discussing and agreeing on boundaries regarding in-law involvement sets the foundation for a healthy family dynamic. Presenting a united front helps establish mutual respect for your family's structure. Creating your family traditions fosters unity and encourages bonding among all members, diminishing reliance on in-law opinions.

It is important to communicate expectations clearly, recognizing that in-laws may have strong feelings rooted in their need for connection. Limiting the information shared with them can minimize unsolicited advice. When conflicts arise, addressing the situation directly yet politely ensures that everyone understands how overstepping boundaries affects the family. If meddling becomes significant, seeking guidance from a family counselor can facilitate necessary discussions. Both partners must support each other, validate feelings, and work as a team to address issues.

Finally, as blending families takes time, patience, and flexibility, together, by prioritizing the relationship and family unit, partners can create a loving, supportive environment where all members feel valued, ultimately fortifying their mosaic family against potential challenges.

Embracing Growth through Adversity

Today, I embrace the adversities I have faced, recognizing the invaluable lessons they imparted. Each challenge has taught me the value of vulnerability and the importance of strengthening bonds with loved ones and myself. My journey in couples counseling underscores the importance of reducing fear in fostering healthy relationships. Confronting fears, whether of rejection, failure, or inadequacy can open pathways to deeper connections.

Mosaic Truth

A mosaic is never built in one sitting. It is shaped by seasons, forged in grace, and sealed by the choice to keep showing up. Imperfection is not a flaw; it is a feature. And love is the grout that holds it all together.

Reflective Questions

- ? What emotional roles are you carrying in your family that might need redefining for the sake of harmony?
- ? How do your expectations of yourself, your partner, or your children need to be adjusted to allow room for grace and growth?
- ? In what areas have you tried to force unity rather than patiently cultivate it?
- ? Where might your family dynamic benefit from more flexibility, more listening, or more emotional availability?
- ? How have you protected or unintentionally poisoned the emotional waters of your home through outside influences or internal narratives?
- ? Are there unresolved wounds or old patterns silently shaping your responses to conflict, discipline, or connection?
- ? What would it look like to see your mosaic family not as a puzzle missing pieces, but as a work in progress being crafted with care?

Key Takeaways

- Mosaic families are not born whole; they are carefully assembled through intentionality, compassion, and persistent presence.
- Success in mosaic relationships is not measured by perfection, but by the commitment to honor each person's story without erasing their past.
- Both men and women have vital, unique roles in shaping the emotional safety of the family, and both must learn to lead with vulnerability, humility, and empathy.
- Conflict is not a failure; it is an opportunity for refinement. When handled with courage and care, it can strengthen bonds rather than break them.
- Emotional intelligence, shared parenting, mutual support, and boundaries are not gendered ideals; they are relational essentials that hold the mosaic together.
- True unity is not about blending identities; it is about integrating differences with respect, curiosity, and grace.
- A healthy mosaic family honors the sacred tension between what was and what is becoming, choosing connection even when it is hard, and choosing love even when it is messy.

Chapter Sixteen

The Pillars of a Mosaic Family

We began this journey exploring the shards of brokenness. Now, we close by discovering the pillars that transform fragments into families. This chapter is not just a summary; it is your blueprint. A mosaic family stands as a testament to resilience, harmony, and love, showcasing that every piece, regardless of origin, holds value and purpose. It is essential to bridge our histories while crafting a vibrant future together, with every shard reflecting our collective journey.

As I reflect on my journey of navigating the intricate dynamics of mosaic families, I have come to identify five essential pillars that foster not only stability but also joy, belonging, and growth within these unique family units. Each pillar stands strong on its own, yet together they form an unyielding foundation that nurtures a vibrant family ecosystem, capable of withstanding challenges and celebrating the beauty of diversity. Here is a recap:

The Pillars at a Glance

Open Communication — Speak truth with love and consistency.

Flexible Roles — Let identity evolve with time and trust.

Shared Traditions — Create rhythms that root everyone.

Empathy & Understanding — Hold space for every heart.

Collective Growth — Support individual thriving for family flourishing.

Let us explore each of these pillars more deeply.

Open Communication: The Heartbeat of Connection

Effective communication is vital for the emotional well-being of any family, but in a mosaic family, it assumes heightened significance. Each member must feel empowered to express their thoughts, feelings, and concerns without fear of judgment. Create a culture of honesty and transparency where feelings can be aired and validated. Regular family check-ins, discussion times, or even fun family activities provide opportunities for open dialogue, ensuring that every voice is heard. If communication is the heartbeat, then flexible roles are the lungs, helping the family breathe and adapt through change.

Letting Roles Evolve: Flexible Expectations

Flexibility in roles within the mosaic family dynamic promotes harmony and understanding. Each family member must recognize that traditional definitions of parent, stepparent, or sibling can be fluid. Encourage individuals to explore their identities openly and allow for a natural evolution of roles. For example, a stepparent might step into a nurturing role, while biological parents establish boundaries that allow all members to thrive. Once roles are understood with compassion, families can begin creating shared meaning, rituals that root us, regardless of where we started.

Creating Shared Meaning: Traditions That Bind

Family traditions serve as the threads that bind us and create a sense of belonging. Encourage the creation of new shared traditions that embrace and celebrate the diverse backgrounds of all family members. Whether it is a weekly family game night, annual trips, or unique rituals that blend both sides of the family's heritage, these traditions foster unity and help build memorable experiences. Even with shared traditions, emotional tensions arise. The next pillar invites us to lead not with judgment, but with presence.

Meeting the Moment with Grace: Empathy & Understanding

Within a Mosaic Family, challenges stemming from varied experiences and histories can lead to feelings of confusion or resentment. Emphasizing empathy helps individuals recognize that everyone brings their emotional baggage into the mix. Each member must strive to understand their own and others' feelings with compassion. This understanding creates a safe space where vulnerability is met with support rather than resistance. Finally, connection deepens when every member is invited to grow, not just individually, but together.

Growing Together, Not Apart: Collective Growth

A mosaic family thrives when each member pursues personal growth while supporting the growth of others. Encourage individual aspirations, participation in activities, and open exploration of new interests. At the same time, create a nurturing environment that fosters collaboration and team building. Validating a person's feelings is an important aspect of emotional support. It involves acknowledging and accepting someone's feelings, thoughts, and experiences without judgment. Celebrate achievements big and small and remember that each step towards personal fulfillment contributes to the overall vitality of the family unit.

To help you visualize the interconnectedness of these principles, the following diagram offers a snapshot of the Mosaic Pillars in action — a compass for your continued journey.

✦ The Pillars at a Glance

Open Communication	Flexible Roles	Shared Traditions	Empathy & Understanding	Collective Growth
Speak truth with love and consistency	Let identity evolve with time and trust	Create rhythms that root everyone	Hold space for every heart	Support individual thriving for family flourishing

What Happens When a Pillar Is Missing?

When communication breaks down, misunderstandings multiply. When empathy wanes, disconnection takes hold quietly. Without shared traditions, we lose our rhythm. Without flexible roles, resentment builds. And when growth is stifled, families stall. Mosaic families are resilient, but even the most beautiful designs need their pillars to be intact to thrive.

Conclusion: Crafting a Masterpiece Together

The journey of building a mosaic family is filled with hope, laughter, and challenges that will ultimately shape an extraordinary portrait of love and resilience. By embracing these five pillars — open communication, flexible roles, shared traditions, empathy, and collective growth — you can create an environment where every member feels valued and empowered to contribute to the family's mosaic. It is this intricate interplay of diverse threads that builds a landscape of connection that can withstand the storms of life.

As you navigate your path towards creating a successful mosaic family, remember you are not simply merging lives but forging meaningful connections that celebrate every story, every experience, and every fragment that makes you whole. Each journey is unique, but together, you will construct a beautiful mosaic that encapsulates the true essence of family.

Life is a mosaic, a breathtaking masterpiece shaped by the diverse experiences, relationships, and lessons we encounter. While often fraught with challenges, the journey toward cultivating a healthy sense of belonging can lead to a space that celebrates individuality and connectedness.

As the founder of *Coached Soul*, my mission is to empower individuals to become their best selves. It is not just about self-improvement; it is about illuminating the paths we tread together. By embracing our unique mosaics and supporting one another, we can become brighter as a collective, inspiring love and acceptance within our mosaic families.

Remember that life is a continuous cycle of growth and realization. We are ever evolving, discovering our true essence.

I hope this exploration has offered insight and encouragement as you navigate your mosaic family. Remember: you hold the power to create beautiful pieces that contribute to the masterpiece of your life. Shine brightly on your journey, illuminated by the love of your mosaic family.

As I bring this book to a close, I would like to acknowledge the profound complexities that mosaic families face daily. My personal marital and divorced experiences, coupled with insights gained from years of counseling and working with families, have led me to understand that no two blended families are alike. Each family forms its unique mosaic of relationships, histories, challenges, and triumphs. While my private practice has provided valuable tools and techniques, it cannot encapsulate the full intricacy of what it means to blend lives, heartbeats, and traditions.

This book has been designed to serve as a guide, a beacon of hope, and a source of practical wisdom for those embarking on the journey of life in a blended family. It is my sincere hope that the insights shared here inspire you to cultivate love, understanding, and connection among your family members. Embrace the imperfection of your journey, knowing that growth often comes from navigating the discomfort of uncertainty.

Remember that thriving in a blended family requires commitment, patience, and a willingness to learn together. Celebrate each milestone, however small, and be gentle with one another during challenging times. The heart of a blended family beats strongest when each member feels valued and accepted, regardless of their past.

May this book serve as a steppingstone toward building the family dynamics you aspire to create, a family rooted in love, resilience, and acceptance. May you find the grace to support each other, the courage to communicate openly, and the strength to embrace each other's unique histories. As you embark on this journey, know that you are not alone; countless families share this experience, and together, we can foster a compassionate community enriched by our diverse stories.

Ultimately, your Mosaic family can be a source of profound love and connection. Let this guide serve as a reminder that you can thrive through faith, understanding, and effort. Embrace the beautiful mosaic that is your family, and may it shine brightly for all to see.

"Healing is not about erasing the past; it is about honoring the scars, reclaiming your voice, and choosing to live forward with grace, strength, and purpose." — Dr. Steve Hudgins

Final Closing Reflection – "The Mug Still Sits on My Shelf"

I kept the mug. The one I shattered.

For a while, I thought I would throw it away. It seemed useless, cracked, fragile, broken in all the wrong places. But something in me knew better. So, I gathered the pieces. Not all of them fit cleanly. Some had sharp edges. Some were missing altogether. I found a way to set them, carefully, slowly, into something new. I sealed it with gold cement grout, not because I thought it could be made flawless, but because I believed it was still worth holding.

That mug now sits on my shelf, not to be used, but to remind me what is possible.

This book began with brokenness, yet it was never about being broken. It was always about the design, the rearranging.

The truth is that what we hold does not have to be symmetrical to be sacred.

Families are the same. They are not fixed images. They are living mosaics, crafted over time, sealed by choice, and made beautiful not despite the cracks, but because of them.

If you're holding pieces right now ...of yourself, your family, your story, do not rush to hide them.

Place them gently. Seal them with grace.

And trust that what you're building, piece by piece, is a work of art.

Healing does not come from pretending the break never happened. It comes from naming it, facing it, and then choosing, day by day, to build something new out of what remains.

Over the course of this journey, I have listened to many stories. Not just clinical case notes or research transcripts, but human echoes of hope, loss, and sacred tension. These voices became the heartbeat of MFST.

Tiffany admitted, *"It took me years to understand how much my childhood trauma shaped how I reacted. By the time I saw it, damage had already been done."*

Joy told me, *"I learned by attending individual therapy that healing must happen before stepping into something new."*

Sarah, after much grief, finally declared, *"I kept thinking I had failed, but then I realized divorce was not the end of my story. It was the beginning of me choosing myself for the first time."*

These are not just reflections. They are roadmaps. Testimonies that healing is possible, not despite the brokenness, but through it.

And now, here is what I know, not as a therapist, but as a man who has stood in the mess of it all.

One night not long ago, I walked into the kitchen and reached for that old mug, the one I broke all those years ago. Its cracks were still visible, the gold cement grout catching the light under the cabinet lamp. And in that moment, I saw my life mirrored in ceramic: not flawless, not fragile, but chosen, restored, and whole in a new way.

This image echoes the Japanese practice of Kintsugi, where broken pottery is repaired with gold, not to hide the cracks, but to honor them. The break becomes part of the story. The restored object is more precious than before.

My family is not perfect. Yours will not be either. But perfection was never the goal. Intention was. Grace was. Love that learns how to hold the sharp edges without bleeding.

That mug still sits on my shelf, not because I need it to function, but because I need it to remind me:

Every piece matters. Every fracture has value. Every story belongs.

And that... is what makes it a mosaic.

So, if you've made it this far, reading, reflecting, remembering, then maybe one final piece remains.

Not a step.

A word.

A prayer.

A reminder of what this journey has always been about.

Let us close this mosaic the way it was built: with intention, with hope, and with a few final words.

Closing Words

You are not behind. You are not broken. You are building something beautiful. This book began with brokenness. Not to glorify pain, but to redeem it.

Because your story is not over, it is being rearranged.

Mosaic families are not "less than" traditional families. They are not fractured reruns of what once failed. They are sacred stories. Stories of survival, redemption, redefinition, and the quiet courage it takes to stay when it is easier to run.

Mark once said, *"I thought my second marriage would fix what was broken in me. Instead, I had to fix myself first."* That is the heart of this book. Not to give you steps, but to hand you a mirror, so you can honor every piece, not just the polished ones.

You are not behind.
You are not broken.
You are building something beautiful.

May your mosaic be shaped by truth, framed by faith, and sealed with love that does not flinch in the face of imperfection. May it whisper to the world that scars are not a sign of shame, but rather a testament to survival.

And may you leave these pages remembering this:

You are not a leftover from someone else's story.

You are not a footnote in a broken narrative.

You are the artist now. You are the story.

And if you remember anything from this book, let it be this:

"A mosaic family is not made from what was perfect—it is made from what refused to be thrown away." — Dr. Steve Hudgins

Mosaic Truth

A mosaic family is not held together by perfection but by pillars of grace, communication that listens, roles that flex, traditions that bind, empathy that heals, and growth that invites everyone to flourish. These aren't just supports; they are sacred acts of love in motion.

Reflective Questions

? What emotional patterns or habits do I bring into my family that need revisiting or reshaping?

? Where in my family do I see beauty forming from pain?

? How can I better honor each person's individuality while nurturing our connection as a whole?

? What conversations need to happen to strengthen our communication and empathy?

In what ways can our family become a living mosaic that tells a story of redemption and resilience

Key Takeaways

- The five pillars of a mosaic family, open communication, flexible roles, shared traditions, empathy, and collective growth, are not rigid rules, but living practices that shape belonging.
- Each family member's journey is valid. Their voice, identity, and needs must be seen as sacred parts of the whole.
- Creating unity does not require erasing differences. It means finding shared meaning amidst complexity.
- Empathy is not just a soft skill; it is the foundation for trust, healing, and connection in mosaic families.
- Thriving as a mosaic family is a daily choice to grow together, honoring both the cracks and the color in each piece.

About the Author

Dr. Steve Hudgins is a Licensed Professional Counselor Supervisor, educator, author, and speaker whose work centers on helping individuals and families navigate life's complex emotional paths. Drawing on his personal experiences, clinical practice, and doctoral research, Dr. Hudgins has dedicated his career to understanding how adversity, family dynamics, and life transitions shape who we become.

After serving in the United States military and later pursuing advanced training in counseling and family systems, Dr. Hudgins developed a strong interest in how families adapt and reorganize through hardship.

His doctoral research examined divorce within blended families. It led to the development of the concept of Mosaic Families, a perspective that recognizes that broken pieces of life can be rearranged into meaningful, resilient relationships. His work encourages readers to reflect on how their own experiences, even difficult ones, can become part of a larger story of healing, resilience, and purpose.

Dr. Steve lives in Oklahoma and continues his private practice, writing, teaching, and advocating for legal changes in the family court system. His faith guides him as he continues to work with individuals and families seeking clarity, healing, and direction on their own paths. He has two grown children and four grandchildren.

www.ingramcontent.com/pod-product-compliance
Lightning Source LLC
LaVergne TN
LVHW020649110826
845149LV00012B/1953

9798999648303